THE
CAR OWNER'S
SURVIVAL
GUIDE

THE
CAR OWNER'S SURVIVAL GUIDE

Robert Appel

Fawcett Columbine
New York

CONTENTS

CONTENTS

■ 2 ■
WHEN THINGS GO WRONG 61

CONTENTS

■ 3 ■

WHEN SHOPPING FOR SERVICE 102

CONTENTS

CONTENTS

■ 6 ■
TO PREVENT PROBLEMS   205

■ 7 ■
INFORMATION AND SUPPORT   228

CONTENTS

THIS IS MY CAR:

Love your car? Of course you do! But do you understand it? Don't be too quick to nod yes. First, take this simple test—it's an excellent opportunity both to see just how much you do know about your car *and* to collect the information you'll need to keep your car "on the road."

Manufacturer: _____

Model: _____

Year: _____

Dealer: _____ Phone _____

Service Manager: _____

Mechanic: _____ Phone _____

The V.I.N. plaque is located _____.

My car holds ____ quarts of motor oil (____ quarts *including* new filter).

The motor oil must meet SAE specification # _____.

The tire pressure recommended by the manufacturer of the car is ____ psi. The maximum pressure each tire can take is ____ psi. The spare should be ____ psi.

The gas tank holds ____ gallons. I can travel about ____ miles on a full tank.

The radiator needs ____ gallons of a 50–50 antifreeze-water mix for a complete flush.

My car's fan is __belt-driven __electric. (Note: electric fans may run even when ignition is off!)

My car uses ____ different V-belts. Their parts codes are _____.

My car uses spark plug type _____. There are ____ plugs in all.

The manufacturer __permits __doesn't permit alcohol fuel blends.

The key tag number is _____.

This car __can __cannot be used to tow a trailer.

This car has __front-wheel drive __rear-wheel drive.

The spare tire is a __regular __temporary type. I should not exceed _____ mph while using it.

My car __does __does not require a special antitheft wrench to change a tire. This wrench is stored in _____.

My car __can __cannot be push-started.

The code number for touch-up paint for my car is _____.

My car __does __does not have an alarm system. If the system goes on accidentally, it can be disabled by _____ _____.

The following items on my car have electronic memory and must be reset if the battery is ever serviced: __radio __clock __trip computer __odometer. My favorite radio stations' call numbers are _____, _____, _____.

If my car is ever towed, the __front __rear wheels *must* remain on the ground.

The fuse box is located _____. Spare fuses are in _____.

The battery __does __does not require added water from time to time.

The headlights are __regular __halogen __quartz-halogen. The replacement part number is _____.

My car's engine has a __carburetor or __fuel injector. The fuel filter must be serviced every _____ miles.

The jack is located _____. It has _____ pieces. The diagram showing how to jack my car is on page _____ of the owner's manual.

The manufacturer of my car __does __does not belong to an arbitration program. If there are problems, the number to call is 1 (_____) _____-
_____.

If my car is leased to me, the lease expires _____. Then I __can __cannot buy the car outright for $_____.

Separate warranties for the following came with my car: __tires __battery __radio __rustproofing __alarm __other: _____. These are kept in _____.

My car __is __is not under extended warranty. It will expire _____ _____, 19____. My policy number is _____.

My insurance company is _____. My policy number is _____. In case of a serious accident I am required to call them at 1 (_____) _____-_____.

I am a member of the _____ auto club. In case of breakdown, the number to call is 1 (_____) _____-_____.

   Don't feel too bad if you had to look up most of the answers—very few people score well the first time they take this test. The fact is, today's cars —and their proper care and repair—are extremely complicated. That's why *this* book was written—it may be the most useful tool you'll ever own!

THE
CAR OWNER'S
SURVIVAL
GUIDE

INTRODUCTION

- Did you know that, in an emergency, you can move a disabled car (with a standard transmission) by putting it into second gear and cranking the starter for short bursts?
- Did you know that there are many automatic-transmission cars still on the road that can be push-started?
- Did you know that there is a product on the market that can inflate a flat tire—at least temporarily—in a few minutes?
- Tell me this, please: If your generator light comes on while you're driving, can you still drive the car for a bit, or must you shut it off?
- Speaking of warning lights, there is a simple way to make sure all of yours are in working order *before* you start a trip. Do you know how?

Cars have changed a lot over the years. Transmissions have gone from standard shift to automatic, and then back to standard again. (Five-speed "overdrive" transmissions are nothing new—just ask the fellow who was driving one back in the 1940s!) The traditional front-engine/rear-drive configuration has given way almost 100 percent to front-wheel drive. Body-on-frame construction has yielded to the new *unibody* design (new in North America, that is, but old hat in Europe). And the monster eight-cylinder motor has taken a back seat to multivalved, overhead-cammed, super-charged four-cylinder engines.

Simply put, the rules of the game have changed. The cars of the 1980s are not quite the same as the cars of any previous decade. Nor should they be treated the same:

INTRODUCTION

- Do you know whether your car can be used to tow a trailer? (Most newer cars can't!).
- Do you know what kind of tow truck to call if your car needs a lift?
- Do you know how much air pressure is right for your tires?
- Do you know what the maximum tire size is you can mount on your present rims?
- Do you know whether your spare tire is a full-sized, a miniature, or an inflatable? Do you know how to mount it in an emergency?
- Do you know the correct way to *boost* your battery—the way that minimizes the likelihood of an explosion, and reduces the chance of a *voltage surge* into your car's delicate computer circuitry?

Don't be surprised—or embarrassed—if you have difficulty with some of these questions: Most folks do.

But embarrassment is hardly the issue here. The issue is money. Hard-earned greenbacks. Not knowing the answers to these questions can cost you big money. There is a billion-dollar car-repair industry just waiting for you to slip up.

To take but one example: constant-velocity joints. These mechanical marvels, known as *CV joints* in the trade, are on virtually all front-wheel-drive cars produced today. Nine out of ten new cars come with them. Their function is somewhat similar to the *U-joints* found on rear-wheel-drive cars —except for three very important differences:

1. There are four CVs per front-drive car, compared to two U-joints per rear-drive car.
2. CVs wear out about twice as fast as U-joints.
3. CVs cost about fifteen times as much to replace as U-joints.

On page 210, I'll tell you how to double-check your CVs and minimize the likelihood of a needless repair.

The Car Owner's Survival Guide is based on a seminar I developed during my fifteen years as an automotive journalist. Unlike the tune-up courses that tell you *how* to make certain repairs or adjustments to your car, *The Car Owner's Survival Guide* tells you *what* to do—and *when.* And, more importantly, *why.*

There is a difference—an important one. As cars become more and more complex, there is less and less that you, the average owner, can actually do to fix your vehicle. At the same time, the marketplace of parts and services competing for your dollar is growing by billions of dollars each year.

There are a lot of people out there who want to help you with your automotive problems—for a price, of course. Whom do you choose? Which services do you buy? What should you pay? Is there an alternative?

The key to answering the questions I've raised is *information*. Information and, if you like, its half-brothers *education* and *intelligence*.

It is possible—and common—to go through life treating your motorcar as the enemy, Darth Vader. The great purple unknown.

That kind of approach works—but it's expensive. A major U.S. government study determined that most consumers *waste* fifty cents of every dollar they spend on cars and car repairs. The problem isn't that work is not done, or that parts are not installed. Rather, it's that the *wrong* work is done and the *wrong* parts are serviced at the *wrong* time by the *wrong* technicians—and at the *wrong* price.

Owning and driving a modern automobile is a major responsibility. It involves complex decision making and choices. Choices that start from the day you buy the car (new or used? standard or automatic? foreign or domestic?), and continue through day-to-day servicing (regular or unleaded? radials or bias? check the oil or change it?), right up until you finally unload the beast (dealer or private sale? best offer or a firm price?).

Want to make the right choices? *The Car Owner's Survival Guide* has exactly what you need: *strategy*. It's a guide to making intelligent decisions, going the most miles for the least dollars, and getting there in one piece.

Surprisingly, many of the questions I've raised in this introduction can be answered by consulting a reference book you already own—the manual that came with your car! (Most people don't really read the manual. Pity!) The answers to most of the rest of the questions can be found in the body of *The Car Owner's Survival Guide.*

No one expects you to finish this book, grab a wrench, and take your fuel-injection system apart. (In fact, the book needn't be read cover-to-cover at all. The chapter heads and index can direct you to the information you need.)

Here's what you should expect: Taking the time to familiarize yourself with your car can make your relationship with your machine a longer one, a safer one, and a happier one. It can also save you buckets of money in needless repairs. This book was designed with you, the reader, in mind. It will not only provide answers to immediate concerns (like how to get a stalled car off the highway) but will also direct you to other valuable information which may be useful "down the road."

I hope you enjoy reading it as much as I did writing it.

Happy Motoring!

Robert Appel
Buffalo, New York

1

WHAT YOUR CAR IS TRYING TO TELL YOU

● **WHEN:** The **air conditioner** delivers only hot air.

■ **WHAT TO DO:** Air conditioners are complex pieces of equipment and *dangerous* to work on without experience. The most expensive repair is replacing the compressor, but this is rare. Most repairs involve finding and fixing leaks, recharging the system with Freon, and correcting the temperature sensors that turn the system on and off. Aside from a few do-it-yourself suggestions (see below), see a professional mechanic.

The basic reasons the air conditioners operate erratically are:

Electrical. A switch may be faulty; a fuse (also called a *thermal limiter*) may need changing; a mechanical overload could be drawing too much power, triggering the circuit breaker; or there could be a simple short or accidental ground. See a mechanic.

Spare fuse?

Owners of older GM models have learned—the hard way—to keep extra thermal fuses for their air conditioners on hand for long trips. Newer models, however, don't use the device.

Mechanical. The compressor could be out of whack; the clutch could be bad; the vacuum-operated controls inside the dash could be leaky, broken, rusted, or frozen; or one of the belts that drives the compressor could be worn, broken, stretched, or slipping. See a mechanic.

Empty System. The two principal ingredients your air conditioner uses to cool things down are oil (for the compressor) and a refrigerant (usually Freon gas) as a heat-exchange medium. Did you remember to run your air conditioner a few times during the winter? You were supposed to: inactivity causes the various seals to dry out—and that eventually causes leaks. Even a properly running unit will lose gas every few years or so. A damaged unit with a severe leak (a bad fitting, hose, or seal) will disable itself almost completely. To help owners check out their systems without fancy equipment, many car air conditioners incorporate a "sight glass."

In case your car is one of the lucky ones, here's a primer on how to read a sight glass: *Condition One:* Clear after five minutes of operation—system is working properly. *Condition Two:* Some bubbling—needs a recharge. *Condition Three:* Large bubbles—needs recharge and possibly repair to correct leak. *Condition Four:* Oily streaks—system is dead. *Call a mechanic now.*

Say good-bye to sight glasses

Sometimes it seems like Detroit doesn't really want you to be able to communicate with your car. Just when consumers were finally beginning to understand what a sight glass was—and how to read it—car manufacturers have stopped installing them. A mechanic I spoke to says that it is still possible to check an A/C system without either a sight glass or special tools—but only if you've got sensitive hands and ten years of experience!

If you have tightened a loose fitting which had caused a leak—see a mechanic anyway. If the leak was severe, it may have admitted moisture into the system. A mechanic will be required to purge it.

HOW TO READ
A SIGHT GLASS

Clear—System OK.

Bubbles—System needs a recharge.

Foam—System needs a recharge and possible repair for leak.

Oily streaks—System inoperative. Call a mechanic.

> ## Danger
>
> Freon shooting out of a pressure valve can freeze and destroy an eyeball or a finger in seconds.

For leaks caused by the normal gradual loss of Freon over a period of months:

1. Use an inexpensive leak detector to verify that the system is in good order (your mechanic should have one).
2. Use an inexpensive recharge kit (complete with the proper gauge) to recharge the unit. These kits are available at most auto-parts shops.
3. Tighten all the fittings and check (or replace) the V-belt.

> ## Tips
>
> If your car has a special thermal limiter or fuse, carry a few spares. These are usually the first thing to check when your air conditioner gives up the ghost.
>
> - If the high-side connection on your air conditioner (see your manual) has a pressure port—*stay away from it. It's dangerous!*
> - Soapy water brushed on the hoses may show up fast leaks. (This same test works on tires.)
> - If you attempt your own recharge, never invert the can of Freon, during the recharge—this can admit liquid (instead of gas) into the air conditioner and damage the unit.

● **WHEN:** You hear noises from your **automatic transmission**.

■ **WHAT TO DO:** The automatic transmission is one of the most complex parts on the car. Many mechanics refuse to even touch them. Depending on the problem, repairs can run the gamut from a simple adjustment or gasket seal ($50) to an entirely new or rebuilt unit ($700). Repairs to four-wheel-drive vehicles cost even more—figure an extra $300.

There was a time, Horatio, when automatic transmissions were practically noiseless. In those days (my age is showing) the companies gave them names like Glideair, Powerthrust, and Whispersoft. While millions of Europeans drove to work in cars the size of shoeboxes, with the gear knob surgically embedded in their right hands, Americans floated to the office in yacht-sized land cruisers with automatic transmissions the size of Volkswagens. In those days actually hearing the transmission was grounds for returning the car and getting your money back.

Those days are gone.

Today's automatics have a *lock-up* torque converter, which constantly subjects the driver to a "thunk" as it engages and disengages. It also makes the engine miss for a split second.

Chuggle?

That's the *official* name for the driveability problems that come with the new lock-up torque converters. They are not exactly a hit with consumers. Owners have gone running to mechanics, dollar bills falling from their mitts, practically begging to have the things unhooked, but that's easier said than done. Some foreign manufacturers copied the American design but with one change—they added a simple switch so the owner could *choose* to turn the thing off if he wished. Also, GM has been experimenting with a siliconebased coupling that is supposed to minimize "chuggle." At the time of writing, this option was being offered only on their top-of-the-line Cadillacs.

OK—what if your transmission is making noises for other reasons? (The most common noise is a kind of whir-r-r, which means that the transmission is *slipping* between gears.) The *only* strategy open to you is:

1. Check the fluid level. If it's low, top it off and figure out where the leak was. (Ask your mechanic for help.)
2. Have the U-joints checked. Bad U-joints can imitate transmission noises better than Rich Little. They are expensive, but cost less than a new transmission.
3. Have the vacuum modulator checked (if your car has one). This is a cheap repair.
4. Give up and go to an expert.

Save your transmission!

If you use your car to tow a trailer and you have a small four- or six-cylinder late-model engine, have an automatic-transmission cooler installed. The transmission you save could be your own.

● **WHEN:** Your car **backfires**.

■ **WHAT TO DO:** Generally backfires are not dangerous. They may, however, cause extensive damage to mechanical systems.

There was a time when backfires were fun—on cars of the '20s and '30s, drivers would deliberately make their cars backfire when they passed a pretty girl, to show their appreciation. This was done with a dash-mounted timing control—a device that is making a comeback in the '80s, but for different reasons (see page 33).

Backfiring is no longer fun. There are two types—both can cause damage. The first type takes place through the air cleaner.

The other, and more common, backfire, takes place in a hot exhaust pipe when an unburned gasoline-air mixture ignites in the muffler.

Most *intake* backfires are caused by faulty spark-plug wiring; either a wire has worn, the wires were attached incorrectly, or a plug wire has shorted or cross-fired (the spark has jumped to the neighboring wire). Changing the wires on your own (a simple job) might do the trick. Otherwise, see a mechanic.

A bad intake valve will also cause intake backfiring. See a mechanic.

Backfiring in the intake (through the air cleaner) is a fire hazard in the worst sense. If the explosion ignites the fuel system, the result is serious trouble.

Exhaust backfiring is not as serious, but it's still a problem. It's not uncommon for a serious backfire to blow the muffler right off the car, perhaps onto a neighbor's lawn. There is also a more subtle type of exhaust backfiring called an "afterburn," which means that small amounts of fuel are being burned in the exhaust pipe. Afterburn is harder to detect than a regular backfire but generally can be identified by a small series of "pop" sounds in the muffler or tail pipe.

Most of today's exhaust backfiring is caused by out-of-whack emission-control systems. Verify that your car originally came with an air pump (also called an A.I.R. system) and off to a mechanic you go.

A faulty ignition system can also cause backfiring. Only a professional with a "scope" can properly do this diagnosis.

Backfiring only when the car is cold is a good indication that the choke mechanism is to blame. See a mechanic.

Finally, a bad exhaust valve can also cause backfiring. This usually shows up only on an engine with high mileage and only during hard acceleration. See a mechanic.

● **WHEN:** Your **brakes** feel funny.

■ **WHAT TO DO:** Adjusting, renewing, resurfacing, rebuilding, and bleeding brakes are all specialized jobs best left to the pro. At the first sign of brake difficulty, the brake-fluid reservoir should be checked and, if necessary, filled following the directions in your owner's manual. This may remedy the problem temporarily. However, regular need for more fluid is unusual—and even this symptom would require the attention of a mechanic.

The job of the braking system is straightforward. When you apply power to the pedal, the brakes should engage on all four wheels with about equal force. This slows you down. If you push extra hard, the brakes should lock the wheels where they are. Locking on ice or bad pavement may result in a loss of directional control (see page 92), but experts agree that locking all four wheels simultaneously may be the fastest way to stop the car.

Power brakes have an extra boost to help them push brake fluid through the lines—vacuum, produced by the engine, is channeled into a special system which greatly magnifies the pressure of your foot on the pedal.

If power brakes suddenly seem hard to apply—the vacuum line is disengaged or the vacuum booster is out of whack. See a mechanic.

Emergency braking

Most modern cars are designed so that, if the power unit fails, you can still brake with good old-fashioned foot-power. Unfortunately, most owners never need to try this until it's too late—and then don't apply enough power when it's needed. Test out your own emergency brake system (on cars with power brakes) by building up speed on an empty road, turning the key to "Off" (but not all the way to "Lock" or you'll lock the steering, and that's *big* trouble), gently pump the pedal once or twice to drain the residual vacuum, and then see how hard it really is to stop your own car!

If the brakes feel spongy or squishy—you've got air in the system, which has to be bled. The leak also has to be located and sealed. See a mechanic.

If the brake pedal goes all the way to the floor, or requires pumping to stop the car—either a small leak in the system is admitting air, *or* a major leak is losing brake fluid (usually at one of the wheel cylinders, or possibly even the master cylinder itself). See a mechanic.

If the pedal pulsates—one of the front discs is out of round. See a mechanic.

If you smell smoke or if one of the hubcaps feels hot—one of the brakes is locked. See a mechanic.

If the car pulls to the left or right when you brake—there is dirt on the linings, one of the pads is worn, or part of the mechanism is jammed or bent. See a mechanic.

If your pedal seems to go too low to the floor, but otherwise the brakes work properly, a simple adjustment on the rear shoes may be all that's required. (You'd have to hoist the rear end to do it, however.) See your manual.

Check your fluids

Don't let brake problems take you by surprise. Periodically, check the level of fluid in your master cylinder following the directions in your owner's manual. Loss of more than a teaspoon of fluid a month is *not* normal; it indicates a leak that must be dealt with. Also, visually inspect the hidden fluid lines of your brake system every now and then by peering under the car with a high-power flashlight. Be suspicious of wet spots (like those a dog leaves on a fire hydrant) near the *inside* of the tires—this is almost certainly a leak at the wheel cylinder. (See also page 209 on brake-maintenance checks.)

● **WHEN:** Your **brakes** squeak or squeal.

■ **WHAT TO DO:** There are three causes of brake noise: dirt (see a mechanic for a simple cleaning), wear-warning systems (see below), and damaged or bent brake parts (see a pro). A high-pitched noise that occurs only on braking usually indicates dirt. A constant high-pitched squeal while driving usually means the wear-warning system has been activated. A low, crunchy growl that intensifies as the brakes are applied indicates internal damage.

The most annoying brake squeal is caused by a built-in warning feature on most modern cars that warns the driver that the front disc pads have worn low and need servicing. Before this warning system was developed, drivers would allow the pads to wear so deeply that the discs themselves (costing several hundred dollars per wheel) would wear along with the pad. Proper maintenance of the pads before they have a chance to damage the discs can mean a substantial saving. See a mechanic.

Other brake noises (squeals, clicks, grinds, thumps) usually mean severe wear or a jammed or broken part. See a mechanic.

On many newer cars, brake noises can be caused by dirt or dust on the linings. This is normal, but annoying. Air-blowing the brakes clean (or using a special chemical conditioner) is not expensive. See a mechanic.

Finally, a trend has developed toward the use of different types of brake linings, usually called *semi-metallic.* These new materials deliver better stopping power and lining wear, but many owners have complained that the new materials are noisier than the old linings they replace. If you're curious, ask your mechanic if your particular make or model uses semi-metallic pads.

Use the right brake pads

Putting semi-metallic pads on cars not designed for them (or putting regular pads on cars that require semi-metallic pads) can dramatically hinder the braking system. Some mechanics have made this change in error—with disastrous results. Find out what sort of pads your car requires and make sure to use the right parts.

There is some evidence that semi-metallic pads cause greater wear on the other brake parts they contact, so that any savings realized on the linings may be wiped out by the cost of replacing the other parts more frequently. This is a controversial point, however—see your mechanic for details.

Got a plastic piston?

Many new car designs feature nonmetal pistons in the front brakes: ask your mechanic to see if this is your situation. These plastic pistons have proved troublesome. Installing a metal replacement part at maintenance time may be a good idea.

● **WHEN:** Your car is **burning oil**.

■ **WHAT TO DO:** Oil "burning" is serious stuff. It means that oil is seeping past worn engine parts, mixing with the air-fuel charge, and burning inside the cylinder. Some canned oil additives may help (see below). For a proper repair, however, some engine disassembly is usually required. "Living with it," by adding oil each week or so, will not damage the engine any further—it may be the cheapest solution to the problem.

First decide if you are truly "burning" oil (letting it enter the combustion process and get burned up) or simply misplacing it. Oil can leak faster than you'd believe. What's more, a tiny leak when the car is at rest with the engine off can turn into a gusher when the engine is on. Usually the fan will blow the oil back under the engine—so this type of leak doesn't leave much trace. If you are *leaking* oil, see a mechanic (and page 34).

If you are *burning* oil, try to figure exactly where the oil is entering the combustion process. Once you know that, the cure is easier to estimate.

Worn rings require almost total engine disassembly to reach, although the parts themselves are not expensive.

If you find that the problem really is rings, consider doing a major engine job, because fixing only the rings may simply lead to other problems as the related parts wear out.

Worn valves require removing the engine head, a job that is slightly less complex, but will still cost hundreds of dollars. See a mechanic for more info.

The problem could also be a broken head gasket (which requires head removal—see a pro), or worn valve guides and seals—which allow oil into the cylinders without any noticeable loss of power or compression (unlike worn rings, which are often accompanied by a lack of power).

Take your tests

Don't guess in the dark—don't let your mechanic convince you to "open her up" (a costly process) without first trying the quick inexpensive diagnostic tests. These include: electronic cylinder-balance test, dry-compression test, wet-compression test, and—for purists— a cylinder-leakdown test. Opening the engine to look for the problem can cost hundreds of dollars, but any of the above tests can be done for less than $20 or $30.

If valve guides or seals are the problem, consider having the valve-stem seals replaced—initially, by themselves; only if the problem persists, should you proceed to the valve guides. The reason for following this strategy is that the seals can be replaced without removing the cylinder head—using an air-pressure technique that most shops are equipped to handle. Taking the heads off to service the guides is three or four times as costly. This problem is very common on today's cars, by the way. It is the result of excessive engine temperatures, which virtually melt down the seals over time. If you do decide to have the seals replaced, ask for Teflon seals.

Avoid commercial additives for oil consumption—these are no more than oil thickeners. The same results can be achieved by switching to a heavier oil.

Is some oil consumption normal?

Yes, indeed, it is. There was a time when fine European cars' manuals would specify how much oil the engine would ordinarily burn every 1000 miles or so—something that most American car manufacturers would consider blasphemy! To protect against internal engine problems, your best offense is a good defense. I recommend frequent oil changes (based on elapsed time, not elapsed mileage) with a new filter every change. If you have a four-cylinder engine and you ever tow a trailer, I recommend an oil "cooler" as well. (It is generally thought that the standard cooler-in-the-radiator is insufficient.)

● **WHEN:** Your car "chugs" (**diesels**) after it is shut off.

■ **WHAT TO DO:** Although generally harmless, every now and then an engine will diesel backward (against the normal rotation of the crankshaft). This condition, although rare, can do extensive damage.

This condition is called "dieseling," because the engine is somehow firing without a spark (the key is off—right?). That's exactly how a diesel engine works: it fires without a spark.

Dieseling is embarrassing, especially on a first date. One solution is to "play" with your car. The dieseling might stop, for example, if you rev the engine just before shutting it off, or, on a manual shift, if you shift to neutral and put the clutch in just before you cut the power.

If "playing" solves the problem, bully for you. If not you may have to:

1. have the ignition timing reset;
2. repair or replace one of the emission-control parts; or
3. (on an older car) have some excess carbon scraped out of the upper cylinder area.

See a mechanic.

Cleaning out the carbon

Newer cars collect carbon in the upper cylinder area quite easily. This can lead to dieseling or, worse, pinging (see below). Periodically take your car out on the freeway and "gun" it (floor the accelerator for a few seconds at a time) to clean out the carbon. Or have your mechanic use an upper-cylinder cleaner (usually applied through the intake). This procedure is inexpensive but may require a new set of spark plugs afterward.

● **WHEN:** Your **engine** knocks or pings.

■ **WHAT TO DO:** Sad to say, pinging on acceleration is quite normal on the newer cars. If the pinging lasts for only a second or two, live with it. Prolonged pinging, however, can damage the internal parts of the engine. See a professional.

Ping is the sound of marbles dropping in a tin can. It comes from under the hood and may only happen for a second or two at a time. It is quite serious and quite common to most cars built in the '70s and '80s. If left unattended, it can cause portions of the pistons themselves to melt inside the engine. Such damage is very expensive to repair.

Do-it-yourself ping check

Verify knocking or pinging by pulling the plugs and looking for the signs of overheating plugs—white tips or blistered electrodes. In severe cases, parts of the plug will have molten fragments of your piston clinging to it.

There was a time when pinging was the equivalent of a social disease for cars. When I was a young lad (the '50s), knocking or pinging meant that your gasoline wasn't strong enough for your car, and that you should switch up to "premium" leaded gasoline. The same reasons still prevail today, but the situation has changed somewhat:

First, today's engines are made smaller and, to work harder, they must be "tightly tuned." This, in theory, means pushing the engine to the point where it pings (that's its most efficient "performance zone") and then easing up just a bit. In reality, however, these tender tuning variations— done lovingly by the factory mechanics—go quickly out of whack in the real world, resulting in pinging.

Second, today's gasolines are like something out of a science-fiction movie. A satisfactory replacement for lead has never really been found (would I lie to you?) and the necessary octane rating really isn't there. Many engines that need higher octane are forced to try to survive on the lead-free stuff—which, according to my car, tastes awful!

Third, the emission controls and computers on today's cars can clog or go out of adjustment—and the *first* symptom of this is usually pinging.

Fourth, pinging can be the result of simple incompetence on the part of manufacturers. There are a lot of cars on the road today that ping because they were designed badly right from the start! Overzealous engineers

V-8 LONGITUDINAL VS.

Comparison of longitudinal and transverse engine layouts.

Not all engines are created equal! "Longitudinal" engines were more common during the heydey of the V-8. Today's 4-cylinder engines are likely to use a space-saving "transverse" mount.

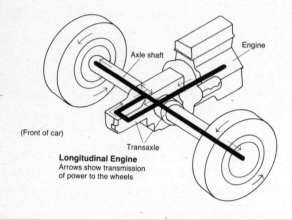

Axle shaft

Engine

(Front of car)

Transaxle

Longitudinal Engine
Arrows show transmission
of power to the wheels

TRANSVERSE 4 CYLINDER

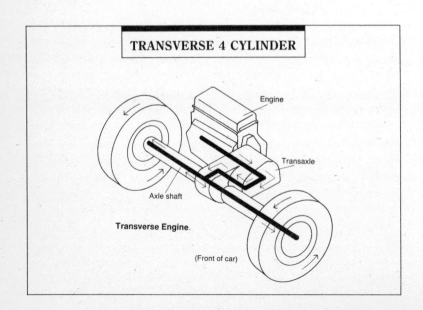

Engine

Transaxle

Axle shaft

Transverse Engine

(Front of car)

created systems that worked on the drawing board, but that ran into problems in the real world. Many cars built in the '80s have had special "factory fix" bulletins, which instruct mechanics how to remedy ping by undoing mistakes made on the line.

Ping got you down?

If all else fails, find out if there is a "factory fix" bulletin outlining some special technique for your car. A good list (only one of many) was published in the January 1985 issue of *Popular Mechanics* (page 82). If your local library doesn't keep back issues, write to the publisher.

Fifth, the recent popularity of turbos has made the problem even worse —if anything will make a car ping, turbocharging will! Most (but not all) modern turbos come with a "ping sensor," which electronically remedies the pinging problem as it happens. If you have a turbo and your car pings, have the sensor checked.

Last but not least are those car buffs still driving muscle cars from the '60s and '70s—these cars will ping all the time unless they get premium leaded gas.

Muscle-car lovers

If your car was originally designed for *premium leaded gas,* you can, in addition to all the fixes described below, try to contact a racing association in your area and see if they have a source of racing fuel. Racing fuel is, more often than not, simply aviation fuel that has been appropriated for racing use, but since there is more than one type of aviation fuel on the market, and it's illegal to sell this stuff directly to car owners anyway, your best bet is a friendly racer.

> ## Warning
>
> There are cans of additives on the market that purport to turn low-octane fuel into high-octane fuel. These are *extremely expensive* and are suspected of causing internal engine damage over the long haul.

If your car pings, there are a number of things you can try to do:

1. If your car takes leaded gas, combine premium unleaded in equal parts with regular leaded. (If you can find premium leaded, grab it!) If your car takes only unleaded gasoline, try premium unleaded. If nothing happens, try changing gasoline brands.
2. Ask your friendly mechanic to retard your timing 2 to 6 degrees. This will lower mileage and performance, but it's a cheap, fast fix for pinging.
3. Consider adding a "ping control box" to your ignition. This will automatically retard timing as needed to deal with ping, and then advance it again. It costs about $150 installed and any good "speed" or accessory shop can get you one. A variation on this is a "timing switch," which you can control manually from the dash to adjust the timing as you prefer. These also cost about $150 installed and allow the car buff a greater degree of experimentation. "Custom-tailoring" your own timing-advance curve on long highway trips can result in high miles-per-gallon numbers that would make even the EPA blush. These things may increase emissions, however.
4. On older high-performance racing engines, some owners have thrown in the towel and had a thicker head gasket installed in the engine, decreasing the compression ratio and emasculating the engine. This is both an expensive and a desperate move. (Note that rebuilding or overhauling a worn engine may lead to pinging because, in "shaving" the block and head, you may be slightly increasing compression and, hence, the possibility of ping.)
5. Have the entire emission system double-checked by a top-of-the-line mechanic. *Some 50 percent of pinging problems are directly attributable to out-of-whack emission controls.*
6. Try a "colder" range of spark plugs (this works sometimes).
7. Your engine may be carboned up, and this may have artificially

raised the compression ratio. (A compression test will confirm this with a higher-than-normal reading.) The best fix is opening up the engine and scraping out the carbon, but this is also costly. Pouring tune-up solvent into a running engine may do it, but BEWARE!— on late-model cars this method may foul the plugs, the catalytic converter, and the "wire sensor" or "oxygen sensor" in the emission system (if there is one).

8. Too much engine oil—believe it or not—will lead to oil foaming and pinging. Check your dipstick.

9. Other things to check for: a bad cooling system, a stuck heat riser, a vacuum leak making the gas-air mixture leaner, a bad head gasket, a restricted exhaust (including a clogged catalyst), a stuck EGR valve, or an improper vacuum-advance part.

10. Water injection systems (ask your mechanic) are wonderful for controlling ping but are complex to install, require regular filling, and may shorten engine life. Ask your mechanic to recommend a good brand.

● **WHEN:** Your **engine** misses or stumbles.

■ **WHAT TO DO:** As a general rule, *all* missing or stumbling is a result of intermittent ignition or fuel-delivery problems. Another rule of thumb that often works is that missing at high speeds is usually ignition-related (try a new set of wires) and missing at low speeds is usually fuel-system-related (the most common fix is a new fuel filter).

Any further diagnosis requires an expert mechanic, usually with a scope.

Do-it-yourself ignition test

Wait for a dark, moonless night and pop open the hood of your vehicle while it's running. (If you have an automatic electric underhood light, disconnect it in advance.) It *may* be possible to pinpoint underhood ignition gremlins by the telltale arcing or blue corona that they give off. This bizarre test could save you hours of diagnostic time. Another simple test is to remove the plugs and look at them. An all-black plug tip (where the others are normal: gray or gray with orange flecks) means that the spark is not reaching that plug. Changing the wire to that plug may well solve your problem.

● **WHEN:** Your **exhaust** smoke is colored.

■ **WHAT TO DO:** Careful diagnosis is required to figure out the cause of colored exhaust smoke. Black smoke indicates a misadjusted fuel system —simple and inexpensive to repair. White or blue-gray smoke indicates internal engine wear, which could require total engine disassembly.

Exhaust smoke doesn't exactly come in a rainbow assortment, but you can get the following shades:

White. Short bursts of white smoke when starting a cold engine are *normal,* and mean that moisture within the system is burning off. A steady billowing stream of white smoke, however, usually means radiator contamination—that antifreeze and water are somehow getting into the combustion chamber. The most common cause for this is a head gasket that warped when the owner allowed the vehicle to overheat. Taking an engine past the red line on the tachometer will sometimes have the same result. This condition can only get worse, not better, so off you go to the mechanic.

Black. Exhaust smoke is black when the air-fuel mixture is too rich— too much fuel. When the choke comes on, it makes the mixture rich for a while, but only temporarily. If the exhaust is black all the time, not only are you polluting the environment (ugh!) but you are burning more fuel than you ought to (ouch!).

The tailpipe test

Have a peek at your car's tailpipe when it's just come off the highway after a long trip. It should be a sandy gray color. If it is excessively black or sooty, you are burning too much gas. Either the choke is not shutting off, or the fuel system is out of whack.

Blue. This one's easy. Blue-gray exhaust smoke means that you're burning oil. (see page 16). That's hardly good news. Check your mirror when driving or have a buddy follow behind you and report. Blue smoke on *acceleration* usually means worn rings. At idle or deceleration it usually means that valve guides and seals are in need of attention. Constant blue smoke means that you are a very, very neglectful car owner. Testing of the compression and cylinder balance by a mechanic can tell more.

● **WHEN:** Your car's **idle** is rough.

■ **WHAT TO DO:** I'm not going to kid you—a rough idle is hard to pinpoint, especially on the new computer-assisted cars. (If the computer is bad the whole unit needs replacing—and only your dealer should attempt it.)

First check the obvious. If the idle problem happens only on cold starts, the choke is suspect. If it happens in the rain, the wiring needs examination. If it happens only after a long drive, the carburetion system should be checked. If the engine has many miles on it, there may be excess gum or carbon in the intake area or the upper cylinders.

If it's a really rough idle and it happens suddenly, maybe a plug wire has shaken loose. Turn off the engine and look under the hood (but keep away from the fan—on modern cars it can start even with the engine off).

A vacuum leak also can cause a rough idle. Open the hood with the engine running and listen for a high-pitched whine. A good mechanic can spot a vacuum leak by ear, and many new vacuum-leak testers are audio-based. The old fashioned dial-type vacuum gauge is useful as well—an increased reading when the suspect hose is pinched confirms the leak.

Finally, if you have not serviced or inspected your ignition recently, one of the plugs may be fouled or shorted—an ignition scope can pinpoint this problem in minutes.

● **When:** Your **instrument panel** says "help."

■ **What to do:** Do you have "idiot lights" or gauges—or a combination? Idiot lights are little red lights that tell you there is a problem long after it's too late to do anything about it. Gauges give much more useful information —if you know how to read them. (If you have only the lights, consider upgrading to gauges. See also page 33)

A SHORT COURSE ON
SOME SPECIAL GAUGES

Voltmeter. There are two different systems that supply power to your car. The first is the battery, which provides the power to start the car; the second is the alternator, which provides ongoing power to the ignition system (and accessories, lights, etc.) once the car is started. What happens to the battery once the car is running? Essentially, it's out of a job—but it does stand by in case the alternator should fail. If its charge is low, it will take some power from the alternator to recharge itself.

If you are lucky enough to have a real voltmeter, check the available current with the ignition key turned on but with the motor off. This will give you a reading on the battery alone. It should read at least 12.5 volts. Next, check the reading with the engine running normally. It should be no more than 14 volts and no less than 12. If the reading is more than 14 volts, the alternator is *overcharging* and may damage the battery. If it reads less than 12 volts it is *undercharging* and your battery may have to provide emergency power (on a temporary basis only). Either situation demands a mechanic.

If you have only a red idiot light, consider investing about $25 for a real voltmeter.

Let's not forget plain old-fashioned neglect!

Many times when trying to track down complex mechanical problems, we overlook the obvious. Battery not holding a charge? Maybe that time you had one too many at a party and left your lights on for two days simply took the zest out of it. Maybe you haven't been minding the water level. Maybe one of your kids poured Jell-O into the cells. Maybe one of the cables is loose—or dirty. Maybe the ground connection (the wire that goes from the negative side of the battery to a clean ground) is loose or dirty. Don't forget: check the obvious!

Oil-pressure gauge.   If your engine is running properly, if there is enough oil, if the bearings are not too worn, and if there is nothing clogging the pump or pickup screen inside the engine, this gauge should read in the normal range (see your manual). If not, *stop the car at once*—driving with low oil pressure will damage the engine faster than anything I can think of.

GAUGES

These simplified illustrations show how to read typical gauges that you may encounter. See your owner's manual for how to read the gauges on your car.

A) *Combination turbo-vacuum*. Section left of zero line indicates level of engine vacuum, which increases as needle moves to right. (Higher vacuum can be related to better mileage.)

Center section indicates degrees of turbo-boost, which increases as the needle moves right. If the needle passes the second line, it indicates a dangerous *overboost* condition.

C) *Water temperature*. A reading between "C" and "H" is normal. See your owner's manual.

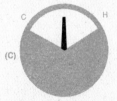

E) *Ammeter*. Needle should be in charge zone (towards "C") about 90% of the time. If the needle is in the discharge zone (towards "D") frequently, battery failure is probably imminent. See a mechanic.

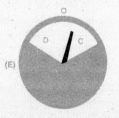

B) *Voltmeter*. A reading between 11 and 13 volts is normal. See your owner's manual for details.

D) *Oil pressure*. A reading between "L" and "H" is normal. An "L" reading at idle—only if the engine is hot—may also be normal. See your owner's manual.

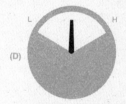

F) *Oil temperature*. This is a newer gauge found mainly on exotic cars. Your engine should not be driven too "hard" if the oil is either too cold or too hot. See your owner's manual.

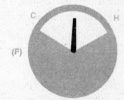

On a badly worn engine, expect low pressure on cold mornings, on long highway trips, at idle, and when using an oil of too low a viscosity.

Driving with insufficient oil in the sump will *always* provide a low pressure reading—but the reading will snap back up if the oil is topped off.

There are additives on the market that will boost low oil pressure, but these are stop-gap remedies at best.

---

*Noise and low pressure—the deadly duo

If you have only an idiot light for your oil, you really don't know whether you have *low* pressure or *none* at all! With some pressure you could—in an emergency—drive a short distance. With no pressure, the engine will be *destroyed* almost immediately. How to tell? A low-pressure light accompanied by a serious sounding noise from the engine means that the game is over—the engine is dying. If there is no noise—and you *must* drive on—proceed slowly to a repair bay.

Temperature gauge. In most cars this indicates the temperature of the engine coolant. Some fancy race machines have gauges show the temperature of the engine oil *or* transmission fluid. Don't confuse one gauge for another!

Let's face it: few cars get into trouble because they get too cold. The most common problem you are likely to have is *overheating*. Overheating is serious stuff. The internal-combustion engine (some call it the "infernal"-combustion engine) can theoretically produce enough heat to melt itself into a puddle. Long before that happens, of course, the pistons will seize in their cylinders and the engine will stop. The only thing preventing a malfunctioning, overheating engine from going this horrible route is *prompt* action by the driver. A temperature gauge (either a dial or a digital readout) can give the owner plenty of advance warning because the needle will slowly creep into the danger zone. The idiot light will give almost no warning at all. One second all seems to be well; the next everything is melted engine. The dial type is recommended. It will cost you about $25.

What if your engine does overheat?

If your car has an old-fashioned belt-driven fan, pull off the road and rev the engine in neutral to cool it. If you have a new thermostatically run electric fan, try turning the heater on to full blast. If either of these remedies seems to make no difference, or if things get worse, switch off the engine and call for a tow.

Two things *not* to do: don't ever try to open a hot radiator to add water. Don't ever try to drive an overheating car the extra mile to the station. (Even if the engine doesn't seize up en route, valve-ring and gasket problems will probably start to appear weeks later.) See also page 73.

Ammeter. Also called a charge-discharge gauge, this works like a voltmeter, only more simply. It simply shows whether current is flowing *to* the battery (when, for example, the engine is running, the alternator is powering the ignition, and an additional trickle of power is being sent back to the battery to recharge it) or *away* from it (as when the alternator is overtaxed and the battery is temporarily helping out). In a properly running auto, the needle would read C for charge or 0 for neutral. A voltmeter is preferable (see above). If the readings are heavily into D for discharge, see a mechanic.

Gas gauge. This tells how much fuel is in your car. Generally it falls to 0 when the engine is cut off—unless you have the newer "zombie gauge" (see page 259). The EMPTY reading usually means you have a gallon or two in reserve—see your manual. Few gauges are really precise—most gauges seem to drain the bottom half of the tank a heck of a lot quicker than the top half. The newer digital types feature a "scale change," which allows you to see just how little gas you actually have left when you are down to your last few gallons. Driving when there is very little gas left ("running on fumes") is risky—stray water can be drawn from the bottom of the tank into the engine, where it can damage fuel components. Air sucked into the line in the same way may damage delicate emission-control sensors.

Vacuum Gauge. Never heard of this one? A vacuum gauge is possibly the greatest one of all, because it is both simple and inexpensive.

All engines (except diesels) produce vacuum. How much or how little vacuum an engine produces, and how the gauge varies under normal operating conditions, can help a mechanic determine the true condition of your engine. In fact, in the days before emission controls, $1.50-per-gallon gas, unibody front-drive econoboxes, and computerized "black boxes," mechanics used to use a five dollar vacuum gauge to diagnose major mechanical ills!

A top mechanic could tell from a few simple tests with the gauge whether there was valve or ring damage inside an engine without having to remove the head—something most mechanics no longer seem able to do!

The major at-home use for the gauge turns out to retrain drivers, to improve their mileage. Driving with one eye on the gauge, avoiding sudden losses of vacuum by easing up on the accelerator pedal, brought mileage gains of up to 30 percent in tests by major oil companies.

The vacuum gauge also proved useful for adjusting the idle mixture on the older cars that permitted this and—in conjunction with a vacuum pump (a $30 gizmo)—complex tests could be done on the emissions-control systems of cars of the late '70s and even some from the '80s. In fact, with a vacuum gauge, a vacuum pump, a tire gauge, and a bicycle pump, the patient, thoughtful do-it-yourselfer might well be able to perform maintenance and repair procedures on modern emission, fuel-injection, and even turbo-charging systems!

Recently, yet another major use was discovered for the omnipotent vacuum gauge—spotting clogged catalytic converters on post-1975 cars. If the vacuum *de*creases as the engine speed increases, you have a blocked converter.

In addition to all the above, keeping a close eye on day-to-day "baseline" vacuum readings (at idle) will allow you to figure out *exactly* when your car goes out of tune (the baseline readings will drop). Last (but not least), a combination vacuum and boost gauge on a turbo-charged car can generally help you control the turbo with accelerator-pedal pressure; you can maximize mileage, keeping the turbo boost in reserve—until you need it!

All right, you say, what does it cost and where do I get one? The cost is about $10 to buy and another $10 to install. If you have fuel injection, figure an extra $5 to reroute some plumbing.

The vacuum gauge is one of the easiest accessories to install. Only two major procedures are required: splicing into an existing underhood vacuum line with a T-fitting ($1), and screwing the gauge onto the dash.

Vacuum warnings

On the most modern cars—with ultrasensitive fuel injection—adding any accessories at all (vacuum gauges included) may affect the fuel metering. Check with your factory representative first (see your owner's manual for a phone number or address). Some little four-cylinder engines produce uncharacteristically low vacuum and require boosters in the engine compartment to run accessories—see your representative for more information.

Turbo-boost gauge. Yes—this one is a bit silly, but if you can afford the $3000 turbo option, you can probably afford a silly gauge that tells you when it's on. (Not all turbocharged cars have the gauge—some have only idiot lights.)

Generally, the only value of the boost gauge is to tell you when the system is overboosting and has to be fixed. (In truth, however, the manufacturer doesn't trust the owner to understand this. Most turbo systems automatically turn themselves off if they go into overboost—see *electronic scattershields,* page 249.) By adding a full combination turbo-vacuum gauge on your own, however, you can not only keep the boost pressure under your own watchful eye but use the vacuum end of the gauge to keep mileage up —the best of all possible worlds!

If you are lucky enough to have a manual shift with a turbo, you can use to gauge to make sure the turbo doesn't come on when you don't want it to. Otherwise, if the turbo is on all the time, as with an automatic coupled with a turbo, you will pay a substantial penalty in gas mileage and engine wear.

Silly gauges and dials. Depending on the make and model of car you drive, there are lots of other gauges that could be trying to talk to you. (Some cars have had gauges that actually *talked,* saying profound things like, "a door is ajar." Consumers universally hated them and they aren't as common anymore.)

You might be told for example that your overdrive is off. On newer cars with automatic electronic overdrive, this means that you have overridden (or "locked out") the overdrive feature. Although the car will seem more spunky on the highway, the mileage will not be what it should be.

If you have one of those "pick-a-suspension" options, you may be told that you are are in the sport-suspension mode instead of regular. If you happen not to be feeling sporty that day, or if your mother-in-law is with you, you can push another button and switch back to regular suspension. Chances are, no one will know the difference—or care.

Your car may remind you that you are due for an oil change (Honda), that your EGR (exhaust gas recirculation) valve needs inspection (BMW), that your window-washer fluid is low (shame!), or that you are late on a car payment or that your cat is stuck in a tree. Frankly, I think all these are a waste of time, but there is no accounting for taste.

A SHORT COURSE IN IDIOT LIGHTS

Battery light. If this light comes on, it indicates that the battery is no longer receiving charge from the alternator (or, in older cars, the generator). The problem is either a broken belt or an electrical failure in the charging system. *Do not turn the engine off,* or you may never get it started again. You can drive for ten or twenty minutes before the current becomes too weak to run the ignition.

Oil-pressure light. Shut off the car as soon as this light comes on. If it only glows briefly at stop signs or after long trips, see a mechanic.

Temperature light. As noted above, this light indicates a serious problem that must be dealt with immediately. Stop your car and turn off the engine. (See also pages 28 and 73.)

Brake light. Depending on the make and model you drive, your brake light may mean you have left your parking brake on (careless, aren't we?) or, *more important,* that you have lost pressure in one of your brake lines. Reduce speed immediately—as you may have little or no braking power left —and get to a garage!

Brake mysteries

Rarely, the brake warning light will come on mysteriously just after some major brake work has been done to the vehicle, although, in fact, the pressure in all the lines is normal. This happens when the mechanic improperly resets the proportioning valve after the job. A repair will take only minutes.

Does it make sense to convert from idiot lights to gauges? I think the answer is yes, all the way. A good mechanic can install a professional gauge package on most cars for less than $100. One caution, however: on computer-controlled cars (most built after 1980) be careful not to discard any wriring from the old idiot-light circuitry. Some of the leads may serve also send information to the computer. Disconnecting these leads will make the car run poorly. If in doubt, contact the manufacturer of the car *or* of the gauge package you want to install.

● **WHEN:** The **instrument-panel lights** flicker or dim.
■ **WHAT TO DO:** The panel lights on virtually all cars are controlled by a variable rheostat similar to that in your living room. First locate this control (see your manual) and make sure it's set to maximum.

The next step is to look at the obvious: your alternator. An alternator that otherwise performs adequately but in fact is slightly undercharging will dim the lights at idle but strengthen them at full or part throttle. If this is the case, consider consulting a mechanic. Repair procedures vary from little things (adjusting the regulator, cleaning the ground) to major parts replacements. If the problem does not get worse, you may be able to live with it for quite a while.

A bad ground wire or a loose housing on the bulb itself may cause erratic performance. This can only be verified by removing the panel and inspecting the bulb (try shaking it gently).

Finally, most instrument panels have their own tiny one-piece solid-state regulator, which can cause all sorts of problems if it goes bad. A replacement is inexpensive but, once again, the dash must come apart (see your manual).

● **WHEN:** Your car is **leaking** its life's blood away.

■ **WHAT TO DO:** Diagnosing the cause of the leak is the first and most important step. Placing a newspaper under the car at night often helps pinpoint the source. Repairs can vary from simply tightening a fastener ($5) to replacing the head gasket in the engine ($500) or rebuilding the torque convertor in the automatic transmission ($800). Auto-parts stores feature cans of inexpensive "stop leak" treatments for most engine systems and—except where contraindicated below—these inexpensive treatments should at least be tried before going to a mechanic. Another inexpensive solution (except for brake-fluid leaks) is to carry around cans of the appropriate fluid and "top off" the leaky system from time to time.

First decide which vital fluid is ebbing away:

Radiator fluid. Losing radiator fluid *can lead to overheating* if not attended to. (Ask for a *pressure test* at your garage to assist the diagnosis.) This mix of antifreeze and water can seep from the radiator or radiator hoses, the engine block, or heater connections (including those *inside* the car). Here's a tip: if rubbed between the fingers radiator fluid leaves a sticky residue. It also smells like bad soup.

Leaks at hose joints mean that the hose clamps have to be tightened. If that doesn't work, either the hose is cracked (change the hose) or the elbow is cracked (call a professional). Block leaks usually require a mechanic. A freezer plug or a head gasket may be at fault. Heater core leaks also require a pro.

Radiator leaks can be repaired. The best repairs are off the car—with the whole radiator being overhauled, rodded out, and refurbished. Some new materials (available at the local parts shops) make it possible to do repairs with the radiator on the car. Try it—it can't hurt. (They work like two-part epoxy glues, require cleaning the application area beforehand, and must not be used at temperatures below freezing.) Leakseal chemicals like Barrs are usually acceptable, but (this is a long shot) may damage something. Pepper, oatmeal, cornmeal, and bran (the traditional home-brew leak sealers) are for emergencies only. They go better in baked goods, frankly.

The leak detector in your medicine chest

Aerosol cans of body or foot powder make great do-it-yourself leak detectors. Clean the suspected component, let it dry, and saturate the areas involved with powder. Within twenty-four hours the source of the leak should be apparent.

Automatic transmission fluid.   This is usually red and oily to the touch. The leak could be internal, in which case you should either call a professional or try a can of a transmission stop-leak formula. Some of them do work for a while. External leaks may be in a fitting, a vacuum line, a sensor, or simply a loose fastener. You won't know until you ask. Occasionally transmission fluid leaks into the radiator through the *cooler*. (The transmission cooler is a special passageway within the radiator for the circulation and cooling of transmission fluid.) A expert can spot this problem by examining the radiator fluid with a practiced eye.

Gearbox, steering gear, rear axle fluids.   Like engine oil, these are black and oily to the touch. Most of these repairs are *not* expensive. Usually a gasket has to be renewed or a fastener tightened.

Power-steering fluid.   Like transmission fluid, this is red and oily to the touch. If you are lucky the problem is only a hose (about $35) or a loose fitting. If you are unlucky and have a newer car with both rack-and-pinion steering (which some say is named after the torture instrument) *and* power assist, you could be looking at several hundred dollars in repairs. Trying a can of stop-leak can't hurt.

Engine oil leaks.   There are hundreds of places that engine oil can leak out of. The easiest to fix is the bottom pan—simply tighten a nut or change the gasket. Next, in order of complexity, come the rocker gaskets (these are hard to get to on the smaller engines), followed closely by the front engine seal, rear engine seal, and head gasket. Sometimes the oil pressure sender—a temperature-sensing device the size of a wine-bottle cork—can cause trouble as well. New products designed to stop leaks in engines work (as do transmission stop-leaks) by swelling old-gasket materials. They may do the job for a while.

OIL LEAKS

Where under-car leaks show up. Front-drive cars do not show the same pattern.

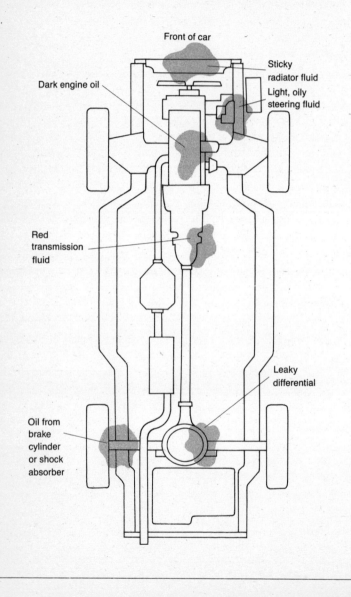

Front of car

Sticky radiator fluid

Dark engine oil

Light, oily steering fluid

Red transmission fluid

Leaky differential

Oil from brake cylinder or shock absorber

Brake fluid. This feels like light oil (but it can blister paint). It usually accumulates around the inner tire area if the leak is at a wheel cylinder.

Don't mess around here, bub. This is your life we're talking about. Anything from a pinhole in a line to a faulty master cylinder to a defective booster unit can cause a leak. Call a pro and get it fixed.

Gas. Gasoline is a thin dark-looking fluid with the distinctive gasoline odor.

Mechanics hate gas leaks. They're messy, smelly, hard to find, hard to repair, and occasionally lethal to boot. Some leak only when the engine is running (this could be the fuel pump or the carburetor) and some leak only when the car is left standing (this usually means a weakness in the fuel line caused by residual pressure in electronic fuel injection systems). New test systems work in a fashion similar to radiator pressure testers—they artificially pressurize the tank and delivery lines. See a professional mechanic.

Water. Whoa!—cars don't leak water. What can happen is the following:

1. Air-conditioner condensation on hot days. This is harmless.
2. Tail-pipe dripping. Newer cars have special drain holes in the tail-pipe to let condensation out before it turns acid. This is also harmless.
3. Water leaking from door or fender after rain. This means that drain holes in the body are clogged. If you don't unclog them soon, you'll find only a pile of rust waiting in the parking spot your car used to sit in.

Plumbers take note:

Teflon plumbing tape, the stuff that plumbers use, works wonders on automotive fittings as well—particularly gas and radiator connections. I've seen five cents' worth of this stuff make the difference between a permanent repair and a temporary one.

● **WHEN:** Your car is **leaking water**.

■ **WHAT TO DO:** Strange but true: cars are not supposed to leak (but many do anyway). The most obvious place for a leak (and the easiest to repair) is at one of the rubber gaskets around the windows, door, hatch, or trunk.

Open all the doors (and trunk, if involved) and inspect all the gaskets. The gasket around a suspected leak may be dry, brittle, cracking, or soggy—all as a result of repeated exposure to water.

No luck? Put a sheet of newspaper around the door (or trunk) and close the door with the paper stuck in between. Try to remove the paper. The area where it pulls away *the easiest* is the place to look at for a leak. (The same test can be done with a dollar bill instead of newspaper. Send the bill to me for inspection when done.)

Here's yet another variation: coat all the black gaskets with a film of spray-on talcum powder, close the doors, put a helper (younger brothers work well) inside the car, and hose down the outside. This test is doubly revealing. First, the seepage should be visible at the leak from inside the car. Second, the powder, when the door is open, will be disturbed at the site of the leak.

What to do when you have pinpointed the leak: If the old weatherstripping has simply come loose, get a quality silicone glue and reglue it. Some experts would also shim it up at the same time by putting a few inches of new weatherstripping (such as the kind made for homes) under the weak area and gluing it in. This will raise the area that leaked and make a tighter seal.

If the old weatherstripping is damaged, the pros say you should replace the entire piece. This is not as easy at it sounds—and often two pairs of hands may be required to set the new piece in place. Your dealer is your best source of weatherstripping—for older cars check specialty magazines like *Cars & Parts.* See page 235.

Leaking around the windshield (front or rear) is a job best left to a pro, and should require removal of the window and replacing the entire gasket. However, kits are available (for under five dollars) which allow you to dig out all the old glue and insert an exceptionally strong temporary seal into the leak area. The odds of these working are 50-50, and the repair will never look really neat.

Get thee to a body shop

If you do go to a pro, remember that you want a body shop, not necessarily a mechanic. If you go to your dealer, he should send the work to his own body shop. Leaks are expensive to repair because diagnosis takes so much time, and because (like rattles in the dash) mechanics don't enjoy the work and often do a less-than-perfect job the first time. If your enthusiasm exceeds your common sense and you do try to remove a windshield on your own, you need: (a) a helper, (b) a special removal tool, and (c) luck. Even professionals with the right equipment have trouble removing modern windshields in one piece.

The final, and most agonizing, leak is at the carpet, usually under the dashboard. First, these leaks, if undetected, can result in rust, rot, and foul odors. In one situation I even saw the moisture interact with the carpet glue to produce mold and mushrooms! Many mechanics say the problem can be traced to a faulty seam or weld under the floor but, in my experience, this type of leak is often made worse by owners who park under shade trees and allow their ventilator ducts to become clogged with leaves or debris. The debris causes the rainwater to seek a new path out of the channel— right into your car! Try flushing the "catchall" ducts on the hood with a high-power hose and see what happens.

● **WHEN:** Your **mileage** isn't great.
■ **WHAT TO DO:** Few cars can actually meet their EPA (or Transport Canada) rating for mileage. In fact, most cars average only about 60 to 70 percent of the manufacturers' mileage claims. If your mileage suddenly gets a lot worse than it has been, however, it usually means that the mixture has richened unnecessarily (too much gas is being mixed with the air). A rich mixture will not seriously damage a car, but it can cost you extra money for fuel, and the ignition system may foul up prematurely.

When people get sick, they usually cut down their food intake. Cars are just the opposite—they begin to take in more gas.

Bad mileage is a sign that something is out of whack. A thorough diagnosis should be made by a professional, particularly on today's emission-controlled cars.

First, check the air-fuel mixture. Try to confirm your suspicion that excess fuel is burning by looking for gasoline (sooty) deposits on the plugs, black smoke coming from the tailpipe, or carbon residue on the end of the exhaust pipe. An *exhaust analyzer* (most garages have one) can check this fairly quickly by detecting the unburned hydrocarbons (gasoline) in the exhaust.

Naturally, do the obvious tests as well—look for gasoline leaks at the tank, at the fuel pump (some cars have two), and at the engine. Smell the oil and make sure that gas is not seeping into the oil through the fuel-pump gasket. Check the hoses and routings on the charcoal canister (see your manual) and make sure nothing is clogged.

The choke system should be given the closest scrutiny. A choke that sticks in the "on" position will go through gas like it was water. (And the car will appear to run well, too). A small thing like a clogged air cleaner will also make the mixture rich enough to cause problems. Change it every 5000 miles.

Is your engine getting hot enough? Short trips on cold days don't give the engine a chance to heat up. Much of the gas enters the engine in liquid form—and excess fuel is used. Malfunctioning emission controls can cause fuel-consumption nightmares. The EGR (exhaust-gas recirculation) system and vacuum-delay system in particular, if clogged, can dramatically raise fuel consumption in city driving.

Suspect the unexpected. Do you have a brake dragging somewhere? Even the parking brake may be stuck slightly—that would certainly ruin your mileage!

If your car is an automatic model, is the idle set too high? That would lead to excessive racing of the motor or "creeping" in the city—which would not only waste gas but also make you use the brakes up faster as well.

On a late-model car that gets bad mileage only on the highway, suspect a problem with the new lock-up or overdrive transmissions. You may end up having to see a transmission expert (See page 133).

Finally, have a look at your own driving habits. Jackrabbit starts and racing to stoplights can only lead to wasted gasoline. Working with a vacuum gauge on the dash (see page 30), drivers have been able to shuck bad habits and reduce gas consumption up to 30 percent!

For more on miles per gallon, see pages 39 and 140.

● **WHEN:** You hear **noises**.

■ **WHAT TO DO:** Noises, like leaks, require careful diagnosis. Generally, the louder and more serious the noise, the greater the likelihood of damaging an expensive mechanical component. Always check under the car first —a dragging tree branch or a fallen muffler can sound a lot more threatening than it really is.

A properly running automobile has been described as a symphony of sound—no one noise should be distinguishable above the others. If you do start to hear things, it's best to find out what the problem is before it's too late:

Underhood whistle (like a teakettle). Have your mechanic check for a vacuum leak.

Underhood banging. Metal parts too close together are the most likely cause. Visually inspect the hoses and clamps for proximity. If the noise is coming from *inside* the engine, you've got trouble with a capital "T" —shut down and call a mechanic.

Underhood knock when driving. It could be ping (see page 18) or it could be a symptom of serious internal engine wear. A likely culprit these days is the fan coming out of alignment (due to a bump or small fender bender) and hitting the components near it.

Underhood rattle. The only thing under the hood that rattles is the engine timing chain. See a mechanic.

Underhood squeal. This is almost certainly a loose belt. Tighten or replace. If the noise comes only when you turn the steering wheel sharply, the power-steering reservoir may be low or the pump unit may need service.

Underhood ticking. This is valve noise, pure and simple. On older American cars, it usually means that the lifter bodies are fouled and need cleaning and replacing. On the newer econoboxes with small engines (and manual valves) it means that the valves are way out of adjustment. You'd better attend to it before you damage the valve train.

Underhood pop.   What sounds like a "pop" on a car is usually the absence of sound (as opposed to a backfire, which is a real explosion—see page 12). Most "pops" mean that, for a split second, the engine did not fire. Ask your mechanic for an ignition checkup.

Dashboard click.   This is usually the speedometer cable. Have it lubricated before it gets worse. Your manual may give you some pointers, but it may require a mechanic (or a circus midget) to get to it. (Newer equipment allows pressure-lubing the cable from the transmission end instead of the dashboard end—see if your garage can do it).

Dashboard rattle.   Lots of things behind the dash can come loose— all too often including the dash itself! These things take hours to find, so decide in advance if you want to spend the time or the money fixing it.

Window whooshes.   Any unusual wind noises coming from around the windows usually means that the window-track mechanism is out of adjustment or that the rubber gasket needs fixing. Oddly, you'll get more satisfaction if you ask a body shop to make the repair than a regular mechanical shop. Try this test: stick a sheet of newspaper between the body and the window and close the window. If the paper pulls out freely, there is definitely a problem.

Tire rattles.   Usually a stone in the hubcap.

Tire thump.   Either a cold spot in the tire from being out all night, a flat tire, or a defective tire.

Wheel clicks.   This could be a bearing or a damaged brake part. This is serious—so go see a mechanic. This can be a particularly complex problem on front-drive cars—see page 210. A steady repetitive click from one of the wheels while driving almost certainly means that you've picked up something in a tire—a stone or a nail is the best guess. Pull over and check it out.

Wheel hum.   If it comes from the rear wheels, this probably means that it's time to take off the snow tires. Anything more serious and the rear axle itself is likely the culprit.

Warning to four-wheel-drive owners

Unusual noises from the *rear* wheels in a front-drive vehicle with four-wheel-drive engagement, or the *front* wheels in a rear-drive vehicle with four-wheel-drive engagement, usually means a malfunction in the four-wheel-drive engagement process. *This could be costly if you continue to drive the vehicle.* On GM rear-drive cars with automatic front hub locks, for example, a clicking from the front wheel during four-wheel-drive engagement means an *incomplete* engagement (or disengagement) of the front hubs. Either try to complete the engagement process (see your manual) or call for a tow.

Undercar thunk. If it occurs when shifting into gear, this usually means a worn universal joint (rear-drive car) or worn CV joints (front drive). This can't get better—it can only get worse. Have it fixed.

Exhaust drumming or amplification. If your car suddenly sounds like you're A. J. Foyt about to cut loose at the Indianapolis 500, you've got a bite-sized hole in the exhaust (probably at the muffler). Off to the muffler shop you go.

Bump, thump, or clunk. Noises that occur only when you go over a bump point to a suspension problem. A part could be loose, broken, bent, or missing altogether. Loose or bent shock absorbers are another possibility.

Nonspecific squeaks and rattles. All cars have these. The newer unibody (frameless) cars have them worse than ever. Learn to live with them.

● **WHEN:** It takes more effort to turn your wheels, even with **power steering**.
■ **WHAT TO DO:** One of two things has gone wrong: either the power steering belt is slipping (tighten or replace it), or the fluid level in the pump is low (fill it, and have a mechanic find out where the leak is).

Pump failures are *extremely rare* in power steering units. They are one of the most reliable units on the modern motorcar. However, the pulley on the pump can get out of line through incompetent or abusive mechanical work, or an accident. If this happens—the first symptom will be V-belts wearing at the pump prematurely—the pump unit itself will eventually fail.

● **WHEN:** Your **radio** gives you the silent treatment
■ **WHAT TO DO:** The radio circuitry (the ground, speaker, and antenna connections) is the most common source of problems. Unless you are good at electrical troubleshooting, invest in a few hours of diagnostic time at an auto-electric specialist.

It's rare for the radio itself to break down—most modern units are made up of solid state electronics that should be good for years. If the problem *is* in the radio, however, remove it and send it back to the manufacturer. Your dealer probably won't be much help—nine out of ten times he'll have to send it back to the manufacturer anyway.

If the radio quits totally, suspect either a power problem (current not coming in) or a ground problem (current not having a path to leave by).

Most radios have two fuses—the first is a conventional fuse located in the main fuse box. The second is a separate "line" fuse located on the power line to the unit. Check that both are working with a probe tester or by substituting a known good fuse.

Is *static* a problem? Try to identify the source of the static by seeing if it's still a problem with the engine turned off (it shouldn't be), or if it's only a problem under certain conditions (during braking, or while using the heater fan), or at certain locations (for example, underground garages).

If the static is unique to a specific location—either don't go there (!) or learn to live with it.

If the static is present with the engine off, suspect a bad ground connection under the dash, a bad ground at the antenna, a short at the antenna, or a faulty (internally shorted) antenna.

If the problem is static when the engine is running, things get a lot more complicated. Manufacturers have designed many types of "static suppressors" into their various models (these could be anything from specially selected ignition wire to finger-sized suppressors hidden all over the car). You can't check these out without first knowing where they are. See your dealer.

An auto electrical expert or a radio specialist may be more valuable here than your regular mechanic. (You can, on your own, use a simple volt/ohm meter to check the ground connection. Look for high resistance, and check for shorts.)

When is a ground not a ground?

Checking radio wiring can be confusing at first. Most people understand that every electrical connection on the car operates on the two-wire principle: one "hot" wire and one ground. The radio is a bit different, because its antenna wire—which runs up from the radio into the antenna mast—also has its own separate ground (usually to the car fender). Therefore, a mechanic checking the radio would first check for a hot wire to the radio, then check the ground connection at the radio, then check for continuity between the antenna wire and the antenna post on the fender (there should be full continuity—no resistance), then check for continuity between the fender and the base of the antenna post (again, full continuity), and finally, look for a short between the antenna post and its base (this should show no continuity—infinite resistance).

Some more tips: Power antennas are a nuisance. If you suspect yours has given up the ghost, replace it with a regular unit. Never overlook a bad connection. Jiggle (I think that's the scientific term) all the wires. If the reception improves, you have located either a bad ground (tighten or resolder) or a bad connection (straighten the pins or use a butt splice and redo the connection).

When a pin is not a pin

Amazingly, the connecting pins on the newer cars are also victims of technological innovation. Since they couldn't make the multi-wire connectors work any *better,* the Detroit engineers made them *smaller* and *more delicate.* When doing any work with the newer multi-pin connectors, invest an extra $2 in a special tool that lets you take the connector apart without destroying it. The other—and more familiar —alternative is to use a "piggyback" splice or connector that simply attaches a new wire on top of an older one.

Finally, the trim screw. All radios have them—and the way to adjust them is to tune in an AM station at the high end of the band (about 1400 kHz) and turn the screw for maximum reception. In real life, however, the trim screw is almost never the cause of the problem.

Rubber warning

Flexible rubber antennas are big news in urban areas because they discourage anti-social types from snapping off your antenna for amusement while waiting for a mugging candidate to drop by. The word on the street, however, is that the cheaper brands don't work particularly well, and that putting a rubber antenna on your $2000 stereo may be the automotive equivalent of shooting yourself in the foot.

● **WHEN:** Your car **rusts**.
■ **WHAT TO DO:** Most body rust is cosmetic damage only, and repair isn't really necessary. However, on a car five or more years old, at least have the floor pan, the trunk floor, and the frame and subframe inspected each year. Rust holes in the floor pan and trunk floor can admit poisonous carbon monoxide fumes. Subframe rot can undermine steering and suspension integrity—with disastrous results!

Before going any further, you've got to understand that I *hate* rust.

My very first car, a new 1971 VW fastback, rusted to death in two years. (I sued the dealer and won. Big deal—I still miss the car.) One of the cars I now own is a 1972 Pontiac LeMans with 110,000 miles on the original engine and suspension. The car gets about 20 mpg (with some modification from me), runs as silently as a Jaguar (I should know—I test them), and uses almost no oil between changes. One problem: I bought it used, and the previous owner had allowed rust to build up inside the panels, under the vinyl roof, inside the frame, under the floor, inside the rocker panels, inside the trunk, and all around the firewall. Mechanically, the car could run for another fifteen years with minimal maintenance. Chassis-wise, I'll have to scrap it in the next year or so, because of rust. (Can it be repaired, you ask? At a cost of seven or eight times what the car is worth, it could be. Ouch!)

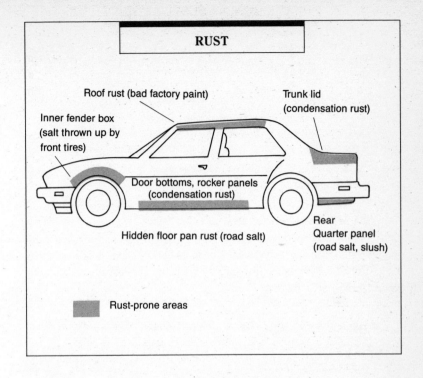

RUST

Roof rust (bad factory paint)

Trunk lid (condensation rust)

Inner fender box (salt thrown up by front tires)

Door bottoms, rocker panels (condensation rust)

Hidden floor pan rust (road salt)

Rear Quarter panel (road salt, slush)

Rust-prone areas

Most people hate rust but don't understand it at all. Look at some myths about rust:

Rust is cosmetic damage only. Balderdash. Rust can undermine the frame on a unibody car and weaken its structural engineering. Rusty brake lines can cut the usefulness of your brakes by over 50 percent—and a rusty gas line can dribble gas. Rusty floor pans can let deadly carbon monoxide fumes into the interior.

The newer cars don't rust. They don't rust the same way, but they do rust. Newer cars use lots of zinc and hot wax (that's good) but the metal itself is thinner (that's bad). Trust me—the new cars *will* rust.

My car didn't rust for the first three years, and then it rusted. That's like saying I was pregnant for a few weeks and then I had a baby. Rusting is a long-drawn-out process; rust starts on the inside and works out. While you're reading this, your car is rusting (rust never sleeps), but the results may not be obvious for a year or two. The trick is to stop the rust early, before it gets a foothold.

Rust is a problem only where salt is used in winter.   Wrong again. There are rustproofing shops doing a thriving business in California and Tahiti. The *Wall Street Journal* identified small areas in Africa and the Middle East as two of the worst spots on the globe for automotive rust. Even the morning dew in a mild climate can collect inside doors and fenders and—over time—cause rust.

I park indoors in winter to stop rust.   That *helps* rust. Ever notice how your windshield fogs up from condensation when you go inside a warm garage on a cold day? That same condensation is taking place on every square inch of sheet metal throughout your entire car. While you are eating dinner, your car is rusting.

I have a plastic car. Plastic doesn't rust.   Congratulations—but your plastic car has a *skeleton* of steel. That rusts. Ever wonder why you can't find a vintage '58 Corvette in someone's barn in Alaska? Think about it. . . .

My car was rustproofed by the dealer. I'm safe.   No, you're gullible. Dealers used to make about a 30 percent markup on cars and, although car prices have gone up (they like that) their margins have gone down (they don't like that). As a result, dealers everywhere have developed protection packages which they sell to starry-eyed buyers seconds after the contract for the new car has been signed. The leading item in the package is usually rust protection. It lists at about $400 but—because the dealer is in a good mood and really likes your face—you can have it for only $300. These treatments consist of about a quart of tar, like material poorly applied by a gas jockey in the back room. The dealer's cost is about $20 and, since he's selling it for ten times cost, he's making back some of the profit Detroit took away. Don't go away—there's more. The tar-and-wax-type treatments dry and flake off over the years. (Did you ever leave a tin of shoe polish open overnight? What happened?) The residue of the coating actually tends to *trap* water and *accelerate rust* from about the fourth year on. Don't you feel silly?

I wax my car often and wash it often. Isn't that protection?
Barely. Studies done with taxi drivers show you would have to wash and
air dry the car almost twice a week for its entire life to end up with any
effective rust treatment.

OK, wise guy, what's the answer? I have maintained for years that
the only effective anti-rust treatments are based on yearly high-pressure
application of an oil-type material that has built-in agents to creep and crawl
and resist drying. In Canada, where this *wet* method (a term I coined years
ago on a national radio broadcast), has finally caught on, many companies
have entered the field and the competition is quite fierce. Look for something similar on sale in your area. Yearly high-pressure treatment (inside the
panels and underneath) with motor oil is not as good as the specialized oil
processes, but it is light-years ahead of the tar and wax processes. *Never,*
for God's sake, use old motor oil—it contains unburned gasoline (a fire
hazard), it's acidic (it'll eat through an open soup can), and—worst of all—
the U.S. government EPA has determined that it is a major carcinogen.

See pages 107 and 126 for more information about rust.

● **WHEN: Screws** are **loose.**
■ **WHAT TO DO:** This is a real nuisance. You reach for the door handle
and it comes off in your hand. Or you grab the armrest and it pulls out of
the panel. Most owners reach for a screwdriver and tighten the screw. If
it tightens, the threads are good. If it doesn't, they're stripped. In the latter
case, consider an oversized screw or a Helicoil brand thread repair kit, or
take the damaged part to a local machine shop for a cheap quick fix. If the
threads are all right, but the screw loosens every few weeks, dab the end
of it with a thread-sealer like Loctite. One drop will do it!

● **WHEN:** Your **signal lights** won't signal.
■ **WHAT TO DO:** If the lamp is totally dead, one of three things has
happened: The circuit to the lamp may have blown, broken, or shorted. This
requires a mechanic, unless only the fuse is blown—see page 81. Next, the
ground connection at the light may have corroded, possibly from water
contamination at the lens. In this case, remove the lens and bulb, sand down
the connector, and check the rubber seal on the lens for water leaks. Third,
the bulb may have simply burned out. (If this is what has happened, replace
it!—see your owner's manual for correct sizes.)

If the signal indicator light on the dash won't flicker, it usually means that either the flasher unit itself is bad (this is an inexpensive repair—the hardest part is finding the part under the dashboard), or that one of the bulbs on the "dead" side—corresponding to the nonflashing indicator—is out for the reasons outlined above. Usually, just changing the bulb will solve all your problems.

Other sticky situations: If any lights are wearing out too fast, the regulator in the alternator circuit is overcharging. See a mechanic.

If the lights are dim or flicker. The alternator is undercharging or there is a bad ground somewhere. If only one bulb is flickering, suspect a loose connection or bad ground right at that bulb.

If the light flashes too slow or too fast—somebody somewhere has mismatched the flasher unit and the bulb it operates. There are both heavy-duty flashers and heavy-duty bulbs. If you use the wrong combination (and there are a few wrong combinations to pick from: regular bulb with heavy-duty flasher, heavy-duty flasher with regular bulb, etc.), the light will work but at the wrong speed. Check the parts codes on your lights and flashers and match them to your service manual.

● **WHEN:** Your car **smells** strange.
■ **WHAT TO DO:** First, check for the obvious (and most unappealing): something could have died in the car (I know of a cat that slept under the engine until the fan caught it), or one of the children could have forgotten some food under the seat, days, months, or even years ago.

Notice a rotten-egg smell when you park? Easy—that's simply your catalytic converter doing its job. Learn to live with it.

Smell rot? That's probably what you have. The carpeting and the under-pad have been known to absorb water and moisture over the years—this process can get a bit smelly. Commercial disinfectant and some new mats should do nicely.

The smell of burnt wiring is pretty distinctive. Theoretically, the fuses, breakers, or fusible links are supposed to see that the wires don't actually melt, but some wires will short and melt anyway. If you find melted wiring, fix the cause first and then *replace* the wires—even if they still work. Don't trust them!

Gasoline is an odor that can't be mistaken for any other. Treat this smell *seriously*, as a broken or ruptured gas line can be disastrous. Diagnosis is complicated by the facts that gas evaporates quickly (without leaving a wet spot), and that serious leaks might not even show a trickle with the engine off (because the fuel line is not pressurized). Here's a trick: Gasoline tends to clean anything it touches, so look for suspiciously clean surfaces. If your car has a carburetor and you smell gas but can't find a leak, suspect that your carburetor needs an overhaul, or that your engine has flooded—see page 72. An inexpensive device has recently appeared on the market that makes it possible to *pressurize* the gas tank—while it's still on the car—and so check for leaks in the lines.

If you've been driving the car hard (substitute the word *torturing* in the preceding sentence), then that bad smell is either a burnt clutch or a burnt brake pad—or both! Lighten up before you break something!

Finally—the smell could be overheating transmission fluid. This stuff has a smell quite unlike anything else on the planet and—once you smell it—you'll never forget it. Sniff the transmission dipstick to verify and then get thee to a mechanic.

● **WHEN:** Your car is hard to **start**.

■ **WHAT TO DO:** Starting problems are annoying but, except for starter "kickback" (see below), they usually mean a maximum expense of $50 to $150 for a new starter, new battery, or overhauled ignition.

Hard starting is the first sign that something in the engine or ignition (or both) is out of whack. The first thing to do is define the problem—when does it occur?

Hard starting in *wet weather* almost certainly points to water in the primary or secondary wiring. The distributor cap may also be involved. Take this problem to your mechanic and, once the problem is solved, waterproof your wires with a commercial plastic or silicone product. In a pinch, an anti-wetness agent like WD-40 spray may get you going.

Do-it-yourself damp diagnosis

Fill an old spray bottle with water and systematically soak down portions of the ignition system—first the coil tower, then the cap, then the secondary leads, then the plugs, and so on. By trying to start the car after each soak, you will be able to pinpoint the vulnerable area fairly quickly.

Hard starting in extremely *hot weather* points to fuel percolation (excessive heat in the fuel lines). In the good old Texas summertime, motorists would start their old Chevys by pouring Coca-Cola over the carburetor and fuel hoses. The cold liquid would usually be enough to turn the overheated gasoline fumes back into a liquid. These days fuel systems are considerably more complex than on an old Chevy—see a mechanic.)

When the car has been standing for some time, chances are the fuel in the carburetor has settled out and the fuel pump may have to turn for 10 or 20 seconds before the fuel bowl is reprimed. This condition is not serious and does not demand immediate attention. (A porous fuel bowl is likely, or perhaps a faulty fuel valve at the pump.)

Hard starting *after taking on gas* often points to water contamination in the new fuel. This is serious; you may have to completely flush out the tank and gas lines.

Hard starting in *cold weather* is tricky, because it combines all the problems previously discussed. The fuel lines could be frozen (try "dry gas," which pulls the moisture from the line), the moisture in the air could be shorting the wiring (see above), or the battery could simply be unable to perform.

Battery blues

Turn on the headlights. Are they as bright as they should be? Now turn the ignition key—does turning the engine over dim the headlights or cause them to go out? No lights or lights that dim mean a battery problem—nothing else can be done to the car until the battery problem is solved.

Finally, never forget the *choke*. Even a cold summer morning can require some engine choking and, if this system is not up to scratch, the car won't start.

Hard starting accompanied by a *strong gasoline smell* means carburetor flooding (a similar condition can happen in a fuel-injected car—even though there is no carburetor). Make sure your starting technique is correct (read your manual) and then check in with a mechanic. For more info on flooding, see page 72.

If the starter sounds like it's chewing ball bearings every time you crank it, you have starter *kickback*—the starter and the engine flywheel are not meshing correctly. *Stop cranking*—damage to the flywheel is much more serious and costly to fix than damage to the starter. See a pro!

The best way to deal with any hard-starting problem is by going to your mechanic and having the repair done before the car refuses to start at all.

● **WHEN:** Your **steering** feels loose.

■ **WHAT TO DO:** Step lively!—loose steering is often the first step towards no steering. Any unusual variation in steering *feel* should be reported to a mechanic. Steering control can be completely lost if the problem is allowed to get worse.

There is a measurement on virtually all cars called *steering free play.* You can gauge it (verify this method by checking your manual) by centering the steering wheel, turning the engine off, and gently twisting the wheel to the left and right until you feel resistance. This is a subtle test—the wheel should turn only about one inch.

If your car fails the free-play test, either the steering gear is badly out of adjustment or the steering mechanism is worn. Loose steering can be caused by other problems as well:

- Over inflated tires
- Worn tie rods, tie rod ends, or ball joints (worn CV joints in a front-drive car)
- Seized components in the steering *box* or rack
- Worn shocks
- Bad alignment
- A front end that's been in an accident.

Excessively "tight" steering can, oddly enough, result from similar causes and lead to equally disastrous consequences. Ever-increasing steering effort is usually a prelude to the steering or suspension mechanism binding or "freezing." Once again, repairs are best left to a pro.

● **WHEN:** The **steering wheel** is off-center.

■ **WHAT TO DO:** It's pretty easy to figure something is wrong when you point the wheel straight and the car heads off at an angle. However, this odd problem usually develops just *after* the wheels have been aligned. It means the job was done badly.

To check for this, make sure the steering is otherwise in good condition. Find an empty, straight, level road without banking (and without snow or ice). While going straight at about 35 mph, release the wheel (do this carefully) and see what happens. If the road has no bumps or irregularities, the car should travel straight ahead for 3 or 4 seconds.

If your car passes this test, take a corner quickly and see if the steering wheel centers by itself, without your having to unturn it after turning the corner. It should center automatically. If it won't, you should suspect a major front-suspension problem in the making or, on front-drive cars, wear in the strut systems.

If your car passes these two tests and recently had an alignment, an off-center wheel indicates that a sloppy mechanic aligned the wheels without making sure that the steering wheel was centered *before* and *after* the job.

Go back to the same shop—it will have to be redone.

● **WHEN:** A **tire** has a slow leak.

■ **WHAT TO DO:** Slow leaks are a pain because, like taxes, they never go away. Getting them fixed is also a chore because, if the leak is really slow, most shops won't be able to find it in the first place.

So here's the scoop: Most slow leaks are either at the *valve* (the short, skinny piece of tubing that protrudes from the tire) or at the *rim* (where the tire fits against the wheel). If you think you have a valve leak, change the valve. What have you got to lose? It's only a $1 part, and you can change it yourself with a small tool that also costs about $1. The valve screws in and out like a light bulb—this simple repair could solve all of your problems. Don't even bother looking for rim leaks. Simply instruct your mechanic to clean the old rim and reseal (and rebalance) the tire. This should cost about $15 and—unless the tire was factory-defective—this should solve your problem.

In any case, don't forget the old tried-and-true test for leaks: the leak tub at your local garage. The tire will be dunked under water; bubbles will show where the leak is.

Defense against flat tires?

As you read this a new product (available under several different brand names) is going on sale throughout the United States and Canada. The product, a liquid tire sealer, is injected into the tire while it is still young and healthy, before a leak develops. The idea is that, if a leak ever develops—even a rim leak—the liquid will seal it.

Do they work? The tire-sealants of the first generation were a disaster—they even ruined the rubber in the tire. The newer ones seem to have licked most of the problems, and several of these companies actually have endorsements from fleet owners. The main —and only—advantage to these products is that you never have to worry about flat tires again. (See page 175.)

● **WHEN:** Your **tires** wear too quickly. Take a moment or two to examine the tread on your tires. Tread patterns are designed to be symmetrical across the width of the tire *footprint.* Any wear variation in these patterns is not normal. Often only an alignment specialist can find the problem. Doing nothing could reduce the useful life of a tire by over half. However, the safety risk from this problem is minimal.

■ **WHAT TO DO:** Tire wear doesn't seem right? Let's consider the question posed by the famous Dr. Kinsey: What is "normal," anyway?

On modern cars, the wear should be uniform across the tread. That is, neither side of the tread nor the center should wear first. Everything should wear evenly. If in doubt, bend down in front of the car and compare the left front tire to the right front. Unusual wear patterns will be obvious.

Tire wear can be affected by a number of factors:

1. The characteristics of the brand of tire.
2. The performance characteristics of the tire (high performance and long tread life don't usually go together).
3. Whether the tire itself was defective.
4. Whether the car has front-wheel or rear-wheel drive.

TIRE TREAD WEAR

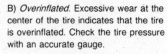

Typical tire tread wear patterns and what they mean. Note that there is no established tread-wear pattern for all-weather radial tires—they are quite unpredictable.

A) *Wear bars*. Excessive wear will expose wear indicators across the surface of the tire. When this happens, it's time to replace the tire.

(A)

B) *Overinflated*. Excessive wear at the center of the tire indicates that the tire is overinflated. Check the tire pressure with an accurate gauge.

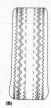

(B)

C) *Underinflated*. Excessive wear at the outer edges of the tire indicates that the tire is underinflated. Check the tire pressure with an accurate gauge.

(C)

D) *Cupping*. "Cups" or "scallops" worn on one of the outer edges of the tire indicate a suspension problem. Have the suspension checked and replace worn suspension parts with new ones.

(D)

E) *Camber*. Excessive wear on one edge of the tire only indicates incorrect wheel camber or misalignment. Have your alignment checked.

(E)

F) *Feathering*. Excessive wear on one edge of *each rib* of the tire (see top edge of illustration) indicates misalignment or improperly set "toe-in." Have your suspension checked.

(F)

Unequal tire wear

Rear-wheel drive cars used to give approximately equal wear on all four tires provided the owner observed normal and reasonable maintenance procedures. This is not true with front-wheel drive. Even assuming a fastidious owner who does everything by the book (particularly this book!), the rear tires will outlast the front by about two to one. One way around the problem (and I'm not sure this really is a problem) is to rotate the tires, but many experts feel that tires "set" on the wheels they are being used for and should *not* be rotated. My advice is to: (a) look after your tires, and (b) on front-drive machines, change the front tires as required. I side with those who think tire rotation is a waste of time.

5. Inflation. Either under inflation or over inflation will cause premature wear.

6. Whether the alignment on all four wheels is correct.

Alignment all around

It's not just the front wheels that need alignment—all four do. In the old days of frame-mounted cars with engines in front drive wheels in back, mechanics virtually ignored the rear tire specifications and consumers never even knew they should be aligned. (I, on the other hand, have had the rear alignment on my classic '68 Cougar checked at least once.) However, with the advent of the new frameless front-engine/front-drive cars, rear alignment has become crucial. In 1985, Ford made history by issuing a massive recall notice simply to adjust the rear alignment specs on their Tempo and Topaz models! If you drive one of these new econoboxes, make sure your mechanic has the equipment to do the job—and get it done each year.

7. Driver habits. (Hard cornering will wear the front tires unevenly.)

8. Whether the front suspension parts are "tight." (A loose part should be replaced since, even if *properly adjusted,* the part will not "hold" an alignment.) Generally, regular lubrication will keep the parts tight, except on the most recent models which no longer have access holes to allow lubrication. (Damned if you do, and damned if you don't!)

9. Whether the car has been in an accident.

Bad news for front-drive owners

As millions more front-drive models hit the streets each year, mechanics are learning things about the design they really didn't want to know. One of the latest bugaboos is that, if the front portion of a front drive car is in an accident, damage to the steering, suspension, or subframe may result, which is either impossible to repair at all or —worse—impossible to repair a *second* time if the the *first* repair was done incorrectly. (More good news: the metal used on today's cars won't take more than one repair without weakening anyway.) If you are not the first owner of your car and the front tires wear poorly even after an alignment, suspect a previous collision. This is serious! See an expert immediately.

Using all-weather radials?

No question about it. All-weather radials—tires that can be used all year long, in summer or in snow—are an idea whose time has come. However, the design is relatively new (five years or less) and some problems are just now coming to light. The main one seems to be uneven wear—unusual wear patterns that do *not* come from any of the causes discussed above, but are simply characteristic of the tire. If in doubt, buy only a name brand like Michelin.

● **WHEN:** Water mists mysteriously on the inside of the **window glass**.

■ **WHAT TO DO:** Some inside condensation on the glass is normal, particularly if you park the car outdoors. However, heavy water deposits especially when the heater and defroster are used often, usually point to one cause—a pinhole leak in the heater-box element, which is allowing radiator fluid to be picked up by the fan and carried through the interior. This can only get worse—see a mechanic.

First, though, make sure that you are using your heater controls correctly. If you have a set marked FRESH and RECIRC (recirculate), then using RECIRC will artificially fog up the inside of the windows, closely matching the symptoms of a heater-box leak! Read your owner's manual!

● **WHEN:** Your **wipers** won't wipe.
■ **WHAT TO DO:** First things first:

Does the wiper motor work at all? If not, the switch may be out, the circuit may be broken, shorted, or improperly grounded, the motor may be jammed, or it may be simply burned out.

Does the motor move the wipers too slowly? If so, I'll bet even money you live in an area where the winters are tough—moisture has contaminated the wiper bushings and the mechanism is seizing. Dissassembly and lubrication can get you back on track.

Spritzers won't spritz? If only one does, the other one is clogged. If neither one does, first undo the hose just past the pump and turn on the switch. If the lines pump out mightily, then the pump is good but the lines are both clogged. Either replace the lines with new hoses and jets or clean them with compressed air, pipe cleaners, and sewing needles.

If the spritzer pump is bad, a new one can be had for under $30—and installation is within the scope of the do-it-yourselfer. If you're feeling particularly tight, there are universal—fit models—which splice in series into the hoses on the original—for under $15—and they work!

Wipers streak? When was the last time you changed them? V-J day? They should be changed twice a year. (That's assuming you want them on the windshield for a purpose other than decoration.) I recommend the *composite plastic* types over the metal in cold climates because the metal ones tend to freeze up. I also prefer changing the blade and refill together (rather than just the refill). The saving is only a few dollars and the blades are tricky to fit.

Wipers miss? The wiper arm (the part with the spring) should not require replacing under normal use, so, before you do something drastic, oil the spring and, using a pliers, *gently* bend the arm toward the glass to get a tighter fit. If that doesn't help, replace it. (It comes off easily and without the need for much force.)

Wipers smear? Either the blade refills are worn or you are using the wrong detergent in the pump. Some brands smear more than others. Are you replacing the blades every 6 months like you're supposed to? (Here's a tip: regular cleaning of the blade edges of the wiper with a cloth and mild detergent will just about triple their useful life.)

Windshield Wax

There is a new product on the market—sold under different names —which treats the windshield to a wax job, supposedly makes the wipers work better, makes it easier to see in the rain, and reduces icing. I've tried the stuff and although it does work it's hard to apply, expensive, and must be reapplied about every other month.

If your wiper hits the window post on every pass, it is possible to remove the arm from the shaft and reposition it slightly so that it doesn't hit. This can be done with only a screwdriver and some patience. If the problem comes back after a day or so, see a mechanic.

2

WHEN THINGS GO WRONG

- **WHEN:** You have an **accident** (whether a serious accident or a minor fender bender).
- **WHAT TO DO:**

1. *Do not panic.* Do *not* leave the scene. Virtually all jurisdictions have laws that seriously punish those who leave the scene of an accident, even if the damage is to property only.
2. Turn the engine *off* (to reduce the risk of a gasoline or electrical fire) unless the car is in the middle of a traffic route where it is likely to be struck. In that case, use whatever means you have (including engine power) to move it. If visibility is poor (at night or at a curve) use flares and your four-way hazard flashers to warn other motorists that there is a problem.
3. Help anyone with injuries to the best of your ability. There is a growing trend away from getting involved with the injuries of others, but this writer says do what you can.
4. Call the police! Give your location and name, and say whether an ambulance is needed. No other details are required at this time.

5. If the accident is serious, call your insurance company. The phone number may be on the *proof of insurance* slip you carry with you. There may be a special number for non-business hours. If in doubt, ask the operator to assist you.

Not insured?

If you are knowingly driving illegally, without the minimum insurance required in your state or province, do not pass GO, do not collect $200, and go directly to jail.

---

6. Take a deep breath. Compose yourself. Now is the time for strategy. Once all the injuries are taken care of, property damage can be addressed. Go over the facts in your mind. What happened? What was the last thing you remember seeing? Doing? If you feel you may in fact have been responsible for the accident, resist the temptation to tell the other driver or the police officer that it's your fault. First, you may be wrong—the law might be on your side. Second, simply admitting guilt will give the insurance company, at the least, a reason to concede your liability during the *settlement* period, and, at the most, to deny your claim *totally*. (Most people don't realize that the vast majority of insurance claims are not decided in a court of law but rather between two insurance agents. Whichever agent has the guiltiest-looking client will probably admit liability, pay the claim, and the then raise the client's rates. Even if that client later changes insurance companies, his record is ruined.)

   There is another good reason to keep your overpowering guilt feelings from the other driver, the witnesses, and the police. The reason is that *anything* you tell these people, no matter how shaken up you are, can be used against you later.

7. Now that you're relaxed, it's time to build your own case. If you're sharp, you'll carry an inexpensive camera in the glovebox and take some pictures of the scene of the accident, the cars, and the damaged area. (The police don't take pictures, they simply sketch. If the other evidence is ambiguous, these pictures may turn the trick and make your case for you!)

ACCIDENT REPORT

DRIVER OF CAR ONE _____

ADDRESS _____

CITY _____

PHONE _____

REGISTERED TO _____

ADDRESS _____

CITY _____

PHONE _____

DRIVER LICENSE SPECIFICS _____

CAR LICENSE PLATE SPECIFICS _____

INSURED BY _____

POLICY # _____

DRIVER OF CAR TWO _____

ADDRESS _____

CITY _____

PHONE _____

REGISTERED TO _____

ADDRESS _____

CITY _____

PHONE _____

DRIVER LICENSE SPECIFICS _____

CAR LICENSE PLATE SPECIFICS _____

INSURED BY _____

POLICY # _____

TIME OF ACCIDENT _____

DATE _____

LOCATION _____

WITNESS #1 _____

WITNESS #2 _____

DRAW DIAGRAM OF   DAMAGE CAR #1   DAMAGE CAR #2

OF COLLISION

SHOWING KEY

STREETS

AND ROADWAYS

Towing a disabled vehicle

Many modern cars require special procedures to be towed safely (see your manual). Towing rates vary widely and some dishonorable operators have been known to take advantage of confused accident victems. If you have to call for a tow, call your local auto club or ask the police for a recommendation.

8. OK—now it's time to interact with the other driver. You are required by law to produce the car's papers and proof of insurance. You don't have to say much else, but if the other driver admits guilt, make a note of it to yourself on a scrap of paper—it could be useful later on.

Front drive car?

Watch out—these are tricky to fix. Many shops don't have the right equipment—or the right training. Insurance companies are aware of the problem, and many will "write off" the car (pay its depreciated value in cash) rather than even try to get it fixed. If your front-drive car is in a serious front-end collision—and the insurance company authorizes repairs—demand in writing: (1) proof that the shop has the equipment to make the repair; (2) proof that the shop has the specifications for your make and model (these are hard to get for some models!); and (3) a list of which parts will be replaced, indicating the price for each part and whether it will be new or used. Once all this is done, have your dealer go over the list and verify that it makes sense. (A friend of mine front-ended an '81 Honda Civic and the insurance company grudgingly had it fixed—but at a cut-rate shop. The front axle fell off the car twice before my friend scrapped the car.)

9. When all the dust settles, you'll be left with one final problem— getting the car back into shape. This simple procedure is becoming exceedingly more complex as spiraling costs make it more and more difficult to get proper work at an acceptable price. If the

accident is serious, you owe it to yourself to get at least two estimates—the first from the insurance company's preferred body shop (or the company's drive-in claim center) and the second from a body shop you pick. It is reasonable to expect that the private estimate will be 40 or 50 percent higher than the company's, but anything more than this is grounds for seeking legal help.

10. Finally, when you get the car back, make sure the work was done properly. If there are problems, complain at once. Here's a list of typical scams pulled in body-shop repairs:

- Junkyard parts used. Bumpers off wrecked cars will rust very quickly indeed.
- Mechanical repairs listed on estimate (such as alignments) never done.
- No re-rustproofing of damaged portions (see page 46).

Can older cars be re-rustproofed?

The insurance companies and body shops say yes, but this writer says no—it's a scam. Trying to use the old tar-wax rust treatments on an old car is like trying to paint an old rusty lawn chair—it looks great for a day, then the paint peels off. In my experience, the only material that works for re-rustproofing after body work is a high-pressure oil treatment.

- Gaskets, seals, and small bits of body trim missing.
- Manufacturer information stickers painted over.
- Electrical wiring not done, or done sloppily. This will cause problems for the next mechanic who has to work on it.
- Headlights not aligned.
- Color-matched touch-up paint not provided to customer.

● **WHEN:** Your **battery** isn't charging.

■ **WHAT TO DO:** Don't turn the engine off if you're having charging trouble—the car may not start again. Diesels, in particular, are sensitive to even the mildest voltage loss and will not start unless the charging system is working perfectly.

A lack of charging may be indicated by an idiot light, a voltmeter dropping below 12 volts on the dial, or an ammeter going into discharge (see page 29). Also, if the headlights or dash lights dim while you're driving, you probably have a problem in your charging system. It means that you are running on reserve power, using the battery's own charge to power the ignition, accessories, and lights.

Turn off all unnecessary power drains. This means radio, heater, air conditioner, cigarette lighter, lights—anything you don't need is expendable. Head for the nearest service bay. On most cars you'll have 10 to 30 minutes of battery power left.

● **WHEN:** Your **battery** is as dead as a doornail.

■ **WHAT TO DO:** Either get a new battery or "boost" your old one. To minimize the risk of explosion, follow the directions given carefully.

First, boost the battery using power from another car. (Never boost a frozen battery, because there is a risk of explosion.) Make sure that you use the proper technique.

The almost extinct and very rare "correct" boost

Boosting a dead battery seems a lot easier than it really is. All you have to do is hook positive to positive and negative to negative and turn the key, right? Wrong! The dangers which can result from an improper boost are: (1) the explosion of hydrogen gas, (2) a fire caused by mismatched cables, (3) a fire caused by accidental ignition of gasoline, and (4) damage to the electrical circuits of the car you're getting the boost from due to current surge.

How to avoid these problems? Use the proper technique:

Bring the two cars close together—but *don't* let the bumpers touch! The car with the good battery should have its engine OFF. (If it's a late model car with computer controls, the ground strap should be disengaged to prevent current surges.) If there are caps on either or both batteries they should be removed and a cloth placed over the cap holes. If the batteries are of the side terminal design, a $2 set of terminal extenders should be attached to give the cables something to grip onto.

The booster cables themselves should be examined and, if excessively rusty, should be replaced with new ones.

Connect the red cable from the positive terminal on the good battery to the positive terminal on the battery being boosted. (It doesn't matter which car you connect first.) Now connect the black cable first to the negative post on the car with the good battery, then to an engine ground on the "dead" car. (The alternator holding bracket is an excellent ground.)

The reason you don't want to go from negative to negative directly is that you may set off a spark which, if it contacts the hydrogen gas that tends to accumulate above the battery, can forever wipe out your chances of having grandchildren. Yes, I know what you're thinking. Most folks do it wrong and most of them live to tell the tale. So what? It only takes one explosion to make you both wiser and sadder . . .

The engine on the "dead" car should then be cranked. But never run the starter over 20 seconds at at time or it might overheat.

Once the car is started, remove the cables in exactly the reverse of the order that you used to hook them up—negatives first, then positives.

Thank you.

Read your manual before boosting

Fancy electronic components can be damaged by even small voltage surges during boosting—this can cost big bucks in repairs. BMW, for example, recommends removing the fuse to the computer circuits before even attempting to boost the battery. Ultimately, boosting will go the way of the dinosaur. Weak batteries will be completely disconnected before they are recharged.

Next, charge the battery. If the battery is not totally dead (you'll need a voltmeter or a hygrometer to tell for sure—the voltmeter should not read below 7 volts; the hygrometer should show at least 50 percent charge), it can be charged with a professional charger.

CORRECT BOOST HOOK-UP

Important: Many post-1985 "computerized" cars may no longer be used to give or receive a boost because of the danger of damaging the computer circuits. (In most cases the batteries must be removed and slow-charged.) Check your manual.

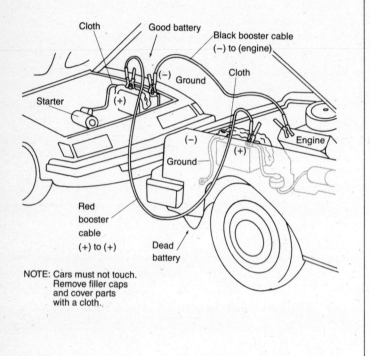

Cloth

Good battery

Black booster cable (−) to (engine)

(−) Ground

Cloth

Starter

(+)

(−) Ground

Engine

(+)

Red booster cable (+) to (+)

Dead battery

NOTE: Cars must not touch. Remove filler caps and cover parts with a cloth.

Charger choices

A professional *fast* charger (6 amps or more) can have your battery up and around in an hour or so—but the strain on the battery could leave it with a limited life expectancy. A professional *slow* charger (or, even better, a *variable* charger, which picks up amps as the battery revives) takes longer, but the result in a healthy, happy battery.

Fraud squad

Some yo-yo tried to sell a device that charged a dead battery by hooking up a long wire to the cigarette-lighter socket of a car with a good battery. (Once the cables are hooked up, you let the car with the good battery idle and, in this way, charge the dead battery.) This clever device consisted of about $2 worth of parts and sold for about $25. The instructions, in small print, pointed out that a really dead battery might require 4 or 5 hours of charging—assuming there was enough gas in the other car's tank. Ouch!

Alternately, you could start your car with a borrowed battery. Keep the following two points in mind: a battery is required only to *start* a car. Once started, the alternator keeps the car going. Removing and replacing a battery can, in most cars, be done in minutes with simple tools.

To borrow a battery: remove the dead battery from your car. Save it, take it to a mechanic, scrap it, or put it on a charger, as you like. Borrow a battery from a good car and hook this one into your own car, and start your car. Finally, unhook the battery and return it—please!

(CAUTION: This procedure, which involves pulling the battery out of the car while it's running, is more complex than it seems. While hooking up or unhooking a battery from a running engine, be careful not to let metal tools or parts complete the circuit from a battery terminal to the car body (or other ground), or from one terminal to the other.)

Now *either* put your own battery back (the motor will slowly charge the battery as it runs over a period of hours) or drive wherever you have to go with no battery at all. The car will run just fine until you stop the engine and have to restart—then you're back to square one!

You might also try to jiggle the connections. Often, an encrusted terminal will cause enough of a voltage drop to keep the engine from starting. Sometimes you can solve the problem temporarily by grabbing a battery cable (near the battery terminal) and shaking it vigorously. A screwdriver thrust between the cable connection and the terminal can also have the same effect.

There might also be an encrusted connection at the *starter motor* (the big device at the end of the positive terminal, mounted on the side of the engine). Shake these connections as well.

Beware battery acid

All batteries contain acid—and acid hurts! Wash your hands after handling battery parts. Be careful to keep the acid off your clothes, or you'll find holes the size of silver dollars in them after the next wash!

● **WHEN:** Your **brakes** fail.

■ **WHAT TO DO:** Virtually all cars have a dual-sump master cylinder, which allows some reserve braking even when a loss of pressure occurs. Also, loss of the power assist on power-brake systems can fool you into thinking the whole system is out. The immediate solution for either situation is simple: push the pedal as hard as you can.

1. Be sure that there is no reserve left at all—*pump the pedal to check reserve braking capacity unless the engine has stalled* (in which case pumping would exhaust the reserve in the vacuum booster and you'd be in worse shape than when you started!)
2. Use the transmission to slow down—whether manual or automatic, shift to a lower gear. (Will shifting an automatic to PARK work? Only at speeds under 5 mph.)
3. Try the emergency brake. If it's properly adjusted (and it *should be*), it will slow you down considerably. If you have the kind with a foot pedal, be careful not to lock the brake on or you'll risk a skid.

● **WHEN:** Your car **breaks down** on the highway.

■ **WHAT TO DO:** In an serious emergency, a standard-transmission car can be moved for short distances by putting it in second gear and cranking the starter for short 10-second bursts.

The difference between a city breakdown and a highway breakdown is that, in a city breakdown, you simply want to get back on your way, while in a highway breakdown, you want to live to drive another day. Here's what to do:

1. Get off the road if you are likely to be rear-ended where you are. Use flares or flashlights as warning lights if you have them. Opening

the hood is a universal trouble signal. Women traveling alone may want to stay inside their vehicle until help arrives.

2. Decide on strategy. If it's a well-traveled road, you may want to flag down a motorist to drive you to a phone, or to the nearest town. Waving is another universal trouble signal. Waving with a towel or rag in your hand makes the message even clearer.

3. Staying in the car has its own risk—it may be hours before the highway patrol spots you. If you have a CB radio, the odds of contacting a trucker or the police (try channel 9) are excellent in most areas. If you don't have a regular CB, consider buying an emergency unit from an electronics store—it could be a lifesaver. It plugs into the cigarette lighter, and the antenna flops on the roof. They're not expensive; I found one on sale for under $40.

4. Finally, here's a tip from a survival course I took: If the weather is life-threatening, if the traffic is sparse, if the car is totally dead, and if you have no signal light—consider making a crude fire in a hubcap from gasoline-soaked rags dipped in the tank. It's warm, it's bright, and it may save your life.

● **WHEN:** Your **clutch** fails.
■ **WHAT TO DO:** If you can get into at least one gear—preferably second —stay there until you reach a service facility.

First, most clutches give some warning before they go—and you should be alert to the symptoms. The most common is a kind of racing between gears (called slippage) that won't go away—even after your mechanic scrupulously adjusts the "free play" on the pedal.

If your clutch fails, you have two choices: to call for a tow; or to shift without a clutch.

This latter technique is tricky, but yes, Virginia, it can be done. It must be done correctly to avoid transmission damage, but, *in an emergency only,* gently push the gear lever against the shift quadrant you want to go into, rev the engine slowly and—with luck—you'll *feel* the opening that you can slide the lever into. (Several friends of mine have demonstrated this technique without apparent damage to anything but my nerves. As I said, save it for emergencies only.)

● **WHEN:** The rear **defogger/defroster** won't.
■ **WHAT TO DO:** In the '70s rear defoggers used a relatively crude fan mounted (or stuffed) into the rear parcel deck.

Crude, yes, but reliable. These things have been known to outlast the cars they came with. The newer types—the fancy wire grid defrosters—are not as durable. Problems with these newer units turn up in:

- The dash switch. (It is a stronger switch because of the high power requirements, and therefore more sensitive. Some have timers built into the circuit. If you have to change a switch, I recommend using a plain toggle switch instead of the timer—the latter is a waste of time.)
- The fuse. (These things use a lot of power and often have their own independent fuse. Check your manual.)
- A bad connection in the rear, caused by rust, normal wear and tear, or abuse. (Rear hatchbacks, especially, take a beating.)
- A broken grid wire.

Can you fix the defogger grid yourself?

Dealers will charge quite a bit to fix your grid. If you are mechanically inclined, you can do it with the help of a helpful kit. If you can't see a break in the wire by eye, get hold of a voltmeter and (with the defogger on) hold a probe on each side of the large vertical line on each side of the defogger. (Switch probes until you get a reading.) A reading of 10–14 volts is normal. Note which side is positive and which is negative. Now, *keeping the negative lead where it is,* move the positive lead to the middle of each horizontal grid line in turn. A readout of 5–6 volts is normal. An erratic reading on a line (either low or high) means that you've found the bad line. Move the probe along the line and the needle will swing at the point of the break. Once you pinpoint the break, simply follow the repair directions with the kit. You may need a photoflood light or some other heat source.

- **WHEN:** Your **engine** floods (gasoline).
- **WHAT TO DO:** You know you've flooded your engine when it refuses to start and reeks of gasoline.

On all cars—wait 3 to 5 minutes. Time works wonders.

On cars with carburetors—try to start it with the pedal to the floor. *Do not pump* the pedal.

On cars with fuel injectors and electronic fuel pumps (see your manual)—find the fuse to the fuel pump and remove it until the car is started, then replace it.

If the flooding is severe, you may have to remove the plugs and wipe the gasoline off.

● **WHEN:** Your **engine** is overheating.
■ **WHAT TO DO:** Stop and evaluate the problem. Particularly on late-model cars, in which the motor is made of lighter, more heat-sensitive alloys, brief periods of overheating can do major long-term damage.

If you have a belt-driven fan, pull over and rev the engine—this should temporarily fix the problem.

If you have the one of the new electric fans, try turning the car's heater up to full blast (this will send some of the heat to the interior, taking some of the stress off the radiator) and, at the same time, get the car out on the highway (the air being forced by the car's speed into the radiator should cool it). If this doesn't get you home, shut down and call for a tow.

Fan fixes

The general feeling about electric fans is that they are absolutely wonderful—until they break down. If the motor itself has failed, there's nothing you can do. If the failure is at the fuse box, a little rearranging of fuses may get you going (pull a good fuse from another circuit and use it temporarily—but make sure the circuit you are borrowing from isn't needed to keep the car running). The most common failure, however, is at the thermo-switch—the switch that checks the temperature of the water coolant and decides whether to turn on the fan. Most designs (except Mazda) have the circuit open (off) unless the thermo tells it to come on. As a result, a defective thermo means no fan—and that could destroy your engine. (The Mazda system leaves the fan permanently on if the thermo fails.) The only Johnny-on-the-spot fix available in the normal design is to find the thermo and short it, using a jumper wire, paperclip, or hairpin, so that it stays on until you can get to a service bay.

A thermostat stuck in the closed position is an excellent example of a $5 part incapacitating a $15,000 motorcar. A quick test is to squeeze the uppermost radiator hose in the engine compartment. If it feels cool to the touch—yet the gauges say the engine is overheating—the thermostat's to blame. Generally this repair will require a tow to a pro.

If things are getting desperate, pull over and let the radiator cool down. Once the temperature drops, pop the cap (be careful!) and add water or antifreeze (ideally, half and half) as need be. Put the cap only half on, so that the system will not pressurize as you drive to the nearest service bay. (If there was a leak, this will minimize additional loss until you get to your destination.)

Finally, check for the obvious: debris or foreign matter blocking the air flow to the radiator. On some sport cars the air-flow design is so tight that a license plate too large could block enough air to upset the radiator and overheat the car. *Nothing* should be allowed to block the flow of air to the radiator.

● **WHEN:** Your **engine** loses power.

■ **WHAT TO DO:** See a mechanic. This problem usually requires professional diagnosis.

There are dozens of possible reasons for the engine to lose power, but here are some of the most common. Investigate the following:

1. *Bad gas.* Did you fill up recently? The new gas may have put water or contamination in the line.
2. *Clogged fuel filter.* You will be able to drive slowly, but not at speed.
3. *Clogged air intake.*
4. *Clogged exhaust.* Do you remember the scene in *Beverly Hills Cop* where Eddie Murphy shoved bananas up the tailpipe of the police car?
5. *Weak fuel pump.*
6. *Bad spark-plug wires.* The engine will "miss" at high speed.
7. *Distributor spark advance not working.* Check all emission-control spark hardware.
8. *Defective ignition "black box."*
9. *Defective automatic transmission.*
10. *Seized brakes.* Check the parking brake in particular.
11. *Interference with throttle linkage.*

12. *Wrong type of gas for the engine.* See page 160.
13. *Engine is overheating and about to seize up.* Check your temperature gauge—and stop the car!
14. *Carburetor float out of adjustment.*
15. *Internal carburetor circuits blocked.*

My best advice—see a mechanic.

● **WHEN:** Your **engine** is soaked (with water).

■ **WHAT TO DO:** If a flood or severe storm may have allowed water into the fuel system, the car *should not be started* but, rather, should be taken to a mechanic, where the critical parts will be disassembled and air dried. Mild water soaking can be insidious, causing a variety of hard-to-diagnose engine problems. Water can create an easier path for electricity to travel on, and thus short major connections.

Generally, ignition systems are most vulnerable after a major soaking. All components that can be reached by hand (plugs, distributor cap, wires) should be removed and air-dried or hand-dried. Next, use a water-displacement aerosol like WD-40 to soak down all of the wiring and ignition connections. (Allow a few minutes for the WD-40 to penetrate.) Then, finally, the engine can be started.

● **WHEN:** Your **engine** stalls.

■ **WHAT TO DO:**

1. Check for unusual conditions that may accompany this phenomenon —strange smells (see pages 50 and 218), overheating (see page 73) —and take the recommended action.
2. Try to restart. If it stalls again, try keeping your foot on the pedal.
3. Is the engine noise—with your foot on the pedal—smooth or shaky? If it's smooth, but stalls as soon as your foot leaves the pedal, then you need to adjust the idle and possibly check the emission hardware. (Air-conditioner solenoids are notorious for causing this problem.) If the engine shakes even with your foot on the pedal, leave your foot where it is for 2 or 3 minutes and see if the idle clears. If it does, you either have a problem with the choke or are burning oil (see your mechanic). If the idle is rough and the car stalls when you remove your foot, you may have a vacuum hose disconnected or a spark plug disconnected or shorted under the

hood. Pop the hood open and see if anything is dangling that ought to be connected. If none of this solves it, the problem is too serious for a temporary fix. See a mechanic.

● **WHEN:** The **fan belt** breaks.

■ **WHAT TO DO:** *Fan belt* is a catch-all term for any belt that drives an accessory with engine power. If the belt to the cooling fan or water pump goes, stop the car and call for a tow. Driving without an alternator belt is not a disadvantage as long as you keep the engine running. Loss of the power-steering belt will make the steering hard to manage until it's repaired. An air-conditioner belt doesn't have to be repaired until it's convenient.

There are belts and there are belts

Let's get our terms straight. Most modern cars have no fan belts—belts that drive the fan off the engine—because most fans today are electrical. However, the engine still drives other accessories by belt—the air-conditioner compressor, power steering, water pump, alternator, and air pump. The belts that drive these are called "V" belts. The discussion here applies to *all* V-belts.

Belts have changed a lot in the last few years. Some are gigantic (such as the Mustang *serpentine* belt) and some are still quite tiny. Some are smooth and some are ribbed because they have to cut a narrower angle. Today, most belts are made of composite rubbers that last longer (the good news), but which don't give much warning before they snap (the bad news).

Got a serpent in your car?

Experts say that serpentine belts are the belts of the future, so you may as well get familiar with them. Small cracks or fractures in the ribs that run across the belt means that replacement is not far away. A smart driver will always carry a spare serpentine belt because if the regular one goes, the entire car is disabled!

OLD FASHIONED VS. SERPENTINE FAN BELTS

Compare the old-fashioned system of fan belts (1) to the newer "serpentine" belt (2).

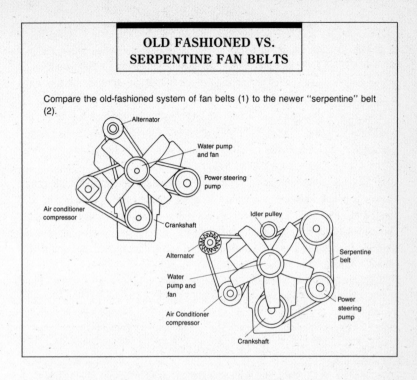

A broken belt can disable a car. Period. Driving without a water pump or a fan is suicidal. Driving without an alternator is bearable for about half an hour. But driving without the air conditioner is not much of a hardship in winter.

First, you should know that you can presumably buy a special kit that permits you to cut a belt to length in an emergency. Personally, I've never seen one, nor do I know of a store that sells them—but I've read about them. I've also read about flying saucers and little green men, but the jury is still out on those. . . .

Another legend says that, in an emergency, you can use panty hose as a makeshift belt.

Also, clothesline or heavy cord will do in an emergency—sort of. Your best bet is to carry a belt or two of the correct size, an extra wrench, and an oversize screwdriver to help set the tension. This last method has several virtues: it's cheap, it's reliable, and—if there is a mechanic nearby —you already have the right part for him to use.

The ultimate solution? Change all the belts every two years and inspect for unusual wear every six months, and you'll never have a problem.

● **WHEN:** Your car is on **fire**.

■ **WHAT TO DO:** Gasoline fires and electrical fires cannot be put out with water. Either use a special extinguisher (see below) or smother the fire with a blanket or heavy coat.

The proper extinguisher would be a recently charged pressurized type with B or C rating. (Type "B" extinguishers are primarily for grease or oil fires. Type "C" is used for electrical fires. Type "A" is for paper-type fires only.) Prices range from $20 to $75.

A portable plastic-encased halon gas extinguisher specially designed for automotive use is also a possibility. The jury is still out on these. On the one hand, they are ideal for automotive fires—and even figured in one of the James Bond novels. On the other hand, the compact plastic units may explode in a crash, and the gas is reputed to be dangerous for humans to inhale. (That's what I call a trade-off.)

Still another possibility is to carry around a large box of baking soda. This is the best, safest, and cheapest fire extinguisher I know of.

Keep the fire out

One final trick: After putting out a car fire, professional fire fighters will snip the negative wire on the battery, *thereby making certain that a short doesn't reignite the blaze.*

● **WHEN:** You get a **flat tire**.

■ **WHAT TO DO:** Can you drive on a flat? Doing so will almost certainly ruin the tire and possibly the rim. If the flat tire is in front, the alignment may be affected as well. In an emergency, a constant speed of under 5 mph is the least damaging.

Your first priority is to get going. That means either calling for a tow, calling the auto club, or changing the tire. If you decide to change the tire, make sure you understand the right way to jack up the car:

- Make sure the car is out of harm's way.
- Chock (wedge a stone under) the wheel diagonally opposite the wheel you'll be working on.
- Make sure you have the proper jack, with all its pieces in working

condition (a piece of pipe makes a handy extension on most jacks —but the force this generates is tremendous and shouldn't be misused).

- Make sure you have a proper spare tire, fully inflated and in working condition. (If you have a temporary or "space saver" spare, read your manual—you'll find it's good only for short distances at low speeds.)
- Assemble the jack and the spare.
- Find the *jack point* of your car. If you're not sure (see your manual) don't proceed until you find it. (On certain GM full-size cars of the late '70s—particularly Cadillacs—the rear bumpers tend to weaken because of accelerated oxidation of the aluminum bumper fittings. GM has never published a complete list of the makes and models affected, but we do know that the bumpers of these cars, if still in service, will not support a jack, so be careful.)
- Jack up the car partway.
- Loosen the lug fittings.
- Complete the jacking.
- Change tires and start to tighten the fittings by hand.
- Lower the car until the wheel touches the ground.
- Complete the tightening (this should be verified by a mechanic with a torque wrench).
- Lower the car, collapse the jack, and (optional) replace the wheel cover.

An alternative to jacking?

Yes, indeed—various manufacturers have come out with aerosol-can tire inflators. You simply carry a can or two around in the glove box (they cost under $5 each). When the tire goes flat, you inject the contents through the valve stem. This *temporary* repair should be more than enough to get you back to civilization. Do they work? In my experience, yes! The TV show *Fight Back!* also had good results with the products. All the brands seem alike, but the Solder Seal product has an especially good reputation.

JACK POINTS

Most full-frame cars can be jacked up at the points marked with squares—while some cars can also be jacked up at the bumper (circles). See your owner's manual for the correct jack points for your car *before* starting. (Note that there are no standard jack points on unibody vehicles.)

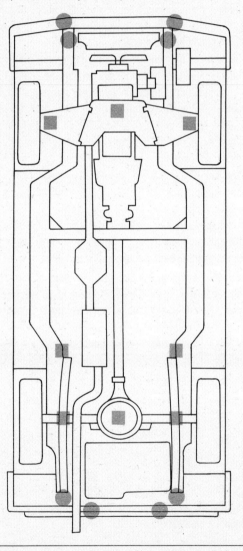

Can all flats be fixed?

Your corner mechanic will try to fix virtually any kind of flat you bring him. Most often, he will succeed. But can *all* flats be fixed? I was taught in car school (yes, there really is a car school) that large punctures or tears in a radial tire, particularly near the flexible side-wall, *cannot* and *should not* be fixed. But today's tires cost over $125 —does this mean we scrap the tire? Well, if your tire did not come with "insurance" (where the cost of the tire is refunded at a de-preciated value toward the purchase of a new one) you might want to consider a serious repair for a serious puncture in a radial (say a break of 2″ or more in the sidewall area). The answer? Find a truck-tire repair specialist trained to handle just such problems, who has the right equipment to do so. The repair costs about $30 in most large cities but, compared to a new tire, that's a bargain! See your Yellow Pages under Tires—Truck Repair.

● **WHEN:** You blow a **fuse**.

■ **WHAT TO DO:** Most of your fuses are in the *fuse box*. Do you know where yours is? The most popular location is under the dash, usually on the driver's side. Other fuse locations are behind the radio and in the kick panels near the glovebox. Some special fuses, such as those for the fuel injection system, may be in the engine compartment itself—see your manual. (*Fusible links* are wires in the electrical system that are designed to burn out in case of overload. In fifteen years of car journalism, I have seen a lot of fuses blow, but never a fusible link.)

Each fuse goes to a separate circuit. Your manual will have a special diagram of these circuits, and most newer cars also have a diagram either on the fuse panel itself or inside its cover.

Fuses are of two types—the older cylindrical type and the new push-pull type. They are not interchangeable, generally, but low-cost adapters allow you to use the cylindrical type in the place of a push-pull.

All fuses are *rated*. As with a house fuse, using a fuse with too low a rating will blow the new fuse, and using a fuse of too high a rating will risk a fire.

The push-pull fuses go in relatively easily (provided you have nimble fingers) but the old cylindrical type should be pried out with a *non-metallic* object (a special fuse-puller is best; a Popsicle stick will do).

You can check a fuse by looking for a gap in the metal link within. (Both types of fuses have inspection slots.)

All this wonderful information about fuses won't do you a whit of good unless you keep some spares in the glovebox. In an emergency, you can borrow a good fuse from the fuse panel to replace the bad one, but you'll have to be sure their ratings are the same—and even then, you'll have to choose: Is the radio more important than the cigarette lighter? Is the horn more important than the license-plate light?

Circuit breakers

Most new cars have circuit breakers instead of fuses. Like those in a home, they can be reset without new parts. Not all breakers are reset the same way, though, so see your manual. On most, you need to *key* the reset button with a small pointed instrument, such as a nail or unbent paperclip.

● **WHEN:** The **gas pedal** jams.
■ **WHAT TO DO:**

- *Do not waste time trying to free it*—that's how accidents happen!
- *Immediately* shift into neutral (whether you have an automatic or a standard transmission).
- *Do not turn off the engine,* as this will disable the brakes and steering on most cars.
- *Do not* go for the emergency brake, as it won't be strong enough to resist the engine.

Once the immediate danger is past:

- Do not use full throttle until a mechanic has had a chance to evaluate the problem.
- Have the linkage in the engine compartment inspected. Look for a seized bushing, rusty washer, or binding pivot.

FUSES

Types of fuses, fuse boxes, and the difference between "good" and "blown" fuses.

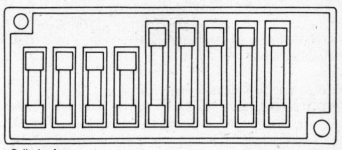

Cylinder fuses

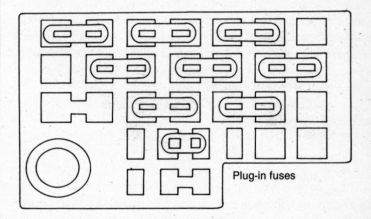

Plug-in fuses

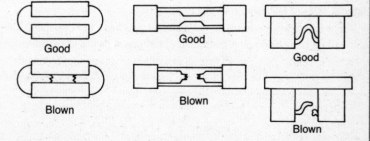

Good

Good

Good

Blown

Blown

Blown

- Check to see if any loose components have fallen into the accelerator linkage.
- Check for loose engine mounts. If the engine moves even a fraction of an inch off its normal position, it may be enough to jam the linkage.
- In the car—make sure the carpet or mat isn't making the pedal stick.
- Check the accelerator pedal itself for rust.

● **WHEN:** Your **headlight covers** get stuck.
■ **WHAT TO DO:** Headlight covers, a big rage in the '60s, are making a comeback in the '80s. The old models were vacuum-operated (the '67 Cougar was the biggest repair nightmare of all) but most of the new ones are electrical.

The "emergency" procedure for each make and model is different. Some require simply pulling a button or turning a screw and then forcing the headlights into position by hand. Some manuals suggest using a jumper wire to bypass what may be a defective switch. If you have one of these fancy setups on your car, check your manual in advance so that you'll know what to do when the "worst" happens.

● **WHEN:** The **heater** quits.
■ **WHAT TO DO:** A loss of heating inside the car is uncomfortable but not serious. The problem can await professional evaluation at your convenience.

The engine produces enough heat per minute to melt itself into a puddle. To prevent that, it relies on a cooling system, which circulates *coolant* (usually half water and half antifreeze) through coolant passages inside the engines. Then the water pump carries this superheated material to the radiator, where the fan-forced air cools it off.

While the radiator's job is to get rid of engine heat, the job of the *heater core* or *box* is to trap some of that heat and use it to warm the passenger area. The heater box works like a miniaturized radiator. It's positioned inside the dashboard so that air driven by a small fan (also inside the dash) can pass over it, collect heat, and warm up the car's occupants.

1. If the heater stops suddenly, one of the control or power cables under the dash may have snapped. Peek under the center of the console and see if anything is dangling.

2. The heater core might be clogged—see a mechanic.
3. The vacuum switch under the hood may have come loose or frozen —see a mechanic.
4. The engine thermostat may have jammed in the open position—see a mechanic.
5. The blower-fan fuse could be out (check the fuse box). The switch could be broken. The fan motor itself could be dead. See a mechanic.

● **WHEN:** Your **horn** jams.

■ **WHAT TO DO:** Your horn actually has *two* switches: the one on the steering wheel that you push, and another relay switch next to the horn itself.

You can usually turn off a horn in one of three ways:

1. Pulling its fuse (see your manual).
2. Pulling the "hot" wire going into the horn (This is *not* hard to find. It's the *only* wire going to the horn.)
3. Removing the horn from its mount so that the ground connection is broken.

Once the immediate emergency is over, a mechanic will have to determine whether the problem was the steering-column switch, the relay, the horn itself, or the wiring and ground connections.

● **WHEN:** A **hose** blows.

■ **WHAT TO DO:** Evaluate the severity of the leak before proceeding. Gasoline dripping on hot engine parts is a severe fire hazard. Radiator hoses are pressurized (like a tire), so even a small leak can empty the cooling system in minutes.

There are two crucial fluid hoses that can cause you grief in the engine compartment: the water distribution (radiator) hoses and the gasoline hoses. Gasoline hoses are smaller and thicker and less likely to blow. That leaves the radiator hoses as the major problem area.

Extra turbo-charger hoses

If you have a turbo-charger, you will find a hose going to the unit which carries pressurized oil to the bearing. Some cars, particularly Chryslers, have a radiator hose down there as well. Inspect these hoses from time to time, as failure to lubricate or cool the turbo bearing could lead to an expensive repair.

If a radiator hose blows, you'll know it—water will gush out, steam will billow, the water-temperature gauge will soar into the red zone, and you'll have your hands full getting the car to a service station. The first solution is to tape the hose at the leak with high-quality electrical tape (use a lot of it—even though it's just a temporary repair).

Also, if the leak is not major, removing the radiator cap will depressurize the system and allow you to limp the car a short distance on the remaining fluid.

If the hose that blows is a heater hose (one of the long skinny ones that go back to the firewall) you have an additional choice: you can tape it *or* cut it and plug it (you'll have no heater for a while) *or* remove the hose section with the tear and loop the good section back to the water pump (again, you'll have no heater for a while).

Are there any other options? I've heard of an experimental product which is sold as a "self-vulcanizing" radiator-hose repair tape. You tape the tear up as you normally would, and then you touch a match to the tape. The heat vulcanizes the repair—and it's fixed. One problem—the product is not yet readily available. Keep your eyes peeled!

If the leak is in a gasoline hose—tape it up with electrical tape and get to a mechanic, pronto.

● **WHEN:** You lock your **keys** in the car.

■ **WHAT TO DO:** If there is one single thing more embarrassing than locking your keys in the car and then having to ask to borrow a coat hanger, I don't know what it is.

Here are your options:

1. Carry an extra key in your wallet or purse. (I do—and I'm not ashamed to admit it, either.)
2. Leave a spare set at the office or at home so you can have someone send the keys over in a cab.
3. If you happen to know your key "slug" number, and happen to be near a dealer who sells your make of car, and you have an honest face and can prove who you are, you can have a brand-new key made up for only a dollar or two. (Don't laugh—this worked for me once.)
4. Carry an extra set in a magnetic box on the car. Thieves love people who do this!
5. Break a window. This approach is messy, and expensive. Car manufacturers politely advise breaking the smallest window, as this is the least expensive to repair. Ouch!
6. Crawl in through the sunroof. (Yes, Matilda, your intrepid author has done this, too.)
7. Use a coat hanger. This is easier said than done. If *you* can, so can *everyone else!* Most cars of the '80s are reasonably resistant to coat hangers, and no one short of a professional car thief can pull this off anymore.
8. Call a locksmith or the auto club. Most locksmiths can either pick the lock or, using a special tool that is supposedly sold only to professionals, can force their way between the window and the door and pop the lock. (I bought one of these by mail—so much for professional integrity.)
9. Call a body shop. First, if there is a way inside the car, a trained body technician will find it. Second, popping the lock with a slide hammer is neater than breaking the glass—and slightly less costly.

● **WHEN:** Your door **locks** freeze.

■ **WHAT TO DO:** There are many overpriced lock de-icer sprays on the market. I'll tell you a couple of secrets about all of them: First, they don't work very well, and second (and most important), they evaporate. By the time you finally need the de-icer, the chemicals are all dried up.

Here's what does work—a match and a key. Heat the key with the lit match, being careful not to burn yourself (wear gloves), and then insert the key in the lock. Presto. And think of all money you'll save on de-icers.

Freeze tip

Regular squirts of a light penetrating oil such as WD-40 in the lock cylinder will make it more freeze-resistant. Don't use anything heavier (such as motor oil) or you'll get in more trouble.

● **WHEN:** Your **oil pressure** is low.

■ **WHAT TO DO:** Stop the car—driving with low oil pressure can destroy an engine.

If you're lucky, a low oil-pressure indication means that you have simply been driving with too little oil in the sump. Check the dipstick; add more oil if needed.

More serious pressure problems usually relate to overheated oil; the wrong type of oil for the car (usually too *thin* a grade); oil that has broken down because it's been in service too long; oil that has become contaminated with gasoline, water, or antifreeze; a clogged filter; a clogged pickup screen; worn bearings; or a weak oil-pump spring.

Stop the car completely and shut off the engine at the first signs of oil-pressure problems. The alternative is to turn your engine into scrap metal.

How low is low?

It is possible (though not advisable) to drive the car for a block or two with "low" pressure (2–4 lbs.) if you go slow. It is barely possible (certainly *not* advisable) to drive with *no* oil pressure. Generally, for cars without an oil gauge, stop immediately at the first sign of trouble. In case of an extreme emergency, however, you can continue to drive as long as the light goes out when you accelerate, and only comes on at idle. See a pro! (Also see page 26 on oil lights and gauges.)

● **WHEN:** You are **out of gas**.

■ **WHAT TO DO:** First, be sure you're down to the very bottom of the tank. (Get out and shake the rear of the car to see if anything is still sloshing.) Next, see if gas can be siphoned from elsewhere. Make extra certain not to get any in your mouth—this stuff is poison. (It's a good idea to carry a self-priming siphon. Car shops have them for under $5.)

Will anything take the place of gas? In one TV series, the hero ran out of gas and used a combination of vodka and moth balls to get the car going. I don't know about you, but this strikes me as a *last resort.*

If you go for gas, be careful with the gas can; the fumes in it can be quite flammable—more explosive than gasoline itself. Some newer gas cans feature a cellular interior that is considered to be much safer.

You should know that on newer cars, running out of gas may severely damage the catalytic converter. On any car, water and debris picked up from the bottom of the tank may foul filters and carburetor or injector circuits. So—be careful not to let your tank get too low. (See also highway breakdown, page 70.)

● **WHEN:** Your car is **recalled**.

■ **WHAT TO DO:** Think of a recall as a chess game. The players are Washington and the car makers. Think of yourself as one of the pawns.

The automobile companies are playing name games these days with different kinds of recalls and not-really-recalls—and it's the consumer who gets the short end of the stick.

Let's distinguish four different kinds of recall:

The genuine garden-variety recall. This usually means a major safety problem in the car. Strict government-approved notification procedures must be followed. The company has to *attempt* to reach all owners, even those who bought the cars used. Repairs are generally made at no charge, particularly on cars with low mileage. Master records kept in Washington at the National Highway and Traffic Safety Administration and Ottawa (Ministry of Transport) are generally available to all consumers. (The U.S. rules on recalls are slightly more rigid than the Canadian.) Over 100 million cars have been recalled since the '60s, so pay attention!

The voluntary recall. This is a new and disturbing trend. Many times the manufacturers disagree with the government as to whether a recall is required. A recall is costly, and the manufacturers tend to rely on one of two incredibly profound philosophical postulates—either that it's *too late* to save anybody else's life, or that the number of people reported killed or injured doesn't prove conclusively that the problem exists in all the cars. To avoid a lawsuit, which can drag through the courts for years while more people get hurt, the government and the manufacturer may agree on a *voluntary* recall, which is not as complex, expensive, or reliable as the regular recall. It is, however, better than nothing. Check with Washington or Ottawa for more info.

The "secret warranty" recall.   This is the "rummage sale" of recalls —anything that doesn't threaten lives directly or fit into the first two categories usually ends up here. (Examples: paint deterioration on certain Nissan cars, faulty transmissions on some GM cars, faults on Cadillac's variable-displacement engine, etc.) The good news here is that the repairs are covered by the manufacturer. The bad news is that they don't advertise or announce the warranty program—and only the consumers who squeal the loudest get the benefit.

The service bulletin.   A lot of cars have problems caused not by the random breakdown of individual parts but rather by *design* defects—the problems came up because the engineers didn't know how the car would behave in the real world. Such things as pinging, no-start, bad idle, highway power loss, rough ride, etc.—all these can be related to *factory* boo-boos —and you need advice from the factory to undo them. Formerly (and this is amazing) the service bulletins with the advice were available only to: (a) the dealers, (b) the manufacturers' zone offices, and (c) major car magazines. What's more, many of these *thousands* of bulletins, issued over the years, were never stored on a computer (although they certainly should have been), and many dealers have dumped their back copies from time to time to make space.

The availability of these bulletins has changed somewhat in the '80s. The Big Three now admit that the bulletins exist (this is a major breakthrough for the consumer), and most car companies will even mail back issues to owners who request them. What should you do if your car has a strange problem that you can't seem to get fixed? Write to the manufacturer and to some of the sources listed in the back of the book (page 234; *Motor Magazine* is exceptionally friendly), and maybe you'll find the enlightenment you're looking for.

> ## Let's hear it for the Freedom of Information Act!
>
> As this book was being prepared, only Ford Motor Company and General Motors had come clean by making their technical service bulletins open to the public. (Ford even lets owners subscribe to the bulletins as they appear—commendable, to say the least.) What if your car is another make? If you exhaust the leads above, you can try a particularly offbeat approach—write the executive secretary of the NHTSA in Washington, requesting copies of the bulletins for your car. Mark the envelope and the top of the request itself with the magic words "Freedom of Information Request." Then cross your fingers and wait ten days for a reply. (A friend of mine who tried this says it really works!)

Confused? You have a right to be: tens of thousands of consumers all over North America are still trying to get various parts of their cars to work. If the problem with your vehicle is really a manufacturer's-warranty situation —as detailed above—arbitration may be open to you. (See page 231.)

Of course, nothing says that your ordinary legal recourses are not open to you. Have you considered small-claims court? (Generally, a small-claims action can be taken in conjunction with an arbitration or secret-warranty claim.)

Still need a shoulder to cry on? Try Ralph Nader's Center for Auto Safety —these guys really seem to care (page 229).

● **WHEN:** Your car **shakes** or **shimmies**.

■ **WHAT TO DO:** A moderate shake or shimmy will not disable the car. You can still drive to the nearest service facility without risk. However, if the problem becomes worse as you drive, if the steering becomes less precise, or if you hear the sound of metal rubbing against metal—stop the car and call a pro.

"Shake." "Shimmy." Sound like '60s dance steps, don't they?

Shimmy (a kind of pulsating sensation transmitted through the steering accompanied by wandering from lane to lane) almost always relates to problems with the front suspension: bad, out-of-balance, or improperly inflated tires, improper alignment, worn, bent, leaky, or loose shocks, worn or damaged (front-drive) struts, worn front-suspension parts, bad bearings, bad (front-drive) CV joints, interference with movement of front-end parts, misaligned steering box or rack, or an improperly adjusted steering box.

A simple test

To see if a bad tire (out-of-balance rim, out-of-round tire) is the source of the problem, temporarily inflate all four tires to about 5 psi above the maximum listed on the sidewall. *Do this only when the tires are cold and only as a temporary measure for the test.* Then drive. If the problem *gets worse,* it's a tire! To find out which, deflate the tires one by one until the problem returns to its normal level.

Shake is more apparent at higher speeds and can include torque problems at any one of the four wheels. It *includes all* of the possibilities above, plus: worn or cracked springs, damaged torsion bars, worn rear-wheel bearings, damaged U-joints, imbalanced driveshaft, problems with the rear axle or (front-drive) transaxle, and problems with the automatic transmission.

Sound complicated? First, have the front end aligned and balanced. Check the tires for unusual wear. If you still have a shake, see a specialist.

● **WHEN:** Your car **skids**.

■ **WHAT TO DO:** Skid control is a skill that cannot be acquired from a book. Familiarize yourself with the theory (below) and get thee to a skid school.

My best advice: Invest a day of your life and a few dollars in a properly run "skid school." Most major cities have at least one school offering this service. Many of the techniques explained below sound good on paper but require split-second timing in real life. And real life is where you can save real lives.

Here's the theory: Most skids take place on braking. Keep this simple rule in mind: If you apply your brakes gently (not to the point of locking any of the wheels) it is possible to both brake and steer at the same time. Unfortunately, the worst skids often happen in panic stops—when the driver unintentionally *locks* one or more wheels and then tries to both steer around the obstacle and brake at the same time. This exercise is contrary to the laws of physics and therefore quite dangerous.

What to do? A well-respected race driver in Canada spent many years and many thousands of government dollars to prove that, contrary to accepted thinking, the fastest way to control a skidding car was to jam on the brakes to lock all four wheels, skid for a bit, unlock the brakes to make steering corrections, jam on the brakes again, unjam, steer, etc. Unfortunately, one problem with this system is that it requires intense training because, if the initial "jam" is not done correctly, the car immediately becomes an uncontrollable missile.

If you're an average motorist—simply keep the following in mind. Braking hard might take away your steering control so, in an emergency, decide whether you want to *steer around* the obstacle or you want to *try to brake.* (Without special training, chances are that you cannot do both.)

Skid tip

In a serious skid in a car with an automatic transmission, if you can act fast enough, shift to neutral. This prevents the rear of the car from trying to "fight" the steering.

Fortunately for consumers, automatic computer-controlled antiskid braking will be on most cars by the end of the decade. (It is now only on top of the line models.) These "ABS" devices work, and they could save thousands of lives. With them, it is—for the first time—possible to brake and steer at the same time.

What about those *pendulum* skids on ice—the ones where you turn one way and the car tries to spin around? In the trade, these are called *oversteer* skids. They are very difficult to control because (1) the steering correction must be done in a fraction of a second, and (2) the first skid will likely be followed by a reverse skid (or rebound), which also must be quickly controlled, by steering the opposite direction. My recommendation: Go to skid school.

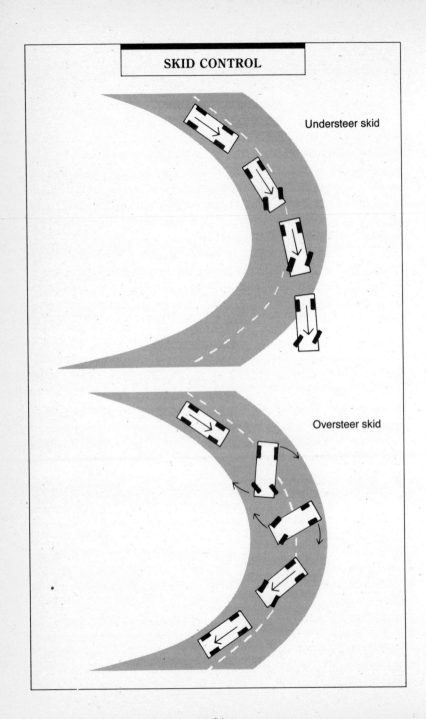

SKID CONTROL

Understeer skid

Oversteer skid

The controversy between front and rear drive

The experts are still arguing about how these two types of power trains affect skids, but here's one fact that everyone seems to agree on. Taking your foot off the gas quickly in a regular rear-drive car may be just the trick to stop the skid, especially if it's your garden-variety oversteer skid. Doing the same thing in a front-drive car is likely to throw you into an uncontrolled *trailing throttle* skid. So—in a front-wheel drive car—never take your foot off the gas quickly, always do it gently.

The last type of skid we have to face is *understeer,* one of the most horrifying. Years ago I was going along an icy mountain road at considerable speed. The road veered to the left and, although I steered correctly, the car headed straight ahead for the embankment. At the last possible second (time moved ever so slowly) the front wheels "caught" and the steering corrected. That's an *understeer*—no response to steering input. What happened to me (I was driving a Pontiac LeMans 1972, a front-engine rear-drive car) was unusual, because this kind of skid tends to happen either on front-drive cars or on rear-engine rear-drive cars like VWs, Porsches, or Skodas.

What to do? Not much, I'm afraid, and you have precious little time to do it. Some experts say *gently* touching the front brakes will transfer weight to the front of the vehicle and make the steering respond.

Another, more risky, strategy is to reach for the parking brake and deliberately throw the car into a spinning oversteer skid—while it's *already* in an understeer skid. The only justification for what seems like a suicidal move is that, if a crash is inevitable, you may want to absorb the impact on the side or rear of the car instead of head-on.

I repeat—for a day of your life and a few dollars, going to skid school is a damn good idea.

● **WHEN:** You are **stuck in the snow**.
■ **WHAT TO DO:** Spinning the drive wheels is an excellent way to put ten years of wear on a transmission in ten minutes. Consider your other options:

1. Get out and assess the situation. Which wheel is stuck, anyway? If both of them are, brother, you *deserve* to be stuck! Got a shovel? Those portable folding jobs are handy to carry in the trunk—the short blade will both pick up snow and crack ice. Clear away the area around the stranded wheel. What about traction? Got any sand? Cat litter? (Not the clay-based kind, though—see below.) Salt? Those metal traction bars with the cleats underneath are wonderful—I recommend them. No luck? Grab one of the rubber mats from the floor and try that.

   Point your wheels straight ahead and put the transmission in DRIVE. Get out of the car, lazybones—we don't need more dead weight. Now push on the door frame while the transmission pushes the car ahead.

2. Turn the wheels straight ahead, give the engine a little gas and pay attention. If the car moves even slightly, there's *hope*. If the car doesn't move and the tire spins immediately, you're stranded.

Don't kill your car

Spinning wheels move at twice the speedometer speed—if the speedometer says 60 mph, that means you're spinning one tire at 120 mph. It won't last long at that speed!

Got a manual shift? Try starting in second gear. You're less likely to lose traction.

Try rocking the car, but keep in mind, my friend, that you are taking *years* off the useful life of your automatic transmission. (Standards aren't hurt as badly by this stuff.)

Running out of ideas? One more time: point the wheels straight ahead, step gently on the gas, and gently apply the parking brake. This will transfer some power to the wheel that still has traction.

3. Even the pros know when it's time to get help. Go to a phone and call in the second team!

All cat litter is not created equal

Clay-based cat litter will absorb water and turn to mush when you need it most. So if you're carrying kitty litter around for emergencies (your cat must think this is tremendously amusing!), try some out on your front walk to make sure you have the right stuff.

Old-timers with a winch are convinced that they can pull their way out of anything—and they are probably right! If you have a winch, you need a solid stationary object to loop a cable or chain around (never hook *to* an object; always hook *around* it). One new product on the market looks like a wheel rim with a rachet mechanism attached. What you do is replace one of the drive wheels with the contraption and then attach your cable between the rim and a stationary object. As the car engine turns the rim, it tightens the line and pulls itself out.

● **WHEN:** Your electronic **sunroof** won't let in the sunshine.
■ **WHAT TO DO:** OK, I know that every moment wasted reading this could be better spent working on your tan, so take note: All manufacturers now have some sort of manual back-up system in their sunroof controls. You'll have to look in your manual or call your dealer, but the procedure usually goes like this:

1. Pry off the access panel.
2. Jam a screwdriver into a special slot.
3. Turn the screwdriver by hand to open or close the roof.

What are you waiting for?—you can still catch a few rays if you hurry!

● **WHEN:** Your car **won't start**.
■ **WHAT TO DO:** In all my years of playing with cars, I've come across only three options that are useful when the car won't start (four, if you count calling the auto club). They are: Jiggle, Boost, and Push.

Jiggle. Many electrical shorts and grounds are both temporary and temperamental. Often the main reason a car won't start is that power is not getting to the starter—maybe there's a bad connection at the battery, a bad ground connection from the battery to the chassis, or a weak connection at the starter. If you can identify the battery and the starter, grab each battery connection in turn and jiggle it fiercely. Do the same for the connections at the ground strap (the cable that runs from the negative battery terminal to a metal ground) and at the starter. Now try to start the car. This works embarrassingly often!

More jiggling

Here's another trick or two: Give the carburetor a good whack with the handle of a screwdriver; if a float in it is stuck, that will loosen it up. Bouncing up and down on the rear fender may free a gasoline intake, that's gotten clogged, especially likely if you were low on fuel to start with.

Boost.   Dead cars that won't respond to jiggling will probably respond to a boost. Do you have jumper cables? You should, you know. They should be of *premium* quality (otherwise they may *melt*) and they should *not* have any rust at the ends. Now find a car with a good battery. Make sure you use the correct boost technique—failure to do so can be dangerous! (See page 83 for details.)

Push.   Can your car be push-started? Here's an educated guess: If it's an automatic, the answer is *no.* If it's a standard the answer is *yes.* (Check your manual to be sure.)

Trivial Pursuit

Can any automatics be push-started? Maybe my age is showing, but yes—most cars built before 1965 can be. Simply pop the transmission into LOW, and off you go!

Here's the correct push-starting technique for standards:

1. Shift to neutral.
2. Get up to speed (10–15 mph).

3. Turn the ignition on.

4. Push the clutch in.

5. Shift to the correct gear (second if you are going forward, reverse if you are—heaven help you!—doing this backward).

6. Cross your fingers and gingerly release the clutch. The car should start.

Disclaimer

I am honor-bound to tell you that push-starting may foul the catalytic converter and that you should really go to your dealer after push-starting and have the converter checked, and, if need be, replaced. If you intend to do this, however, call me first. I have some swamp land in Florida you may be interested in. . . .

Why did the car conk out in the first place? Don't forget: preventive maintenance is as important as corrective repair. You don't want to go through all that again, do you? When talking the experience over with your mechanic, try to pinpoint the symptoms you experienced when the car wouldn't start.

A car needs the following five things to start correctly: *spark* (ignition), *gas,* adequate *compression* in the cylinders, an operational *starting system,* and the correct operating *temperature.* Let's examine them:

Spark. Is the ignition in good repair? A scope test will tell you. Perhaps it was only a temporary problem. Maybe water or moisture shorted out the distributor cap. If a mechanic had been with you when your car refused to start, he would have pulled off a plug wire, stuck a key in the end, and held the key about half an inch from the engine while you turned the starter. If a strong, healthy white spark had leaped forth while the engine turned, he would have assumed the ignition was in reasonable shape.

Gas. Are the carburetor and fuel pump working? Is the filter clogged? In the old days (before electronic fuel injection) it was possible to lean over the carburetor and see if fuel squirted into its throat as the accelerator was depressed. Now this is often not possible. At the other extreme, the smell of gas in the air indicates flooding. See page 72.)

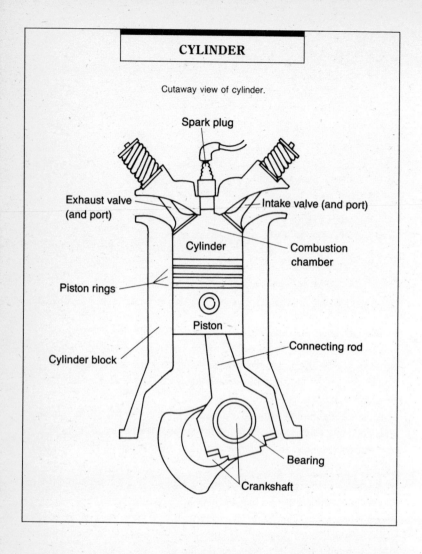

CYLINDER

Cutaway view of cylinder.

Spark plug

Exhaust valve (and port)

Intake valve (and port)

Cylinder

Combustion chamber

Piston rings

Cylinder block

Piston

Connecting rod

Bearing

Crankshaft

Compression. Compression depends on the ability of the internal engine parts (valves and piston rings) to seal tightly. In the old days, weak compression often caused starting problems. This is less common with modern engines.

Starting system. Is the starter cranking normally, or can you hear it straining? Don't overlook the battery as a possible cause—perhaps it's not sending enough current to the starter.

Grounding the ground

One of the single most overlooked maintenance items on cars more than five years old is a periodic cleaning of the connection where the battery negative cable runs to ground. The connection may become blocked by almost invisible corrosion—which could cost you hundreds of dollars in analysis and repairs before you pin it down. On one of my cars, a well-meaning mechanic sold me a $200 timing-chain overhaul before realizing that there was excessive resistance at the ground. Fixing *that* was a five-minute job.

Operating temperature. If the engine is too cold, the fuel will liquefy and the engine will not start. If the engine is too hot, its pistons will seize or its fuel will vaporize prematurely in the fuel line or in the carburetor and so be unable to reach the engine.

How's your camshaft?

A camshaft is an innocent-looking engine part which, because it is nestled right smack inside the engine, is extremely expensive to replace. In the days of the old cast-iron V-8s, these parts were good for a hundred thousand miles (at least). Replacement (they cannot be repaired) was rare and failure was usually due to abuse. All that has changed in the cars of the '80s—modern cams are lighter, more delicate, and very sensitive to wear. They are—sad to say—becoming one of the most frequent causes of a hard-to-diagnose starting failure. The symptoms are: (a) hard starting, (b) uneven, labored cranking that picks up and slows down, and (c) unpredictable and irregular readings in a repeat series of compression checks. See a mechanic.

▪3▪
WHEN
SHOPPING FOR
SERVICE

● **WHEN:** You need an **alignment**.

▪ **WHAT TO DO:** There are four different alignments that are important to your suspension and steering:

The first is the alignment of the car itself, panel to panel, front to back. On older cars this alignment was maintained by a full underframe, but on the newer unibody (frameless) cars a severe sideswipe might throw the whole car out of alignment. When this happens, all the other alignments (below) will be inaccurate, because, essentially, they have no baseline to relate to.

The second is the alignment of the steering column and steering hardware within the body. Older frame-type cars usually had a steering box bolted right to the frame, so that this was never a problem. However, the newer frameless cars use a complex steering system (called rack-and-pinion) which has no frame to attach to. A severe bump can knock the steering mechanism out of alignment so that no amount of ordinary mechanical work can fix it.

Note that these first two alignments must be correct before the wheels can be aligned. (Only a properly equipped body shop with the correct body specifications and trained personnel can verify the above alignments.)

The third alignment is your average wheel alignment, the one that used to be on special for $9.98. Except that there is nothing "average" about wheel alignments anymore. First, they are done (on the newer frameless cars) to all four wheels, not just the front two. Second, the manufacturers, in their infinite wisdom and tireless search for a cheaper manufacturing process, have eliminated two of the three normal adjustments in the front alignment. (*Toe* is still adjustable on most cars; *caster* and *camber* may not be.)

This sounds great in theory, but in practice, mechanics are finding they need these missing alignment ranges to correct for bad driving habits, uneven tire wear, manufacturers' error, and prior fender benders that have affected the chassis.

What to do? Even though caster and camber are theoretically not adjustable on the new cars, some companies have designed contraptions that *force* and *bend* the suspension components so that you can in fact adjust what was supposed to be nonadjustable. These things are selling like hotcakes.

One problem, though: the manufacturers of the cars say that using these new tools to force-align the wheels may weaken the front end and endanger the owner and passengers. The manufacturers of the tools have reacted by putting labels on the tools that say that they are not supposed to be used to force-align front end parts—which is, of course, exactly what they are for.

Again, what to do? If the front steering feels wrong (the car wanders, the steering wheel feels loose, the steering wheel doesn't center, the tires wear unevenly) find an absolutely A-1 shop. Do not trust your car to an amateur. And if you are ever in a fender bender with a frameless car, double-check that the car is fixed correctly before approving the work.

The fourth, and simplest, alignment is that of the steering wheel itself. It's simple—the steering wheel should point straight ahead when the two front wheels point straight ahead. If this is not the case—and on many cars it isn't—then it's a safe bet that, in the history of the car, at least one wheel alignment was done by a lazy mechanic who didn't center the steering wheel before starting the job. The next time you have a wheel alignment done, have the steering wheel centered at the same time. No extra charge.

Fraud squad warning

A ripoff that began in the '60s is still prevalent to this day—alignment shops that "lowball" the price of the alignment so they can sell you replacements for front-end parts that don't need replacing. Today's alignments should cost $30 to $60, so beware of anything cheaper. There is no free lunch.

A tip

A good alignment shop will check shock absorbers, springs, and even tire pressure before starting the job, and will test-drive the car both before and after the work. If you don't get full service, don't patronize the shop again.

Does this inspire confidence?

Many shops now feature $20,000 chrome-and-steel computer-assisted alignment racks, which look *great* even when sitting still. Here's a good question to ask your friendly mechanic—when was the last time the machine was recalibrated by a manufacturer's rep? Recent spot checks show that half of the machines are seriously out of whack. If the machine isn't reset at least once a month, it's probably wasting everybody's time.

● **WHEN:** You are looking for an **auto club**.
■ **WHAT TO DO:** There are two kinds of auto clubs: (1) the big guys; and (2) everybody else. The big guys (American Automobile Association [AAA] in the United States; Canadian Automobile Association [CAA] in Canada) are the kings of the hill. You may not like what they charge, but they provide the fastest, widest-ranging service around.

The little guys (some of whom are not so little—many are affiliated with major oil companies) offer a lot of services the big guys don't (including some really silly ones, in my opinion) and may charge a bit less. Be careful —there are no bargains out there. The contract should be read with a magnifying glass before you sign. (Be *especially* careful of clubs which promise to let *you* pick the tow and pay you back. The list of exemptions in the contract will probably be as long as your arm.)

● **WHEN:** You need to choose a **body shop**.

■ **WHAT TO DO:** With the possible exception of auto electronics, no other area of the car business is going through worse growth pains than the body-shop business. The advent of frameless unibody front-drive cars was the death knell for the smaller marginal shops that lacked the capital to buy the right equipment and the personnel trained to use it properly. Even a relatively simple change like the new clear coat top finishes the manufacturers are using requires better spray equipment, spray booths, and a cleaner, more efficient shop than many smaller outfits can provide. Also, many unscrupulous operators are using used parts from "chop shops" while charging the insurance company (or the customer) for new parts. You cannot afford to pick a bad shop, or let the car be towed to whatever shop happens to be closest. Demand credentials, references, and proof of integrity.

Here's a rundown on how to deal with the different possible situations:

Collision (with work paid for by insurance). Have the insurance company's estimate double-checked by at least one other independent source (insurance companies understand that damaged cars need to look good, but hidden mechanical damage is a mystery to them—talk to a good mechanic). Insist that whether the parts will be new or used be put in writing. If mechanical parts are to be changed, ask for the old ones back. Add the phrase, "subject to inspection of car after repair" to everything they put in front of you to sign. If you are driving a new front-wheel-drive car, verify that the shop has the proper equipment and body specs to work with. When you get the car back, leave nothing to chance. Try all the doors and windows. Run it through a car wash to test for leaks. Check the hood and trunk latches. Try the door locks. Go for a test drive. Check for steering and alignment problems—it's *your* car: does it handle like it used to? Have all worked on areas re-rustproofed (see below). If there is overspray on the glass, the tires, or the trim (there usually is) insist that it be removed while you wait. Finally, ask to see the car from *underneath*. Look for bad welds, holes, or signs of used parts. (A friend of mine with a low-mileage front-wheel-drive car had a junkyard front axle put in—and the insurance company went along with it!) If things are not entirely to you satisfaction—call a lawyer.

Collision (without insurance).   It's a sad commentary on the industry that if you are paying for the damage yourself—and you make that fact crystal clear to the body man—your estimate will be considerably less than it would be on an insurance claim. (Although the actual fee paid by the insurance company would be even lower still, because the body man would expect the adjuster to bargain down from the high estimate!)

Simple Repaint.   A repaint (without body or rust repair) puts the consumer in the strongest possible bargaining position. Virtually any shop —including the ones that won't survive to the '90s—can do the job with equipment on hand. Get a lot of estimates and pick the best one. Resist the temptation to do the prep yourself, even though some shops will go as low as $99 if you bring the car in already prepped. The reason? A badly prepped car will not show the new paint as well as a professional job. Want to take pride in your vehicle? Go the extra nine yards.

Want free drinks for the rest of your life? Car paints have become very, very complex in the last few years. Even the most hardened car jock probably won't know a urethane from a nitrocellulose lacquer. Commit the following information to memory and then bet the guy sitting next to you that he doesn't know what kind of paint is on his own car.

Nitrocellulose lacquer was the great-granddaddy of the paints. Its advantage was that a tremendous shine could be achieved—with many separate coats and lots of buffing. The paint was not particularly strong, however, and is now used mainly for classic-car restorations. Oil-based enamels were popular for a while but are considered difficult to work with compared to today's more modern formulations. The advent of plastic (acrylic) was a big breakthrough in car paint. General Motors developed an acrylic lacquer in the '50s that is still used on some models. Alkyd enamels, however, are the single most popular group of paints currently in use. Their main advantage is that they're *cheap* (can't put it any more plainly that that, can I?); their main disadvantage is a long drying time. The drying problem has been circumvented by "spiking" the paint with isocyanates as hardeners. These last combinations—the spiked alkyds—are currently number one on the market. If you are *shopping* for a paint job, pay for something that will perform. Acrylic enamel is one notch better than the spiked alkyds, and an acrylic enamel spiked with isocyanate is a pretty good paint. The only paint on the market that beats that—the king of the paints, if you please—is "true" polyurethane, the polyurethane enamel that does *not* have isocyanate hardeners in it. A true polyurethane can cost at least double the price of a simple alkyd.

Paint tips

1. It's the preparation of the body, the cleaning of the old paint, and the choice of the primer that really determines how the final job will look.
2. Those "lifetime waxes" are a nuisance and require special chemicals to remove them properly.
3. The hot-selling new clear-coat paints are generally a good investment. If the underlying coat is a metallic paint, they are almost a necessity.
4. New paint should not be waxed or washed for at least a week. With cheaper paints, you should wait even longer.

Want to go fancy? Consider changing the initial color of the car to something sexier. This will cost about 20 percent more, because extra sections of the car (the trunk and hood) will have to be painted. Give some serious thought also to the new clear-coat technology. This stuff works—it produces a sharp paint job with durability and good resistance to dirt and ultraviolet contamination. Applying the clear-coat does, however, require better-than-average equipment, spray booths, and expertise.

Rust repair. There are two kinds of rust repair: (a) quick and dirty, and (b) the right way. Over the years, consumers have been slowly educated to say key words when asking for rust work: like "using metal please" or "file down to bare metal." Unfortunately, they don't understand the meaning of the magic words they are speaking and—even more unfortunately—the body man often nods sagely and does the "quick and dirty" job *anyway.*

Never forget: Rust is like tooth decay. The decay *must be* removed before the tooth can be repaired. Almost all rust problems develop from the inside out. The real rust will never be seen until the panel is removed. Welding (the correct way to replace metal) will further weaken the old metal unless a preventive is applied after the welding (see page 46). Rust that returns after body work is called "rebound rust."

Here's the best strategy: All old rust must be punched or cut out. "Sanding down to bare metal" is a meaningless phrase because the rust is coming from underneath—there is nothing to sand down *to*. The new metal should be cleaned, treated, primed, and painted. About twenty-four hours after the work is done, the panel should be oiled from underneath.

The customer is always wrong

Ever stop to think about what rust is doing underneath the car? On a frame car it could be rotting the frame from the inside. On a frameless car, it can do its nasty work on the sub-frame channels and suspension moorings. It is possible to spend several thousand dollars in rust repair on an older car and end up with a car that looks showroom-new—but it will be a death trap for its occupants. Why? because body shops typically will not do structural or underbody rust repair (as inexpensive as it may be) unless *specifically* asked by the customer. So ask.

More miracles

There are a number of converter chemicals being advertised as having the ability to neutralize rust, stop it cold, and stabilize the metal that was formerly rusting. Sound too good to be true? It may be. Most of these products are intended for external steel structures like bridges, storage tanks, grills, and catwalks—where they do a pretty decent job. A few unscrupulous companies, however, are recommending these products be used *inside* automotive panels where rust, moisture, and dirt are working their way throught the tiniest cracks and crevices. At this point, the converter chemicals are a waste of time.

Excited about fiberglass?

When fiberglass replacement panels hit the market about ten years ago, everyone thought they were a dream come true. They were cheaper than steel, they would never rust, and they were easy to find for most makes. Today fiberglass is still here, but it's hardly the rage. What happened? Reality set in—while the fiberglass fenders were cheaper to buy, the installation, prep, and painting cost as much as steel panels. True, they won't rust, but neither will steel if treated properly. And finally, crash protection—they don't have any. Using fiberglass panels on unibody cars originally designed with steel can make the vehicle dangerous in the event of a crash. Also, many suppliers have entered the market with replacement steel fenders for popular makes and prices have dropped. So forget fiberglass—it's an idea whose time has passed.

What about re-rustproofing after the repair is done? It sounds great in theory, and a lot of shops will be happy to take your money for the service, but there is a catch—it won't do a bit of good. Traditional tar-wax rust treatments simply won't stick to older, dirty metal or even to the welding work that's left after rust repair. The only thing that works—and can add to the useful life of the job—is an oil process. (See page 46.)

Other services.   Most quality body shops can offer the following services—or can subcontract them out:

- Replacing vinyl roofs (not expensive except for sanding down the damaged areas under the old one).
- Upholstery repair (as folks hang on to their cars longer and longer, this is becoming a thriving business).
- New vinyl striping or custom pinstriping.
- Banging the dents out of hub caps. (You have to ask for this one!)
- Frame repair (for rust).
- Door, hood, and trunk alignments.
- Fixing window leaks.

- Changing locks.
- Installing side mirrors.

● **WHEN:** You need a **brake shop**.

■ **WHAT TO DO:** As often happens in the car business, even simple things can become enormously complex. Brakes are an excellent example. Generally, renewing and replacing brake pads and shoes is a simple chore. Yet, if you lack the experience and expert eye that comes only from having done the job hundreds of times, you could miss something important during the job. And that error could kill somebody.

So—take this as a given—we need brake shops and mechanics that are experts at their craft.

Now for some basic economics—where's the *real* profit? A shop that makes its income on brakes alone has to have a nice comfortable profit margin or it won't survive. Yet it also has to have low prices or it will not be able to compete.

Enter the *low ball*—an advertised price for a brake job that sounds too good to be true. It is. Once the shop gets its hands on your car, they'll find that the discs need truing (or replacing), the drums need turning, the fluid needs flushing, a cylinder needs replacing, and a caliper needs rebuilding.

Bang!—there's the missing profit.

In my younger days, I used to write "renew pads only—no parts" on the work order for my brake job. The shop would inevitably get upset and tell me that there was no warranty on the work, and that I was at my own risk.

Obviously, I am still here to tell the tale. Yet the brakes of today are not as simple as the brakes of yesterday. They are smaller, so they work harder and get hotter. Different linings are used. Some calipers (boy, is this dumb) have plastic pistons—which jam if you look at them cross-eyed.

For a brake job on a modern car, deal with the best shop you can find. Insist on a test drive, and have all the parts put on the bench and measured. If something is out of spec (out of the range of specifications set by the manufacturer), replace it. Go even further—have the fluid flushed and bled every twenty-four months whether the mechanic recommends it or not. (The stuff absorbs water—and that can damage the system over time.)

When your parking brake gets loose—and they all do—have it adjusted. It's not an expensive repair. Also grease the thing before winter so that it doesn't freeze when you need it most.

The $64,000 question

Memorize this phrase: *"How much wear is there left on the lining, please?"* Say it a few times so you'll get it right. Most brake specialists can tell at a glance how long it is until you really need a brake job, but if you don't ask, they won't tell you. Brakes are not something you renew every twelve months, or only when a major problem develops (by then it could be too late). Have your brakes inspected every six months—and repeat the phrase you memorized above. They may charge you a few dollars for the inspection (the wheels may have to come off) but it will be money well spent.

A word to the wise

The semi-metallic front pads being used with increasing frequency on front-drive cars (see page 15) are unforgiving—the wear on other brake parts must be within certain specifications or the new pads will damage the rest of the system. If your mechanic recommends semi-metallics, make sure the rest of the system, rotors especially, is also properly checked.

● **WHEN:** It's time for a **car wash**.
■ **WHAT TO DO:** There are three types of washes: mechanical, pressure, and hand washes.

Mechanical washes. This is the most common type—these are the barnlike affairs with the large twirling brushes. Obviously, speed, economy, and convenience are the main advantages. Paint experts maintain, however, that the rotating brushes leave fine scratches in the paint every time they are used, and that continuous use, over a period of years, will take paint right off the car.

Also, some of the older washes use recycled water—a dubious practice in winter, because the salt content of the water will increase and residues could end up in critical body areas.

Beware the so-called "hot wax" feature—this is not a real wax at all, but rather a temporary water-dispersal agent that is mainly a profit-maker. (Besides, if the car before you got the "hot wax" treatment, so did you!)

On many of the smaller cars, the rollers on the brushes can damage windshield wipers, particularly on the rear hatch.

The best part of the automatic washes? The tire grabbers and scrubbers —they do a fine job!

Pressure washes.   The "imitation" pressure wash can be found in most cities, where for a few quarters car owners can rent a high-pressure water-spray gun and hose down their own car. Rating: not bad. Bring some soap and a hand mitt, and you'll really be getting a good wash.

Real pressure washes are harder to find. Call a truck-fleet operator and find out where he goes. We're talking *macho* pressure washes, real John Wayne stuff. Not expensive, either.

Hand wash.   Nothing could be simpler, right? Wrong. There are dozens of ways to do a hand wash—and even the experts don't agree on all points. The best of their tricks:

1. Never wash in direct sunlight.
2. On the window glass, use water as hot as you can stand and buff with newspaper.
3. A soft wool mitt is best for scrubbing.
4. Use a *mild* detergent. Even dishwasher detergent will do a great job.
5. Using a window squeegee to scrape off excess water will speed up drying. Follow up with a chamois.
6. If the old wax is still there, rub lightly with a very soft dry towel once the car has dried to bring back the shine.
7. Both vinyl roofs and magnesium wheels deserve their own very special detergent. (Dishwasher liquid will do in a pinch. A toothbrush—one you no longer use—can really help with mags.)
8. Spray "after-washes" like Armor-All are great, but are too expensive.
9. Small scratches can be "rubbed out" with rubbing compound, but if you overdo it you'll do more harm than good.

10. Vinyl roofs and mag wheels also deserve their own special waxes —especially the mags, because they are especially prone to corrosion.

● **WHEN:** You want **detailing** on your car.

■ **WHAT TO DO:** Detailing is an art. For a few hours' labor and a few dollars (under $50) a detailer can take a ten-year-old car that would look at home on a scrap heap and make it look like an award-winner. Detailers use:

- Wax to make the outside look good
- Rubber cleaners and glazes to make the tires look great
- Chemicals and steam to scrub down the engine
- Special paint and paint guns to repaint the engine and radiator
- Special clear lacquers to make the rubber hoses look new
- Cleaners to care for the rugs, and dyes to cover bad stains
- Vinyl kits to fix tears in the vinyl
- Special upholstery cleaners

Where do you find detailers? Look in the Yellow Pages under "Car Cleaning," try some trim shops, and, if you get desperate, phone a large used-car dealer and ask him to refer you to *his* detailer.

● **WHEN:** You want a **diagnostic center**.

■ **WHAT TO DO:** Diagnostic centers were big business in the '60s. Many of the oil companies got into the act and introduced special bays with the latest in modern test equipment. For a mere $19.95, it was said, the very darkest of your car's secrets could be revealed. The rest is history. People started to notice that: (a) the same car came back with completely different reports from different centers, and (b) even a brand-new car couldn't sneak through for only $19.95—usually $119.95 was more like it.

Customers stayed home with one hand clutched firmly over their wallets. Most of these shops have been converted to car washes or storage space.

So where do you go for a good diagnostic job? The AAA and CAA (see page 228) have—in certain areas—arranged for at-cost diagnostic testing for members. Try this route first. In terms of sheer *volume* of test equipment, your friendly dealer has the latest and the fanciest stuff—he's the only one who can afford it! (Always get a second opinion if the repair cost quoted is high.)

Your own personal mechanic is still your best way to interface with the repair trade—cultivate his friendship, his love, and introduce him to your daughters. He is worth his weight in gold. (See page 119.)

Do-it-yourselfers

The following "tool chest" of diagnostic equipment is not expensive and will help you test for 75 percent of the problems your car is likely to come up with: a radiator pressure tester, a gas-tank pressure tester, a battery hygrometer and voltmeter, an antifreeze strength tester, an electronic ignition tester, a spark-plug (neon) tester, a continuity tester, a "hot" probe tester, a compression tester, and a vacuum gauge tester.

● **WHEN:** Your **engine** needs a new lease on life.

■ **WHAT TO DO:** Off to the engine rebuilder you go. Engine rebuilders are doing fine; thanks for asking.

First, as cars approach an average retail of $15,000 (try to say that and smile at the same time—bet you can't!) it seems more and more reasonable to rebuild an old engine for $1500 and use the change to make a down payment on house, or perhaps pay for Johnny's college.

The engine rebuilders are also thriving on the new econobox cars with their high-revving overhead-cam engines, aluminum-alloy composition, and owners who don't know the difference between a spark plug and a taco chip.

In perusing the minutes of the annual meeting of the American Society of Engine Rebuilders (1983) I noted that these businessmen were especially pleased about what happens when the weather gets cold and owners (using too thick a motor oil for the temperature) get into the car and zip off to work without letting the oil pressure build in the valve area. Engines were seizing up all over the country. And the engine rebuilders were loving every minute of it.

Do you need a rebuilder? If old Bessie is belching blue smoke and making *pocketa-pocketa* noises, you do. If the valve compression is so low that you can barely start the car or climb a hill, you do. If your mechanic (the one you've permitted to date your daughter) says it does, you probably do.

Tip #1—Don't do half a job. The major expense in engine rebuilding is the labor. Once it's open, you may as well change everything that moves inside it.

Tip #2—Don't try to save money by doing the engine removal or disassembly yourself. Unless you are a Grade A mechanic (you've been keeping secrets from me!) there are tricks to the job that you can't even guess at. At least, if the rebuilder makes a mistake, the labor is guaranteed as well.

Tip #3—Pick your rebuilder carefully. Ask around. In the trade, the rebuilders are known by their failure rate. ("Oh, Joe down the street? Only had to send back six of his jobs. Sam? Sam's engines never run right until he's had them apart three or four times.")

Tip #4—If you want any customizing done (see page 129), such as a special cam or oversize pistons, discuss this before the engine is apart, not after. Agree not only on price, but on brand names and warranty as well.

Alternatives to rebuilding

Rebuilders are the best solution, but not the only one. You can "swap" engine sections for commercial rebuilds (mass-production rebuilds of someone else's engine). Many parts and machine shops offer this service; even chains like Sears maintain a "swap" connection. Nor must you go for a whole engine—you can pick only the valve train (the head), or simply the piston assembly ("short block"). Commercial installation can be arranged at the same time, but the warranty will never be as good as for a custom rebuild. Also, scrap yards ("parts recyclers," as they now call themselves) also have lots of low-mileage engines in good running condition—and the price should be quite reasonable indeed.

● **WHEN:** You need **insurance**.

■ **WHAT TO DO:** Insurance is a subject so complex that I could write a separate book about it.

Let's take it one step at a time:

Do you need it? All states require some kind of insurance. The differences in no-fault laws determine which types (first-party, liability, etc.) are mandatory *and* whether you can use the courts to recover damages in spite of the no-fault law. In any case, you are advised to carry *extra* coverage such as comprehensive, collision, and medical. (Ask your local broker for details.)

What are basic types of coverage?

1. Third-party—bodily. This looks after the claims of others whom you hurt with your car.
2. Third-party—property. Similar to bodily, but looks after damages to physical objects, not people.
3. Collision. Covers damage to your own vehicle. May or may not have a deductible (an amount you have to pay in cash if you are at fault). One advantage is that, even if the claim itself takes a long while for the adjusters or the courts to settle, you can claim under this to have your own vehicle repaired almost *immediately.*
4. Medical. Covers the driver and passenger in your car at the time of the accident.
5. Uninsured motorists. This is becoming more and more important. In areas where no-fault does not reign, you may have to look to the personal assets and insurance coverage of the driver whose vehicle hit you if he was at fault. This coverage foresees the day when the driver will be insured inadequately or not at all.

Insurance Tip

Underinsured coverage (where the party at fault has some coverage but not enough) is, in some jurisdictions, *not the same* as simple uninsured coverage. The agent, who makes precious little profit on selling it, may hesitate to make the suggestion. It is therefore up to you to be certain that your coverage includes *both uninsured* and *underinsured* coverage.

---

6. Comprehensive. Covers mainly fire and theft. This is the catch-all, even covering things like stone damage in windshields. Note that you must have a police report to claim reimbursement under theft insurance. Fire claims demand proof of an actual fire ("no flame, no claim"). Items *not directly related to the operation of the car* (like that $2000 portable computer you carry with you) are not covered unless specifically named under a special rider; it's often better to cover them under a home policy.

Do you want to go directly to an agent of a particular company or an independent broker? This is an awkward issue. Some companies encourage you to come directly to them, give you competitive rates, and then try to get all your insurance business. (Not surprising, since car insurance is hardly a source of profit for insurers these days.) There's only one problem: although all companies provide more or less the same coverage at more or less the same price, they differ widely in *service, speed,* and the *friendly* processing of claims. Therefore, you really want either to pick a top-notch car insurer right off the bat (check back issues of *Consumer Reports*) or, better yet, you want to pick a top-notch broker who is intimately familiar with the pros and cons of the various companies and will do the choosing for you. I favor the broker.

Is there any competition left?

According to recent studies, at least twenty states in the United States still have freely competitive pricing systems for insurance, which can lead to aggressive discounting if the customer contacts three or more companies. In other words, it still pays to shop around.

Does it matter whether or not you live in a no-fault area? Yes, very much—and you have a moral obligation to yourself and your family to find out how the system in your state or province works. At the time of this writing, twenty-seven states in the United States and several provinces in Canada have introduced some form of no-fault. All no-fault is *not* the same. In some instances, additional private insurance is required. In some instances lawsuits under no-fault are outlawed and in some cases they are not. In some cases the problem of a motorist who is hit by an out-of-state motorist can be a nightmare without some form of uninsured-motorist coverage (see above). So do your homework now, before it's too late.

Does the kind of car you drive affect the rate? Yes, indeed, but it's a little late in the game to change that, isn't it? The companies play rate roulette from year to year, constantly changing their minds about which vehicles they feel are higher risks than others. Some rules of thumb—sports cars of any kind are higher risks, "muscle" cars from the '60s are higher risks, cars that are in demand by car thieves (BMWs, Corvettes, etc.) are higher risks, and small econoboxes that do poorly in crash tests are higher risks.

When I shop around, what am I shopping for?   First, for the best service and second, for the best discount. Discount programs vary from company to company. They can be given for everything from a safe driving record and a driver's-education program to such things as:

- A good antitheft system
- No smoking
- No drinking
- A really conservative vehicle (a four-door station wagon means big savings!)
- More than one car
- Student away at school
- Car pool
- Farmer
- Good student
- Senior citizen
- Passive restraints
- Female, age 30 to 64
- Government employee
- Company fleet program

Any more tricks to watch out for?   Yes, some companies, concerned about inflation, are issuing only six-month policies. Consumers are often tempted by the initial savings (after all, they are paying a bill only half as big as they expected) but don't realize that the company will be sliding in a price increase at every renewal. I don't care for this trend at all.

Also, there is a controversial legal issue as to whether the insured is duty-bound to notify the company about accidents he has during the term of the policy that might affect his rate. Say, for example, you are insured under a low safe-driving rate and get into a fender bender that is your fault. Rather than claim under your policy (and risk a rate increase) you pay the other guy out of your own pocket. Are you obligated to report the accident to your insurer and catch the increase anyway? Some say yes, some say no. Some companies will send questionnaires out from time to time asking for ecent accidents or recent traffic violations. Fibbing on these might be more han enough ground to void your policy. Also, in jurisdictions where drivers' :ecords are publicly available for a fee, most companies will do a periodic spot check to see what's really going on. (See also page 61.)

Antique-car owners

There are policies available for a second (or third) car that is more a collectible than a day-to-day runabout. Special insurance policies from companies offering this kind of coverage are quite reasonable— usually less than $200 per year per car. *But read the contract first—* you may be restricted as to how many miles you can drive. You may even be given a phone number to call in advance of an outing. The information you provide the agent could be critical: whether or not the car is modified, for example. (Most insurers get nervous about insuring '60s muscle cars that have been modified for race use— understandably, of course.)

Recently upgraded old Bessie?

Watch out—the thousands of dollars you just poured in may disappear if an accident occurs before you notify the company that you have made the investment. Two options: either try to get a rider for "replacement value" on the policy which virtually entitles you to another car of the same condition, *or* ask for an independent appraisal of the newly overhauled car and pay for protection equal to the appraised value. (See your agent for details. Procedures vary from company to company.)

● **WHEN:** You need a good **mechanic**.

■ **WHAT TO DO:** Did you know that there is less than one mechanic for every hundred cars on the road? And that every car on the road is wearing out every time it is driven—and even when it isn't?

Let's describe the perfect mechanic:

He would be an expert at his craft and be able to work on *any* car regardless of make or year.

He would have all the electronic gizmos to work on, diagnose, align, and otherwise communicate with the cars of the '80s. The equipment would be recently calibrated (alignment shops take note!) and in a good state of repair. He would know how to operate the equipment correctly, the first time, without help from the manufacturer's representative.

He would have a good shop library—technical manuals, specification sheets, parts interchange manuals (*Hollender*), electrical and vacuum routing guides, technical bulletins, etc. He would subscribe to a *current* information service like *Chilton* or *Motor.* He would have a line on local shops that specialize in getting used (junkyard) parts for all makes and models, especially older cars.

If he does not have specialty alignment, radiator, muffler, brake-refinishing, and engine-rebuilding equipment right there on the premises, he would have subcontract arrangements with quality local shops. And *he* would stand behind *their* work as well.

He would have access to Original Equipment Manufacturer (OEM) parts suppliers other than the dealer. He should pass some of this discount along to his regular customers—at least 5 percent.

Insurance Rules?

A lot of that nonsense about insurance rules forbidding customers from going into the service bays is just that—nonsense. Customers should be advised of the safety dangers (oil, grease, sharp objects) —and then be given the option of proceeding at their own risk. However, most shop owners have experienced the proverbial "obnoxious customer" who hovers over his car like a pregnant hen and pesters the mechanic with silly questions. All customers are *not* like this—but just one or two a month can be pretty scary. Ergo— the great insurance lie. Not permitted in the bays? Nonsense: it's only that the mechanic prefers to work alone. Serious owners (*my* readers, God Bless You) are advised to request permission to enter *at their own risk*—and to resist treating the mechanic like a giant Panda in a California zoo. An honest shop should not object to this request.

He would be located conveniently near a bus route (unless he had a courtesy car) and would have lots of parking.

He would book appointments in advance. A regular customer with an emergency would be entitled to rush service.

He would let you go into the service bay to watch your car being worked on, but at your own risk.

He would have written records, so he can keep track of regular customers. (These records can add to the resale value of your car!)

He would—this is the mechanic's golden rule—only replace parts that required replacement. He would perform only services that were necessary. He would keep old parts to show you the problem. He would test-drive the vehicle before and after the repair. Where there was a choice of repair procedures to take, he would explain the options and give you the choice. He would charge for time actually worked, not book time.

Estimates?

State and provincial legislators are making a big thing about estimates these days, but I think that this is a case of the tail wagging the dog. Many jobs are almost impossible to estimate until the parts are disassembled. Forcing accurate estimates is a crude method of trying to make dishonest mechanics *resemble* honest mechanics. Most of the tradespeople I interviewed were of the opinion that, under the new laws, *all* estimates would be deliberately on the high side and, if the repair came in cheaper than estimated (as most would) there would an irresistible temptation to ask for the *higher* amount.

He would do oil changes while you waited and—instead of reading a girlie magazine while the oil dripped out—he'd inspect the underside of the car for problems.

He would carry only products he believed in—not the stuff the oil company shoved down his throat.

If a job was too difficult for him, he'd say so.

He'd have a half-brother (or other relative) working at one of the big dealers so he could keep up with the latest repair problems and other gossip.

He would accept personal checks from regular customers without making them feel like axe murderers.

Does such a lad exist? Probably not—but here are some clues to help you find him:

Does your mechanic take the refresher courses that are offered by the major manufacturers, plus aftermarket companies like Moog and Champion? No? Get your car out of there fast—without these courses, it's almost impossible to keep up with the new technology.

Get recommendations from friends (the ones who know something about cars), taxi drivers, cops, limousine drivers, the auto club, local reporters, and other mechanics. (Finding a "mechanic's mechanic" is real coup!)

Avoid locations on major streets with a captive audience. These guys will lose their competitive edge in no time.

Also avoid shops that are always empty. These guys make their money by separating the occasional customer from his occasional money.

Ever hear of the broom test? One car writer swears this works—find out where the shop broom usually is and see if it's in its place. If not, go elsewhere. The reasoning, I think, is that a shop which can't even keep track of its broom might have greater difficulty taking apart (or putting back together!) someone's engine.

Call an antique-car club. They know secrets about cars (and mechanics) that most of us can only dream about. Call your insurance agent and see who he uses. Call the insurance adjuster for your insurance company (even if he has no idea who *you* are) and ask him where to go. These guys know who to trust—they have to, it's their job.

An old idea that still works

Get together six or seven friends, relations, drinking buddies, etc., all of whom have cars that they want well serviced for the next few years. It helps if everybody lives in the same area. Next give yourselves some kind of dumb name like Hell's Kitchen on Wheels and register yourselves as an organization at the local courthouse. Now approach a well-recommended shop (found using the clues above) and suggest that your club will give him *all* the work on *all* of your cars, including *all batteries, tires, mufflers,* and other repairs, provided he gives all the members: (a) discounts for cash, (b) on-the-spot service, with no waiting, and (c) unwavering honesty—as within the guidelines above.

Mechanics, Care and Feeding Of

1. Treat them like people. They are.
2. Let it be known up front that, if satisfied, you will buy everything there—including tires and batteries. They might cost a bit more, but you'll make it back in service.
3. If it's not an emergency, ask them when they would prefer you come in for service. They'll love you for it. (Tuesdays are usually the best time for most shops.)
4. If you are pleased, send them your friends. This will also benefit everybody in the long run.

Here's help

A list of certified mechanics in your area is available free from the National Institute for Automotive Service Excellence, 1825 K Street NW, Washington, D.C. 20006. (Don't expect miracles, though; many excellent and honest mechanics don't take the time to write the qualifying tests!)

A credit card with your interest at heart?

Recent consumer legislation has made it advantageous to charge mechanical repairs to your credit card, provided that the mechanic you frequent is local—usually within 100 miles of your home. The advantage is that you may not have to pay the bill if the repairs were badly done. Contact the Federal Trade Commission (FTC) for details.

● **WHEN:** You need a **muffler**.

■ **WHAT TO DO:** Most drivers still aren't completely certain what a muffler is. When interviewing the founder of one of the largest muffler chains in the country, I asked what he did. "I sell silence," he explained. "People hear a strange noise under their car, the noise is unpleasant, they come and pay me $75, and the noise goes away." That, I'm told, is how millionaires are made.

Frankly, most muffler shops today aren't too bad. The quality of the products has increased dramatically. (Some outfits were purchased by the companies that made the mufflers they installed—quality went through the roof!) Prices are good, although not by choice. The fierce competition in the industry keeps them that way. Service is usually good and prompt, the warranties are strong, muffler diagnosis and installation is a relatively simple affair, and the washrooms are clean.

Here are some things to watch out for:

- Partial warranties that cover the muffler, for example, but not the labor or fittings.
- Parts that are changed when they don't need changing. Claiming that the pipes are worn (or "soft"), many shops will try to replace the whole system. This is a needless expense. Unless you trust the technician completely, have only the damaged sections replaced. (Everything wears out over time, even automotive journalists.)
- Catalytic converters might be pushed because the profit margin is high.
- Other items that the shop "happens" to have in stock. They will be pushed too—tires, shock absorbers, and springs are most common.

The new high-performance "turbo" mufflers are often not available at the muffler shops due to low demand and low profit margins. This is a shame, because the data indicate that a well-designed muffler with low back-pressure under highway conditions can improve both mileage and power. (Ask your local speed shop for assistance—the top brands are Thrush and Cyclone.)

● **WHEN:** You need an **oil change**.

■ **WHAT TO DO:** Lots of folks change their own oil. Once, while signing books in Buffalo, I was asked a few questions about engine oil by two charming elderly ladies, either of whom could have been Whistler's *grand-*mother.

Their car was a '72 Delta in pretty good shape, and they wanted to know if it was important to change oil frequently.

"Yes," I said. "Oil changes are important. And they're not expensive, either."

"We know," replied the distinguished duo. "We do it ourselves."

Change your own oil? Congratulations. You are saving a couple of dollars on materials and labor (no more), and you are exposing yourself to one of the dirtiest and most unpleasant jobs in the car business.

Most mechanics have scars on their right little fingers, burned on hot exhaust manifolds when trying to pull the filters out of the jam-packed engine compartments of small cars. It's almost impossible to stay clean during an oil change—but you should: In 1985 the U.S. government declared old engine oil to be a major cause of skin cancer and published some unpleasant photos of what happened to mechanics who let the stuff collect on their hands.

Change your own engine oil? You have to be out of your mind.

Here's the mechanical scoop:

Frequent oil changes are required on virtually all cars on the road. Smart motorists (cab drivers, police, limousine drivers, and readers of this book) change by calendar, not by mileage. The newer higher-revving overhead-cam alloy engines need more frequent changes—not less. (GM increased the recommended frequency of oil changes for its expensive new C-cars in 1985). An oil and filter change is recommended every three months, regardless of mileage. Oil breaks down and gets contaminated even while sitting in your driveway.

Not all brands of oil are alike—and there is much controversy as to which kinds last longer. If you follow my advice and change every three months, this won't concern you, since virtually all oils labeled SF or SE (check the top of the can) can do at least three months' work without breathing hard.

Not all multigrade formulas (10/30, 10/40, 15/30) are alike in terms of staying power. In 1985, GM shocked the industry by essentially declaring 10/40 an unfit recipe for oil, regardless of brand. Apparently, it breaks down too rapidly in the crankcase. Again, changing the oil every three months—like clockwork—can bypass this problem.

Filters should always be changed with the oil regardless of what your neighbor or high-school teacher tells you. Today's filters are smaller than ever. They clog more easily. An ounce of prevention is worth a pound of cure—for sure. Manufacturers have made sincere attempts to produce a higher-quality, longer-life filter (Monroe) but Joe Public didn't give a hoot. As a result, *all* filters are about equal in quality and price and should be disposed of with each oil change.

The oil should be changed when hot because it flows better. It should be changed by draining the crankcase—not by siphoning it out of the dipstick hole, which doesn't get the sludge out.

Pre-flush

Special cleansers that you put into the crankcase about thirty minutes before the oil change to "flush" the crankcase are a good idea, but shouldn't be overdone. Once a year is about right. (See page 143.)

The gasket on the drain screw is the single most overlooked part of an oil change—it should be renewed with each change. These gaskets are inexpensive—though hard to get for some foreign cars—so pick up a handful at your dealer. In a pinch, a temporary gasket can be formed from the ever-popular multipurpose silicone gasket glue.

Oil additives are of questionable value. I've come across only one that has a real track record. See page 142.

Finally, peering into the oil-filler hole with a flashlight will give you a good indication of the condition of the inside of your engine. You should see shiny metal, not sludge or rainbow varnish.

● **WHEN:** You need **rustproofing**.

■ **WHAT TO DO:** Traditional commercial rustproofing is based on tar-wax sealants which are injected blind inside panels and allowed to dry.

Generally, one injection treats the car for life, although some shops scam the customers by asking for a yearly "inspection." (How can you inspect what you cannot see? Panels are not taken off during these inspection, nor are fenders and doors removed—so what is being inspected?)

These treatments have a host of drawbacks:

1. Large areas of metal inside the panels (where you cannot see them) are missed. Only owners unlucky enough to need to remove their panels for collision work after the rustproofing have ever noticed this.
2. The stiff, rapidly drying materials do not get into the really tiny cracks and crevices. This is doubly unfortunate, because rust *starts* in the cracks and crevices and works outward.
3. After the third year, the material dries, cracks, and deteriorates.

(Ask any body-shop technician or car mechanic what he thinks of rustproofing—he'll laugh.) Unfortunately, most of these treatments, being solvent-based, can be applied only to new metal—so reapplication is a waste of money.

4. This is the most shocking point. Areas where the traditional "dry" coatings deteriorate tend to *trap* moisture, so rust will penetrate *these* areas faster than the areas that were not treated.

The solution?

In Canada, I was responsible for a new type of rust-protection system based on yearly high-pressure oil-based treatments of the inner panels and underside of the car. The treatments, which cost about as much as a yearly tuneup, are slightly messy and virtually 100 percent effective against rust for as long as you keep your car. They also effectively retard the spread of existing rust on older cars, something the old-fashioned dry treatments can't do at all. My own process is sold under the trade name Protectoil but, based on the Canadian experience, other companies can be expected to enter the fray as demand heats up.

I had my car rustproofed—am I safe?

No, dummy, you are *not*. A sad kind of brainwashing has been going on. North American automobile owners are conditioned to look at rust as something that is inevitable—notwithstanding the promises of the car companies—and at rustproofing as something you buy simply to feel you've done the right thing, but without really expecting it to work. Many relatively new "rustproofed" cars on the road are rusting inside the panels right now. The rust will begin to peek through in a couple of years—and that will be too late. If you want to verify this, have a body shop remove a door panel or fender—and take a look.

Two special cases: Older cars and cars that have had body work. A sad limitation of the older tar-wax treatments is their complete ineffectiveness at rustproofing older cars. When cars have recently had body work, the rust will very often quickly attack at the welds used to patch the old metal—body men call this "rebound rust." The only solution seems to be oiling. (See above and page 46.)

● **WHEN:** You're checking out the **"shine" shops**.

■ **WHAT TO DO:** Slow down—many a consumer has been separated from his money because he wanted a sharp-looking car but didn't exactly know how to go about getting it.

Yes, the new paints (especially the base-coat–clear-coat combinations) are more durable, but some finish protection is still required. Yes, the new synthetic coatings are quite wonderful, but more from the applier's point of view (they're easier) than from the car's (they don't *last* significantly longer). And yes, environmental contamination and ultraviolet light (from the sun) are still a car's worst enemies, next to rust, of course.

No, there is no such thing as a lifetime wax. (Please don't run to your desk and pull out your warranty. I didn't say that no one is *selling* them—simply that they don't exist.)

> ## Fraud squad
>
> Lifetime waxes are another great scam whose time has come and gone. True, the car never needed "waxing" after the first treatment. But in the fine print of the contract was a requirement for a yearly refinishing with a special chemical that looked, smelled, and seemed to all the world like wax. It's been said before: the only thing that lasts for life is your mother-in-law.

Yes, waxing is addictive. Once you start to wax your car on a regular basis, you have to continue or you lose the protection.

No, the new synthetic finishes are not especially compatible with the old natural (carnauba) finishes. Best *not* to mix and match brands.

Yes, your neighbor has been using the same brand of wax since *Leave it to Beaver* went off the air, and his car looks great. Scary, isn't it?

What can I say? There are almost as many brands of waxes on the market as there are cars. Most, by the way, are not true waxes but contain a "polish" or abrasive agent that cleans off dirt and oxidized paint. If you wax frequently, you won't need much abrasive.

Red cars "come back" the best, even after much abuse. Black cars are the most sensitive to improper waxing—if you omit a square inch somewhere on the car, your girlfriend will see it from 100 yards.

Never wax too big an area at a time—the base chemical will dry and become hard to remove. Never use regular wax on vinyl tops—they require special treatment. The same is true for mag wheels, and for "blackout" trim.

What do I recommend? Consumers Union, publishers of *Consumer Reports,* did some testing and fell in love with a product called *Rain Dance* which is made by DuPont. It's a pretty good product. The consumer TV show *Fight Back* once tested a product called Nufinish—they were pretty pleased as well, so there's an alternative for you. (Nufinish contains more abrasives, however.)

● **WHEN:** You are checking out a **speed shop**.

■ **WHAT TO DO:** Strange but true: In my fifteen years in the business, I have never known anybody who was a regular patron of a speed shop, yet these shops are everywhere and represent a billion-dollar industry. Stranger yet is that most of these shops do not install parts themselves (though all can refer you to an installation mechanic). That reinforces the idea that those who patronize these shops are quite capable of doing their own work.

Since all speed shops carry the same products (yes, indeed) you had better look for the best price and the best service. In particular, the willingness of the counterman to listen to your problems, assist in diagnosis, and make sure you get *all* the right parts *the first time* is very important.

Here are some examples of the things you can buy at speed shops:

Fancy nonsteel wheels.   The less the unsprung weight at the wheel, the better the car handles (hence the desirability of a lighter, nonsteel wheel). Most buyers of nonsteel wheels don't know what unsprung weight is, but buy the things because they look nice. (Be careful to choose a rim size and offset that will *not* destroy your bearings—the counterman will help.)

Performance parts.   Companies like Edelbrock, Holley, Crane, and Moroso make replacement parts that can replace every single piece of the engine that came with your car. (This was demonstrated once on a Chevy 350 engine, I believe.) Why would you want to do this—for more power, for better fuel economy, or because you're completely nuts?

Performance improvements.   This can be a big step up—rather than simply replace existing parts with higher-performance parts, let's add parts that weren't there to start with, shall we? Things like turbochargers, superchargers, and water injectors fall into this category. There are dozens more.

Glamour parts.   There is no accounting for taste, as you know, and speed shops can sell you nonfunctional chromed oil-pan covers, chromed axle covers, chromed rocker covers, chromed doorknobs, and chromed speeding tickets.

Fixits.   If you take the time to go through a speed shop catalog you'll find lots of little goodies that may be used to correct deficiencies the manufacturer built into the car. One good example of a speed-shop part is the Carter ping eliminator, which works by electronically retarding the timing to get rid of the annoying ping on late-model cars. This useful device should be available in *all* auto-parts shops—but isn't.

Economy improvers.   Because of the changing times, I list this as a separate heading, but it's very close to the first category above. Many speed parts (the Edelbrock SP2P intake manifold is a good example) are targeted more toward owners looking for better fuel economy than for more performance—though the performance will be there too, I promise.

Gadgets.   Include unusual tools, antitheft devices, and other paraphernalia.

● **WHEN:** You are looking for a **tire shop**.
■ **WHAT TO DO:** Everybody sells tires these days—Sears will even mail them to you, if you wish. Still, you're better off with a pro.
   A professional shop will:

1. Test-drive your car to check for alignment and suspension problems.
2. Explain the various sizes, widths, and types of tire that will fit on your car.
3. Offer some form of factory warranty, hopefully covering *road hazards.*
4. Remove your old tires, clean the rim, and check for bent lips.
5. Mount the new tire without harming the bead.
6. Install a new valve.

What is a road-hazard warranty?

A lot of bad things can happen to tires that are not the fault of the manufacturer or of the owner. Punctures, blowouts, curb damage, alignment problems—what do you do when these prematurely retire a $150 tire? The answer is road-hazard insurance, a special kind of warranty that allows you to replace your damaged tire with a new one for a nominal fee—even though the manufacturer is not at fault. *Not all companies* offer this plan, so you have to ask and shop around!

7. Dynamically balance the tire. The new computer balancers are best, provided that they either recalibrate themselves each time they are used *or* are recalibrated by a technician once a month.
8. Mount the tire, tightening the lugs with a torque wrench in the proper sequence.
9. Provide a valve extension if needed.
10. Replace the hubcap without squashing it to a pulp.

Other services a good shop will provide:

1. Leak-tank diagnosis and plug repair of tires. (If you want a patch repair instead of the cheaper and quicker plug repair, you should consult a truck-tire specialist—see page 81.)
2. Alignments.
3. Mounting tires on custom alloy rims, using special equipment.
4. Checking for out-of-round tires with the proper equipment.
5. Repairing wheel-cover rims (if they don't stay in place).
6. Inspection of your good tires for unusual wear.
7. Changing tires at the end of the season.
8. Storing your out-of-season tires.

● **WHEN:** You need a **tow.**
■ **WHAT TO DO:**

Don't panic! Calling the nearest or most convenient service could turn into a nightmare. Are you a member of the auto club? If so, call them first.

Another good (but desperate) move is to call the local or state police and *beg* them to recommend a good service. Not that all towing shops are bad apples (far from it), but there are enough troublemakers out there to give the others a bad name.

Here are the problems to watch out for:

Outdated equipment. Approximately 15 percent of the cars on the road today should not be towed with anything except the new "wheel lift" trucks. *Most shops do not have this equipment.* Cars like the Nissan 280 ZX, Mazda RX-7, and many another with an exceptionally low chassis or fragile plastic fender parts risk *major* damage if towed by the wrong equipment.

Wrong procedures. Front-wheel-drive cars should not be towed with their front wheels on the ground except in an emergency. Even then, precautions should be taken (limited distance, transmission in neutral, and low speed). The same applies to rear-drive cars (including rear-engine, rear-drive cars like the Volkswagen Bug) being towed with the back wheels on the ground—it's a no-no. (Improper towing can be especially damaging to the "transaxles.") *Never* under any conditions tow a car with a transmission or differential case that is empty of fluid.

Repair-shop roulette. Some shops have a "sweetheart" deal with certain repair shops—they will tow only to that shop. Many such shops are noted neither for their mechanical expertise nor their sense of charity to strangers.

Overcharging. Here's a rule of thumb as valid today as it was in 1920. *Before they tow, the cost you should know.* "Surprise" charges can be very unwelcome. Remember, tow charges are *not* generally standardized.

Caution to owners of four-wheel-drive vehicles

On these vehicles, no matter which end you lift, you may still be forcing drive-train components at the other end during the tow. Read your manual—you may find that the way to tow safely is to (a) tow short distances at low speeds, or, (b) use dollies under *both* front and rear axles, or (c) disassemble the propeller shafts before towing.

TOWING

Proper towing. The basic rule in towing is "never tow a car differential-side down." The illustration shows the proper way to tow a rear-drive car (with the differential in the rear). If the front end of the car is damaged so that the car can't be towed with the front-end wheels on the ground, a dolly should be used to keep the differential off the ground. The same is true for front-wheel drive cars—keep the front end off the ground. For four-wheel drive—see your manual.

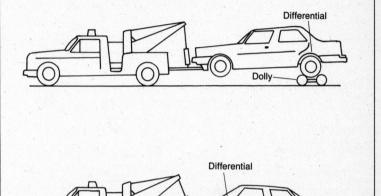

● **WHEN:** You need to find a **transmission shop**.

■ **WHAT TO DO:** You don't have to be J. P. Getty to see the predicament these shops are in—they sit there with a few thousand dollars in inventory (all of it rebuilt transmissions) and a few bored transmission-installation technicians, and then in *you* roll cheerfully asking them to check the strange noise under the car.

The strange noise may well have been a gopher trying to eat your catalytic converter, but sure as shootin', by the time you drive out of the bay you'll have (a) a new transmission, (b) a pretty new warranty, and (c) a hole in your wallet.

The automatic transmission is still the single most complex piece of mechanical equipment on your car. I agree that it's better to replace than repair them when they act up, but still you must be absolutely sure that the problem is a major one.

■ 133 ■

I recently had a transmission leak on my '72 Pontiac. My own *(wonderful!)* mechanic could not find the problem. I badgered him until he told me about a transmission shop that he (sort of) trusted, and then I scooted over. At the transmission shop, I repeated that I wasn't interested in a new unit, simply in repairing the one I had. I also made it clear that I was a referral from a mechanic he dealt with. The problem turned out to be in the seal around the sending unit to the vacuum delay. Fixing it cost me less than $10. I sincerely believe that if I hadn't made a fuss, I would have had trouble. Incidentally, that unit has over 105,000 miles on it today and still functions perfectly.

Some transmission trivia:

- Many newer units actually leave the factory with the *shift points* (the points at which the transmission shifts up or down) incorrectly set but, since most owners don't know what a shift point is, nothing is ever done about it.
- The newer lighter units are hypersensitive to overheating. Install a transmission cooler ($75) if you ever haul a trailer.
- The fluid and filter should be changed every two years. On older vehicles, where the fluid has never been changed, varnish and other deposits from the over-used fluid may have lodged themselves in critical sections of the unit. New fluid *may* loosen up these deposits and allow them to circulate through the system, where they *may* cause damage.
- If the radiator clogs on an older vehicle, it could affect the cooling of the transmission and turn a $50 repair into a $700 repair.
- Transmission antileak additives actually seem to work and are worth the $5.
- Most units don't have "band" adjustments anymore, but check your manual just in case.
- Overfilling the transmission with fluid can damage it.
- The fluid level should usually be checked with the car on a level surface with the engine on and the unit in DRIVE (but check your manual).
- "Shift kits" (available from speed shops) change the valve units and shorten shift intervals. They are expensive, work well for about a week, and then kill the transmission. (There is some controversy here, however, and some experts feel that the better kits may actually increase transmission life.)

- Fancy in-car shift knobs which make your car resemble the inside of a 747 do no major harm if properly installed.
- There still are basically two kinds of transmission fluid: type F for Ford and another for everyone else. *All brands* are basically the same. At the transmission shops, you'll see that all of their fluid comes out of the same drum!
- Some post-1985 models require a new, third type of fluid that's incompatible with the first two. Check your manual.

● **WHEN:** You are looking for a **tune-up specialist**.

■ **WHAT TO DO:** Hold your breath for this bombshell: *most modern cars don't require tune-ups.*

Cars from the '50s, '60s, and early '70s required tune-ups about twice a year.

Modern cars—with leadfree gas, fuel injection, catalytic converters, computer-controlled spark and timing, and silicone-jacketed wires—can go about 15,000 miles between spark-plug changes and several years between "tune-ups"—in the traditional sense of an ignition-system overhaul.

So we have two situations: If you have an older car with a carburetor, leaded gas, and point-controlled ignition, follow this program:

1. Change the plugs and points at least once a year, more often if you drive more than 12,000 miles a year.
2. Change the cap and wires every two years.
3. Overhaul the carburetor every 50,000 miles and clean it "on the car" once a year.
4. Have the car checked with the scope each time you go to the shop, to spot electrical problems and bad wires. Change the high-tension wires every two years anyway.
5. Service the air and fuel filters (also the PCV valve) twice a year.
6. Follow the manufacturer's recommendations on valve adjustments.
7. Don't forget the other checks: the brakes in particular. Tighten the hand brake as need be.
8. Pressure-test the radiator once year.

On more modern cars:

1. Before you do anything else, start with a scope test and an exhaust analysis. Pull one or two plugs at random to check for unusual wear.

2. Inspect all under-hood vacuum tubing and fittings. Do a leak test using a vacuum gauge or sonic leak finder.

3. Service all filters as needed. Do other mechanical checks at the same time (adjust the valves if required, pressure-test the radiator, check the brakes).

What's a valve adjustment, anyway?

Millions of cars on the road—mostly four-cylinder econoboxes—need a periodic valve adjustment (which costs about $50), but the owners of most of these cars don't know it—or even know what a valve adjustment is. Don't set yourself up for a needless engine teardown —check your owner's manual right away!

Valve adjustments are required to maintain critical valve-port clearances in the upper part of the cylinder. A badly adjusted valve may warn you by tapping or clicking (if the setting is too *loose*), but if the setting is too *tight*, you won't know about it until the valve burns or mushrooms.

---

4. If all the above check out, there is no need for further work. Do *not* buy plugs, wires, caps, or other ignition parts needlessly.

Historical footnote

Let's face it—tune-up specialty shops are no longer useful. Any ignition work you need can be handled by your friendly mechanic— see page 119. One note of caution, however: your mechanic *must* be familiar with the emission-control hardware on your car or no amount of tinkering with the plugs and wires will make it run right.

● **WHEN:** You need **vinyl repair**.

■ **WHAT TO DO:** Let's take a hypothetical situation: a sloppy mechanic sits in a brand new $20,000 car without taking the screwdriver out of his back pocket and accidentally rips, tears, and scuffs the fancy vinyl along the seat, door panel, and dash.

Can this be fixed? Yes—a professional vinyl-repair person using a wizard's chest of glues, dyes, and spray paints can fix the whole thing up *like new* for under $50.

On the other hand, an amateur, using one of those $5 kits sold in auto shops and a borrowed laundry iron, could ruin the car so badly that not even the manufacturer would recognize it.

Which would you choose?

Where to find vinyl repair:

- Yellow Pages under "Vinyl."
- Yellow Pages under "Glass and Trim."
- Some body shops.
- Some used-car detail shops (see page 113).
- Some large furniture stores.
- Rent-a-car service areas.
- Antique-car clubs.
- Call the AAA or CAA.

New product

Many vinyl dashboards eventually crack and fade badly. These are hard for even the vinyl wizards to fix. A product new in the mid-'80s was a dash "wig" that fits over the old dash. The reviews on this item aren't all in yet; check with local body shops and trim shops for more information.

Vinyl care

Detergents are not kind to vinyl. The best treatment is to wash it with a mild *soap* with warm water, let it dry, and "finish" it with Armor-All or an equivalent. If the cleaner you use makes the vinyl "squeaky" or sticky to the touch, it's too strong.

● **WHEN:** You need a new **windshield.**

■ **WHAT TO DO:** Not all windshield problems are incurable. Many bullet-hole-type cracks can be fixed as good as new (or better) without having to replace the glass. The process pioneered by a company called Novus, uses modern epoxies and heat. I've seen the results and they're excellent. Home kits based on this process are available in auto stores (these don't require heat for curing) but in my tests they don't make the grade. Where can you get this done in your area? If the Yellow Pages won't help, ask your insurance agent. Since this process cost less insurance money than a new glass, most agents will be happy to cooperate. (If you strike out, phone the Novus head office directly at 612-944-8000.)

Replacing windshields is truly a specialty. It's also a fairly quick and clean process and—if you book an appointment in advance—there is no reason why it can't be done while you wait. The typical procedure goes like this:

1. Remove the old glass with a special seal-breaking tool. (Don't be surprised if the old glass cracks in the process. The fancy tools don't always work!)
2. Clean the mating area.
3. Clean the new glass and apply cement.
4. Pop in new glass. (This is usually a 2-man job.)

Any problem areas? The windshield-wiper system and trim sections may have to come off. If these fitting are rusty, you could have a problem. If your old glass had a built-in antenna, make sure the new one does also. You should inspect the plug-in connector at the same time.

Who pays for all this fun? Usually, your insurance company—subject to a small deductible that's your own responsibility. (Business is so competitive these days that many places will quietly "eat" the deductible themselves, a practice which is of questionable ethics.)

It's a good idea to run the new glass through a car wash after a day or so (with your car attached) and check for leaks.

● **WHEN:** You think it's time to **winterize** your car.

■ **WHAT TO DO:** Hold on, fellow. Let's talk this thing out. Winterizing doesn't stand for much anymore.

In the old days, cars didn't use antifreeze all year long, so as winter approached, the water had to be drained from the block and fresh antifreeze had to be added. Multigrade oils were not invented yet, so the oil had to be replaced with a thinner grade so that the engine could turn over easily in sub-zero temperatures. (The same applied to the differential and transmission—you needed thinner oil.) The thermostat in the cooling system had to be replaced as well—for a "hotter" model that kept the engine working harder in winter, providing heat for occupants. Older cars had a WINTER and SUMMER setting on the accelerator linkage (which had to be reset), and the choke needed an adjustment for winter as well. Sometimes a well-intentioned mechanic would richen the carburetor mixture as well, just to be safe. Ignition parts in those days didn't last long, so a tune-up was often squeezed in, and, finally, changing the summer tires to winter snow tires rounded out the final bill.

Today's cars are different:

- They use the same thermostat year round.
- They use the same oil year round.
- The ignition parts do not need changing.
- The carburetor (if you have one) does not have *any* adjustments for winter.
- Many cars have all-season radial tires.

So what is winterizing all about these days?

- Make sure the ignition and battery are in good working order so that the car will start when you need it most.
- Wax the exterior finish before winter.
- Stock up on winter doodads like ice scrapers, traction aids (the metal cleats are best), and an extra set of mittens and scarves.
- Yearly pressurized oiling inside the panels and underneath is recommended.

4

WHEN SHOPPING FOR AUTO PRODUCTS

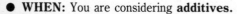

● **WHEN:** You are considering **additives.**

■ **WHAT TO DO:** Additives are a multimillion-dollar business. For a long while, the car companies turned up their noses at additives, but today, rather than miss out on a good thing, they are selling their own brands through dealer parts counters. (Some aren't bad, either—GM Combustion Chamber Cleaner is an A-1 product.)

Additives come in many flavors. Let's look at a few:

Gas Additives. Well, first you have dry-gas, which is actually methyl alcohol. Yes, it works in small doses (about 8 ounces per tank) and yes, it's cheaper to buy this stuff in a hardware store under its chemical name. Much cheaper, in fact. Dry-gas is useful not only in winter, when water could freeze in a fuel line and clog it, but also in summer to keep condensation problems at a minimum.

Next, we have upper-cylinder lubricants, also called "top oils." These materials (similar to diesel oil) are meant to lubricate the critical upper-cylinder areas of the engine and were once, before the advent of computerized cars, pretty well thought of by mechanics. On the cars of the '80s there is some concern that upper-cylinder lubricants are not compatible with catalytic converters and that they may cause problems in delicate fuel injectors.

Next, we have cylinder cleaners and de-gummers. Gasoline turns gummy as it decomposes and can, over a period of years, clog up carburetors and even manifolds. Poor combustion in the cylinders can leave carbon deposits which raise the engine compression and lead to pinging and dieseling (see page 184). These products, added to the gas, are supposed to de-gum and de-carbon. They do work fairly well, but (a) are expensive, (2) won't work miracles on a seriously neglected engine, and (c) may foul plugs, emission valves, oxygen sensors (wire or plug type), and catalysts. Check your manual or call your dealer before using. (There are also products which combine upper-cylinder lubricants and combustion chamber cleaners. *Read the product label!*)

Lastly, we have additives which are supposed to give you better mileage. These are particularly unusual because most "better mileage" products are designed to be added to your oil, not the gas. The gas additives claim to increase the combustion efficiency within the cylinder. Do they work? One brand that I know of actually did improve mileage in tests, but also damaged the engine. (No names, please, there are lawyers in the room.) You're probably better off avoiding these.

Diesel fuel additives. There are many different kinds of diesel fuel additives available. The most popular claim to: (a) keep diesel fuel from gelling in cold weather, and (b) prevent fuel contamination and breakdown. Read your warranty before using these products. Some diesel engine manufacturers forbid the use of any additives, with the possible exception of bactericide/fungicide products.

Transmission additives *(for automatic transmissions)*. Again, there are many brands and many claims made for them. The majority are designed to stop leaks by softening up or swelling internal seals which may have become brittle. (Most "power steering" additives work in the same way.) These usually pretty harmless.

Transmission additives *(for manual transmissions)*. Most of these are friction reducers, similar to those you add to engine oil to improve mileage.

Battery additives. These are sold as a means of restoring power to old batteries. With all due repect to the snake oil salesmen who hawk them, most don't do much.

Radiator additives.   There are several main types:

The first, *water pump lubricants,* won't help much. A properly maintained *antifreeze* mixture (you're supposed to flush and fill this every two years, or had you forgotten?) will contain this anyway.

The second type, *additive restorers,* are supposed to supplement the antifreeze additives that have been made ineffective by time and hard work. Again, the logic behind these products is correct, but if you are flushing-and-filling like you are supposed to, you won't need these.

The last group are the leak sealers. Most (not all) work by clogging up the leak with fine material or cement. Since it is relatively expensive to replace a radiator (or to repair it—because you have to remove it from the car before you can work on it) most mechanics will try a leak sealer before deciding to rebuild a radiator.

Windshield-washer additives.   These are usually just high concentrations of detergent. Try a few brands until you find one you like. No additive on the market will improve worn-out wipers, however.

Rear-axle additives   *(for rear-drive cars).* Again, most are friction-reducers designed to improve mileage. (See next.)

Motor-oil additives.   Here we go again—a book could be written on this subject. Motor oil is a billion-dollar business worldwide. One might expect (foolishly) that customers would have enough confidence in the manufacturers to trust their cars simply to regular oil changes (every three months regardless of mileage—see page 213) without the need for additives.

No such luck. Nobody trusts anybody anymore, and additives are big business these days.

The first and most popular type are the VI improvers (thickeners), which simply thicken the oil so that, on a worn engine, the oil won't flow past the rings as fast, and the pump will be able to hold pressure better when the motor is hot. Bearing noises are quieted as well. (In the old days, when I was a lad, bananas in the crankcase served the same function.) There are many different brands of this stuff that make many claims on the label, but you can spot them easily by shaking the can before you buy. This stuff is as thick as molasses and simply won't move even when you agitate it. Mechanics consider them temporary remedies at best, but—aside from accentuating any problems you have in starting in the cold—they can't hurt. The best-known VI improver is the original formula, STP.

The second group is the detergents. Your oil *already* has detergents in it to start with. The working theory here is that you, the thoughtless owner, have not been changing oil often enough and that a lot of crud has built up inside the cylinders, at the valves, and along the rings, so your oil needs extra detergent to clean everything up. There is some respect for this theory among the mechanics I polled, so, if you are so inclined, give it a try. Side effects seem minimal, although the oil will quickly be contaminated from all the freed-up sludge and should be changed a few days after use of the detergent.

Not quite an additive

Crankcase flushes are new on the market and are gaining favor with mechanics. These are not really additives because you must drain the crankcase (and change the oil and filter) minutes after use. What they do is quickly remove many years' worth of accumulated sludge and "varnish" from poorly maintained engines. They provide good value for the money—but removing all that sludge may reveal other problems that the varnish was masking.

The last group of oil additives is also the most controversial. These claim to provide better mileage by somehow reducing the internal friction of the engine and enabling it to produce more horsepower with less gasoline. Products such as these would also benefit gear boxes and rear axles on rear-drive cars—if they worked.

Do they work? According to the U.S. government, which tests all major gas-saver products each year or so, none work. Period. Who am I to argue with the U.S. government? Well, I found one product which has not only garnered some pretty impressive media endorsements (*Popular Mechanics* thought it was the cat's pajamas) but has some pretty impressive independent data to back it up it as well.

The additive Tufoil, invented by a reputedly eccentric American inventor, supposedly reduces friction inside your engine by means of tiny Teflon particles held in suspension. We already know that Teflon is one of the slipperiest substances on the planet (Teflon-coated bullets can pierce bullet-proof vests). One of the biggest hurdles to developing a formula was to keep the stuff floating in suspension so that it won't clot with itself and gum up the engine. The Tufoil people have reputedly achieved this by a special patented charging process. You treat your engine with about 8 to 15 ounces to start, then about 8 ounces every other oil change. The proven benefits seem to be: (1) about 8 percent better mileage, (2) a dramatic increase in cold-starting efficiency, even in subzero temperatures, (3) a smoother-running engine with reduced tendency to ping, and (4) longer overall engine life, even in subzero climates.

● **WHEN:** You need a **battery.**
■ **WHAT TO DO:** There are three kinds of batteries:

The old-fashioned add-water-once-in-a-while types. Actually these are pretty reliable if you maintain them, and will generally take more abuse than the newer reduced-maintenance types.

The reduced-maintenance kind. These are of different internal construction and don't require water as often, although there is some provision for adding water. They cost more than the regular type and usually have a built-in color-coded specific-gravity tester to tell you the state of the charge, and whether or not the unit will accept a recharge. (See your owner's manual to read the color code.)

True maintenance-free batteries. These have no provision for adding water, are the most expensive of the bunch, and will generally give excellent service until you abuse them by leaving your lights on overnight or by letting your defective alternator overcharge, at which time they will be forevermore useless.

There are basically three places to buy batteries:

Retail stores. Regardless of how many places sell batteries, only a handful of manufacturers in the world actually make them, so it's a safe bet that many brands are equivalent. Match the rating you need to your car, make sure there is a warranty, and, if free installation is included, take it. (Batteries are heavy!)

CAP TYPE VS. SEALED BATTERIES

Old-fashioned filler cap and newer sealed cap type batteries.

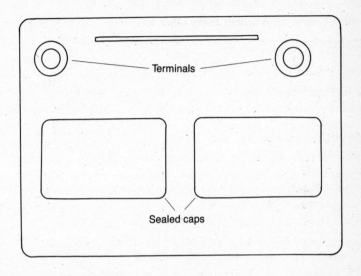

Terminals

Sealed caps

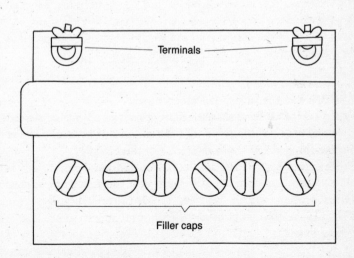

Terminals

Filler caps

Battery rebuilders.   Only large cities have these. Prices and warranties vary. See your Yellow Pages.

Scrap yards (a.k.a. parts recyclers).   What happens to all those fresh young batteries in late-model wrecks? They end up in cars like yours, if you're sharp. Prices vary, usually no warranty.

Protect your investment

Battery chargers work by converting household current to direct current so as to keep the battery fully charged. For example, if you use the vehicle sparingly, you might want to use a "trickle" (lo-amp) unit to keep the battery healthy. These units cost under $30. Some easy-to-use models can be plugged into the electrical system directly through the cigarette lighter. They must be left on for at least twelve hours at a time to have any effect. (In contrast, high-amp chargers can recharge a dead battery in mere hours, but there is evidence that powerful chargers can shorten battery life.) The new maintenance-free batteries are particularly sensitive to overcharging so, ideally, select a unit that automatically reduces charging current as the battery charges. (Expect to pay more for this feature.) Always follow the directions for hookup that come with the charger. Incorrect installation can cause the same sort of explosion as an incorrect boost start—bad news any way you slice it! As with boosting, never charge a frozen battery; if there are vent caps, remove them before starting to charge.

● **WHEN:** You are looking for **cheap parts.**

■ **WHAT TO DO:** Be reasonable. If you are driving a BMW or Mercedes, the odds of finding cheap parts are reduced—to say the least. (The odds of finding cheap *anything* are reduced with these cars!)

On the other hand, if you are driving an American product, or a very popular Japanese product, the odds improve. If you are driving a common American product from the '50s, '60s, or '70s (particularly a Chevy with a V-8 engine) the odds go through the roof.

Where to look:

Dealer.   Ha-ha. Just kidding. Nothing at the dealer is cheap. Even the price of ashtrays goes up daily on the inventory computer.

Corner auto-parts store. This guy probably buys his parts through a long chain that begins with the manufacturer (an "aftermarket" manufacturer, that is) and goes through one or two warehouse distributors and a jobber to boot. Even at that, his prices may beat the dealer.

Mass merchandiser and mass mail-order. Good bet, if you don't mind availability problems on certain parts. These guys have good prices all the time.

Scrap yard. Excellent prices, but a nuisance. Even the trend toward radio-dispatched parts and computer searches hasn't changed the basic fact that most of these guys are just plain unfriendly to deal with. (On the other hand, when's the last time you asked a yard operator to lunch?)

"Part Mart" locaters. Aha!—some light on the horizon. These guys are a new wrinkle in the business, and welcome too. They run storefront operations that are clean and friendly and chockful of recycled parts—but their main value is their "little black book" of yard operators in the area and their willingness, for a reasonable fee, to phone around and find your part for you. Recommended.

Cars for sale—parts only. If you have the space, buy a spare car and keep it as a source of parts.

● **WHEN:** You need a **child's safety seat.**
■ **WHAT TO DO:** Children's safety seats come in three basic types: *Infant* (up to 20 lbs.), *Convertible* (for infants or toddlers up to 40 lbs.), and *Toddler* (for 20 to 60 lbs.).

There are many styles and brand names within each type. You should avoid models produced before January 1981, as these may not meet current government standards. For test reports on seat performance, contact:

National Child Passenger Safety Association
1705 DeSales Street N.W., Suite 300
Washington, DC 20036
(202)429-0515

Once you've bought the right model, the next step is installation. If the seat is to work properly, you must follow the installation instructions carefully—not only the ones that come with the seat but also those from the car manufacturer. (See your owner's manual.) Most late-model cars have pre-drilled bolt holes to facilitate installation, but to use these you must first know *where* they are and what *size* bolt to use.

Once you have all this information, you can proceed.

Never cut corners in this type of installation—the savings just can't be worth the risk!

Should you ever remove an installed child's seat, be sure to plug the bolt holes with silicone—otherwise they may admit deadly carbon monoxide from beneath the car.

● **WHEN:** You want a **citizens' band radio.**

■ **WHAT TO DO:** Hang on to your hats—here's the official pronouncement: The CB craze of the '70s is officially over.

It is no longer considered trendy, hip, fashionable, or sophisticated to get a car CB installed and use it to:

- Call the wife before coming home to dinner.
- Call the girlfriend before calling the wife.
- Call strangers and pretend you're a six-foot Texan with jaw disease.
- Spend hours listening to total strangers do all the above.

Yes, real truckers still use CBs to talk to each other, but they are certainly not as friendly to strangers as they used to be. The CB madness of a few years back scared the heck out of them!

Why would you want a CB? Some of the advantages are:

- Someone to call in case of emergency.
- Highway patrol will monitor Channel 9.
- Weather and traffic reports.
- Possible radar warnings from well-meaning sociopaths.

How much do they cost? Prices have dropped—prices with installation included are less than $100.

Theft factor? Not the problem it once was. Car thieves like to be in fashion too, you know.

Any special brand? The brands that survived are all pretty equal. Uniden makes a nice model that keeps the guts of the thing in the trunk and all the major controls on the mike. Although I don't think theft control is an issue anymore, the advantage of the hideaways is that they don't take up much dash space, which, in the newer cars, is at a premium.

Antennas? Yes—folks still like to rip off CB antennas. Must be a primal urge of some sort. Spend the extra dollar and get the break-apart type, which you stow in the trunk when not in use. Some flexible rubber types are coming on the market, but word on the street is that most of the cheaper ones don't perform and the ones that do don't justify the high cost. (I've seen a "hidden" antenna in mail-order catalogs that installs under the dash using the existing connections to your AM radio. The retail is about $15, which means you're really buying an item with a wholesale worth of under $5. As expected, early reports are not totally enthusiastic.)

"Hey, good buddy. I was rocketing down I-90 with a song in my heart and the pedal to the metal when my baby blues gave me the news there was a bear in the air. I shifted the tranny, moved my fanny, and put out a 10-33 to my lawyer friend Danny." Yes, friends, it is still possible for grownups to talk like that on the CB. Here are the "top twenty" call codes:

10-1	Unable to copy
10-2	Signal OK
10-3	Stop transmission
10-4	Message received
10-6	Standby
10-7	Leaving the air
10-8	In service
10-9	Repeat please
10-10	Standing by
10-13	Weather/road report
10-16	Pickup expected at _____
10-18	Checking in please?
10-19	Nothing to report
10-20	My location is _____
10-24	Assignment complete
10-27	Moving to channel _____
10-33	EMERGENCY!
10-36	Time check
10-77	Nothing on air
10-100	Rest stop

● **WHEN:** You want to **customize** your car.

■ **WHAT TO DO:** After you've exhausted the local speed shops, you'll find that the most exotic parts are available by mail only. Try J.C. Whitney and Rick's (Kansas City) for openers. Attend a few car shows and swap sources of supply with other owners.

CUSTOMIZING SOURCES

General customizing:
Cal Custom
23011 S. Wilmington
Carson, CA 90745

Mr. Gasket
4566 Spring Rd.
Cleveland, OH 44131

Performance improvements:
Crane Cams
100 N.W. Ninth Terrace
Hillandale, FL 33009

Moroso (great catalog!)
Carter Dr.
Guilford, CT 06437

TRW
8001 E. Pleasant Valley Rd.
Cleveland, OH 44131

Isky Cams
16020 S. Broadway
Gardena, CA 90247

Oil and transmission coolers:
Hayden Coolers
1531 Pomona Rd.
Corona, CA 91720

General shopping:
Sears
303 E. Ohio St.
Chicago, IL 60611

Whitney's (#1 in the
  business)
1917 Archer Ave.
Chicago, IL 60680

Wards
6200 St. John
Kansas City, MO 64123

Rick's
2754 Roe Ln.
Kansas City, KS 66103

Exhaust headers:
Hedman Headers
9599 W. Jefferson Blvd.
Culver City, CA 90230

Hooker
1032 W. Brooks
Ontario, CA 91761

Japanese car parts:
Interpart
100 Oregon St.
El Segundo, CA 90245

CUSTOMIZING SOURCES

European car parts:
MG Mitten
36 S. Chester
Pasadena, CA 91101

IECO
1431 Broadway
Santa Monica, CA 90404

Carburetors:
Holley
11955 E. 9 Mile Rd.
Warren, MI 48090

Gauges:
VDO
116 Victor
Detroit, MI 48203

Superchargers:
B&M
9152 Independence
Chatsworth, CA 91311

Ignition:
Accel
Box 142
Branford, CT 06405

Jacobs
3327 Verdugo Rd.
Los Angeles, CA 90065

Shocks and struts:
KYB
901 Oak Creek Dr.
Lombard, IL 60148

Spoilers:
Kamei
300 Montowese
North Haven, CT 06473

Turbochargers:
Ak Miller
9236 Burmudez St.
Pico Rivera, CA 90660

Intake manifolds:
Offenshauser
5232 Alhambra
Los Angeles, CA 90032

Edelbrock
411 Coral Circle
El Segundo, CA 90245

● **WHEN:** You want a **defense against radar.**

■ **WHAT TO DO:** Is police radar fair? Pull up a chair and let's talk this out like sensible adults. Are the speed limits fair? Do *most* people travel *under* or *over* the limits? (The answer is *"over."*)

So why do the police pull over? The ones driving far in *excess* of the limit, the ones driving *moderately* in excess of the limit, or simply *anyone* they catch speeding on the day they are out trying to make their quotas? (The correct answer is a *combination* of all three situations.)

Yes, Virginia, there really are quotas. There *have* to be because: (a) speeding tickets are a nifty source of municipal revenue, and (b) most municipalities tend to spend more than they make (except possibly for Horse's Paw, New Mexico), and (c) the cost of the radar and the training it takes for the cops to use it—or abuse it—is yet *another* expense.

So Mr. Police Officer is out there doing his thing and you get picked up on the radar. What to do?

Drive slower in the future. A good idea, but, as I said, most folks "speed" most of the time. The real trick is *avoiding* radar traps rather than driving more slowly than the rest of the traffic you're traveling with.

Fight the ticket. Another good idea, but very time-consuming. (The best book on this costs about $30 and can be purchased from the Electroalert Company, a manufacturer of radar detectors. See below.) Thinking about going to court and defending yourself? Been catching up on all the old Perry Mason reruns, have you? You had best do *lots* of homework before the trial date. Some unusual uses of radar that might help get you off are:

- Speeding unverified by visual sighting can be inaccurate (radar can clock trees going down the highway at 30 mph).
- Radar not properly tested or set up (subpoena a copy of the instruction manual).
- Radar set up on an angle greater than 30 degrees to the road (leads to something called "cosine error").
- Radar set up too close to power lines, bridges, and tunnels (which can confuse the radar).
- Radar beam width was wider than the operator thought and could have picked up traffic going the other way (an interesting defense —all too often true).
- The suspect vehicle (that's you) was traveling within 100 feet of a larger vehicle traveling faster, and the radar was unable to distinguish between the two.

Before you try any of these, talk to a lawyer. Otherwise you might anger the judge and get sent up for life.

Buy a detector. Good news—radar detectors are a big business worldwide, and some excellent designs are on the market. Although price is not dropping as fast as expected (most top models cost several hundred dollars), the units' size is decreasing everyday. Most of the newer models can even fit in a shirt pocket—which raises some awkward constitutional "search and seizure" questions in those jurisdictions where the detectors are illegal. Also, the newer models, having better discrimination, rejects signals from other detectors. (If your detector goes off for ten minutes straight while you are on the highway, the same thing is probably happening to the poor guy in the car next to you!)

Brands I can recommend are: Electroalert (for starting the whole thing); BEL (a Canadian company that is very competitive and produces some very advanced stuff); and Escort (overpriced but unequaled in after-sales service). A final tip—most units come with detailed instructions describing how to tell from the warning signal where the radar is coming from. The instructions are complex but worth reading.

The odds

Here's the scoop—if you get ticketed and fight it, the odds are *against* you. You lose! The trick is not to get ticketed in the first place. Most radar infractions are based on a proximity of an eighth of a mile or less! Why? Because even the police would have trouble distinguishing radar signals further out—*don't forget they're supposed to back up each "electronic" reading with a visual fix* (although whether they do it all the time is debatable). If you have a detector, it can easily give you over a mile of advance warning—even more if the radar signal has lots of trees and other things to bounce off before it gets to your detector. But what if you have no detector? Keep your eyes peeled for radar-equipped police cars off the shoulder in the distance. If you see radar —*slow down*—because radar cannot fix on a rapidly decelerating object. Stay near large trucks or any other larger vehicle that is going at a rate you can live with—the readings will be jumbled. If you are alone on the road and entering a blind curve—*slow down*—those are the number 1 choice for radar traps.

The address for the Electroalert office (these are the people who can provide reams of data to help you win your court case) is:

Electroalert
4949 South 25A
Tipp City, OH 45371

Electroalert also makes the Fuzzbuster brand detector and has been super helpful in fighting antiradar-detector laws throughout the US.

The famous Escort machine is available from:

Cincinnati Microwave
1 Microwave Plaza
Cincinnati, OH, 45272

The BEL people have not one but two toll-free numbers: 1-800-268-3994 (in Canada) and, 1-800-835-4054 (in the US).

Want to turn invisible?

It is possible to alter the radar profile of a car by wrapping the nose in various insulating materials, but it's a lot of work and your car will look strange. If you are really serious, write to the Library, *Car & Driver* magazine (3460 Wilshire Blvd., Los Angeles, CA 90010), and try to get a copy of their experiment with radar masking. The only *other* way to beat radar—aside from turning invisible (and if you can do that you probably don't need a car anyway) is to make a broadcast unit that sends *false* signals to police radar—or jams the radar entirely. (In other words, you are really going 110 mph but you are electronically sending a message to the police radar that you are only going 55 mph.) Are such devices legal? no, not really, but it *is* possible to order plans to build a jammer (check any car magazine for these ads). At least one company has attempted to sell "broadcast" devices that operate by transmitting "noise" to the two frequencies used by police radar and blank out the signals. (Note that you can't use a detector *and* a jammer together, since the jammer would blank out the detector as well. Pick one or the other.)

● **WHEN:** You're shopping for **diesel fuel.**

■ **WHAT TO DO:** Read your manual carefully. Pay special attention to what additives, if any, you are permitted to use. (The two most common additives on sale are to prevent gelling in winter and to prevent bacterial contamination.) Find out what steps you are supposed to take to keep water out of your fuel and follow them—some filters require frequent changes.

Quick tips

Having a machine shop install a drain plug in the fuel tank will permit periodic draining of water, since the water is heavier than the fuel. This is an old Air Force technique—and a good one! (Parts source for do-it-yourselfers: Peake, 16615 Budd Rd., Poolesville, MD 20837)

Stay away from heating oil. It's not pure enough, and it's illegal. (If you are caught, there are fines.)

The *correct* fuel for virtually all diesels is number 2. Problems can, however, develop in cold weather if the fuel starts to "wax" or "gel." One solution is to install an in-line fuel heater (standard on most modern cars), although this is not enough to prevent the problem from taking hold in the tank ahead of the gas line. In that case, during cold spells, use *either* number 2 diesel sold as "prewinterized" at the pump, *or* number 1 diesel all by itself, *or* equal parts of number 2 diesel and any one of the following: kerosene, number 1 diesel, or nonpremium gasoline. Note, however, that using anything other than straight number 2 diesel will probably cause lower performance and mileage.

See your manual for more details. Using these "basement brews" regularly could do long-term damage, and blending gas with diesel fuel makes quite a flammable mixture. Some old-time garages mix oil with diesel fuel in the mistaken belief that they are helping the engine. Using an oil-diesel blend on most modern cars can hurt the fuel system and void the manufacturer's warranty.

Don't forget that water is the enemy of the diesel engine—either install a drain plug at the bottom of your fuel tank or change the filter frequently. Some newer designs have a built-in hand pump that permits the owner to forcibly expel water from the filter. Remember, diesel oil is *harmful* to rubber. Keep it away from hoses and belts, *please.*

Tank full?

Diesel oil foams when pumped into your tank. This may cause the gauge to read full when there is still room left in the tank. Wait a few minutes and then pump some more in.

● **WHEN:** You want to prepare an **emergency kit**.

■ **WHAT TO DO:** I know space is at a premium in new cars, but a smart motorist will have a few odds and ends tucked away for the hard times.

I suggest storing your kit in a high-quality plastic laundry basket. They are light, well ventilated, and unlikely to bang around the trunk. The plastic is also fairly resistant to extremes of temperature. Things to include:

- Chocolate bars are a good emergency food—and they last for years.
- Candles and waterproof matches. "Survival" candles are designed to burn a long time and provide an emergency heat source.
- Blankets, gloves, and an extra sweater.
- A towel.
- A simple tool kit: a screwdriver with multiple bits, an adjustable wrench, pliers, scissors, tape, some extra screws, hose clamps, an extra distributor cap, a spare radiator cap, an extra spark plug, a flashlight (a combination incandescent-fluorescent, with flasher, is best). The spark plug can be used to test the ignition quickly—remove the wire lead from an engine plug, put the lead on the spare plug, and touch the bottom of the plug to an engine ground. If no spark is visible when cranking, the ignition is out.
- A shovel, preferably collapsible, and an aid to traction (metal cleats are best).
- Distilled water (for battery or drinking), a quart of oil, a quart of antifreeze (makes two quarts of radiator mixture), a reserve of window washer fluid, a pint of brake fluid, a can of radiator stop-leak, a container of dry-gas, and a quart of transmission fluid (which will also serve as power-steering fluid).
- One complete set of spare V-belts that fits your car.
- A battery-operated air pump *or* two cans of aerosol tire inflator.
- A siphon with a bulb starter and a safety-approved cellular gas can.

- A large box of baking soda, to be used as a fire extinguisher.
- A short length of pipe to extend your jack handle.
- A can of WD-40 or equivalent (can be used for drying wet ignition wires to assist starting—or as penetrating oil).
- A spare windshield wiper with blade already inserted.
- An ice scraper (a credit card will do in an emergency).
- An emergency roof-mounted CB radio (will take up about as much space as a box of facial tissues).
- A high-quality set of booster cables—$20 minimum. (Many cheaper brands will let you down when you need them most.)

● **WHEN:** Your **engine** has cold feet in the morning.

■ **WHAT TO DO:** Need an engine heater? Do you have an electrical outlet handy? Yes? Then proceed as follows:

Leave a 100-watt bulb burning in the engine compartment overnight. This —the cheapest route of all—will provide just enough heat to the battery and engine to get you going in climates where winters are not terribly cold. The installation can even be done by your four-year-old who's studying to be a sumo wrestler—and one 69-cent bulb lasts about one winter (the extension cord is an extra cost).

Where winter is a serious business, a core-plug heater (a.k.a. *block heater*) is the answer. It costs only about $15, but there is a catch— installation is tricky and could run you another $30. This is the top-of-the-line cold fighter. Plug it in overnight or, if you're a perfectionist, set up a timer to turn it on three hours before blast-off in the morning. Some of the fancier models have a light to indicate whether they're working. Here's a tip: the power demand is so great on these (like a kitchen toaster) that, if it's in working order, you'll see a tiny spark from the electric plug when you push it into the socket. Make sure the female receptacle at the car end is secure—and use WD-40 occasionally to clean out the salt and dirt that will accumulate. Aside from the plug, these things have no moving parts and— once properly installed—may outlive the car.

Next in order of usefulness is the heater-in-the-water-hose trick. This gizmo replaces the large heater hose that goes between the radiator and the engine, and has an electric heater inside. I prefer the block heater, myself.

The simplest heater is also the least useful. A dipstick heater replaces the oil dipstick and heats the oil. This model, as the name implies, is intended for dipsticks.

Again, for mild winters, a battery blanket ($10) may be simplest. Funny thing, though—they *look* simple to install, but they're not; usually the battery must be moved from its tray. If you go this route, I recommend a $5 battery holder that allows you to move the battery slightly more easily. If the battery feels like it's made from lead, that's because it is.

Modern science strikes again!

Consider for a moment the block heater described above. The hardest part of using it was the installation—we had to make sure it stayed put on the side of the engine, where it was needed. A new product makes it easy—it couples a strong electric heater with a powerful magnet base—which secures itself to the engine block or oil pan (not aluminum, though) without fuss, muss, or bother. Cost is about $30; its versatility (it can be used for other cold problems as well) probably justifies the expense.

● **WHEN:** You want **gadgets.**

■ **WHAT TO DO:** While you're reading this, an elderly gent named Louie Mattar is probably cruising through the southwestern states with a very special car indeed. This particular vehicle, which has won about every customizing award you can shake a stick at, is a modified 1947 Cadillac that not only has your basic custom goodies like flush toilet, television, and wet bar, but also incorporates a curious hydraulic contraption which, in the event of a flat, allows the driver to change the flat while the car *maintains highway cruising speed.*

The point is—you can do anything to your car you darn well please. Your pleasure is limited only by imagination, financial resources, manual dexterity, good taste, and the current catalog of your favorite custom supplier.

Some items to consider:

• Custom tires, mag wheels, low-rider shocks that bounce the chassis up and down at the touch of a button.
• Regular exhausts, custom exhausts, sidepipes, headers, turbo-type muffler, scavenger systems, reverse headers, chrome exhaust extensions, and custom resonators. (Let's not forget straight pipes and glass packs.)

- Regular seats, bench seats, reclining seats, power seats, manual seats, adjustable seats, inflatable lumbar supports, seats that turn into floors, floors that turn into seats, rumble seats, reverse seats, and seats that turn into beds (I'll take the fifth on those).
- Sunroofs, moonroofs, electric roofs, one-way roofs, T-roofs, roof racks, convertible tops, interchangeable tops, gull-wing doors, aircraft doors, kick panels, running boards, tire carriers, "continental" trunk lids, and trunks that reach out and shut themselves.
- Seatbelts that stretch out and hand themselves to you when you sit down.
- Underhood marvels like braided stainless-steel hose, Army-Navy–type screw fittings, high-rise air cleaners, low-rise air cleaners, ram inductors, superchargers, blowers, six-packs, air injectors, fuel injectors, water injectors, resonators, sidewinders, double-pump carburetors, oversized pistons, hot cams, cold cams, and strawberry jam.

Or, even more exotic possibilities:

- Volkswagens with Rolls-Royce radiator grilles.
- Exotic kit cars daringly mounted on old VW or Honda chassis.
- Rear-view mirrors that sense when the car behind you has its "brights" on and comport themselves accordingly.
- Blinking cars, chiming cars, talking cars (will someone please invent a car that lets the owner record his own messages?).
- Cars with Pac-Man dashboards—which cost $2000 and are hard to see in the daylight.
- Electric mirrors, heated mirrors, heated seats, seats with timed heaters, wind-up clocks, electric clocks, digital clocks, clocks that turn on the radio, radios that find their own music, radios that know when you're not the rightful owner, and windshield washers that turn themselves off after three perfect wipes.
- Warning buzzers that tell you that you forgot your key, that your engine is too hot, your engine is too cold, it's icy outside, your turbo is about to explode, your emission system needs service, your fuel is low, your headlights are still on, and a door is really ajar.
- Cruise control calibrated so that each tender exertion of your baby finger on the button raises the speed exactly 1 mph, no more and (scandal!) no less.

- One-tone horns, two-tone horns, horns that go "ah-ooh-ga," horns that play *Melancholy Baby,* horns that would raise the dead, and horns not even truckers would be caught dead with.

- Cups with dripless tops so that you don't spill the coffee before you drink it.

- Ice scrapers that have mitts attached so your hands don't get cold. In a pinch they can be used as puppets in the school play.

- Headlights that can see around corners, headlights that turn around corners, headlights that would scare off Darth Vader, and headlights that turn themselves off if you get mugged and can't reach the switch.

- Ashtrays with little fans that suck up cigarette smoke (and then get cancer and die?).

- Air changers, air filters, air ionizers, air scents, and "imitation new car smell" (an intriguing combination of glues, plastics and solvents —you can get high just reading the label).

- Digital fuel gauges, digital water-temperature gauges, digital oil-temperature and -pressure gauges, digital tachometers, digital speedometers, digital odometers, digital voltmeters, digital mileage gauges, digital clocks, digital signal-lock radios, digital CBs, and hideaway radar detectors ("Why, officer, how should I know why the Kleenex box has wires coming out the back?").

If you have a weekend with no plans, get some catalogs (page 150) and find out more. . . .

● **WHEN:** You are trying to pick a brand of **gas.**
■ **WHAT TO DO:** Confused? I don't blame you. The gasoline business has really become pretty confusing over the last few years. In the beginning there was:

Leaded regular.   Good stuff. Without it there would be no motorcar at all. The original "pioneer" fuel. The lead acts as an inexpensive octane enhancer, engine lubricant, and despoiler of the air. Leaded regular begat:

Leaded premium.   More lead meant more octane, and more octane meant that the compression of the engine could be higher. Oddly, many *small* high-compression European engines from the '60s needed a fix of this stuff as badly as the oversized muscle cars that dominated the American scene. And then came:

Unleaded regular. When this stuff first came out, one American writer suggested that this was "Not good enough for my lawn mower," and he may have been right. It lacked not only lead but *enthusiasm* as well. And they charged us more for it, to boot! (It did keep the environment cleaner, however.)

Unleaded super. They couldn't use lead (that much was clear,) so they boosted the octane using other ingredients, and raised the price yet. (Are you beginning to see the pattern?) It came as something of a shock to folks who were having trouble finding leaded super that unleaded super, which cost more, didn't perform as well.

Half and half. A popular blend of unleaded super and leaded regular will produce a potent near-imitation of leaded super, it turned out. This is also very useful for folks with older engines that *needed* lead (for upper valve lubrication in most engines produced before 1972) and yet also need a higher octane rating.

Methanol-ethanol blends. Just when things finally started to get simple, two new problems arose. Both ethanol and methanol blends currently sold in North America use these alcohols to "water down" the gas slightly and so reduce manufacturing costs. (Arco Oil, in particular, has a big stake in this type of fuel technology.) The problem is twofold: first, some gas companies are *not giving the consumer a heck of a lot of warning* that he's buying this stuff (you almost have to read the fine print on the pump) and, second, car manufacturers *don't like this stuff* and can get quite nasty about *paying off warranty claims* to consumers using it. (Methanol has the potential to be far more damaging to fuel-system componenets than ethanol, but the gas companies are trying to fix this by using more anticorrosive agents with the methanol. Many experts are unconvinced by this logic, however.)

A rule of thumb

If you must use an alcohol blend from time to time, make sure it's *ethanol,* not methanol, and *even then* make sure that it's no more than 10 percent ethanol by volume. *Methanol* blends are to be used only in an emergency. Even so, check that the methanol blend is sold as "containing anticorrosive agents"—to reduce methanol's natural corrosive action. Generally, if the methanol is more than 5 percent of the mixture by volume—regardless of whether the anticorrosive agents are added—*do not use it under any conditions.*

The situation for new-car owners can get quite touchy, particularly if the consumer is using the stuff unintentionally and the manufacturer (Porsche, for example) has vetoed the use of alcohol blends. Read your owner's manual *and* read the gas pump labels carefully!

No-name gas

When you drive by Joe's Discount Gas, do you ever stop to wonder if Joe makes the stuff in his basement while watching the Red Sox? The answer is no, he doesn't; he buys from a major refiner (likely one of the Seven Sisters, as they are called). He buys their surplus at a savings—which he passes along to you.

● **WHEN:** You are checking out **gas-saving doodads**.
■ **WHAT TO DO:** Let's be brutally frank. Most don't work. That's not to say they don't do something subtle and interesting to your car (most do), but simply that they don't save much gas. Particularly, they don't save enough gas to repay their purchase price.

There are a number of types available:

1. Exotic gadgets that you blend, splice, or otherwise intermingle with the fuel lines or carburetor, including the infamous "cow magnet." There is no evidence that these work!
2. Water injectors—much more effective at ping control (page 18)

than at saving fuel. These may cause long-term damage to internal engine parts. Many shoddy brands on the market. Installation and *constant refilling* with water or special (and expensive) chemicals are required.

3. Air-conditioner cut-out. There is a device called Passmaster that cuts out the air-conditioner compressor when the engine is under stress. The U.S. government has agreed that the device *can* cut fuel bills when the air conditioner is used frequently.

4. Better-"breathing" intakes and exhausts. These save fuel but it can take years to recover the initial investment.

5. Aftermarket carburetors—Holley, for example, may save fuel (if driven gently) but again, the investment is hard to recover.

6. Aftermarket ignitions can improve overall engine performance but the fuel saving is in doubt.

7. Dash-installed timing controls. These were originally designed to control pinging, but owners who use them to improve mileage on the highway (in violation of EPA specifications) are reporting interesting results. Any speed shop can order one of these for you.

8. Exterior air dams provide only a small savings in fuel, which doesn't justify the expense.

9. P-metric radials. Higher inflation pressures make for easier rolling —ever notice that a bicycle pedals harder when the tire is low?

10. Fuel pumps with built-in regulators. One Italian firm makes a big deal out of these, but the results are still nothing to write stateside about.

11. Additives. The only one I like is Tufoil (see page 143).

12. Dash-mounted vacuum gauge. This is not truly a gas-saving device but rather a useful tool for retraining bull-headed leadfoot drivers. Remarkable savings of as much as 30 percent have been seen with these.

13. Cruise control simply allows the driver to relax and ease up on the gas during long trips. Can be added to almost any car on the road quite easily. Recommended.

14. Overdrive transmission (for a car that didn't come with it) will not generate enough savings to pay for itself.

- **WHEN:** You are considering adding **headers.**
- **WHAT TO DO:** Headers are one of the most-misunderstood and least-

appreciated aspects of the modern car. *Headers* is a nickname for all ex-tended tubular multipipe exhaust-scavenging systems which, when in-stalled, can increase engine efficiency and therefore horsepower production and fuel economy. Like the newer, more efficient intake manifolds on the market, these things assist engine breathing and are quite worthwhile.

The disadvantages are: high initial installation cost (and possible difficul-ties on some models), the need for air-fuel readjustment after installation (except on fuel-injected models), possible problems due to extra heat buildup in the engine compartment (silicone-jacketed wires are advisable), noise, and the fact that they can wear out prematurely in cold climates.

If you live in a warm climate, headers are worth considering. Your speed shop can give you all the details. And don't worry about the noise—proper installation can produce an end result no louder than your present muffler system.

The great debate as to whether headers pay for themselves in terms of better gas mileage is still unresolved. Ask ten mechanics and you'll get ten different answers. Chat with the experts—the guys who race for a living —and they tell a different tale. Of course headers work. Simply make sure you get the best ones (all brands are not equal); make sure their design and size are professionally mated to the rest of the exhaust system, possibly including special new mufflers, pipes, and crossovers (reversion reducers); make sure the headers are not warped from the factory (many are); make sure the nearby wiring can handle the extra heat (if not, upgrade to solid-core wire with silicone insulation), and make sure that the carburetor mix-ture matches the new headers. If you do *all* that—they will work!

Header coatings

Special coatings are available at most speed shops to keep the head-ers from rusting externally (although short-range city driving will rust them *internally*). Although porcelain is the most common, the best coatings (the ones that outlast cars) are complex, and may require a side trip to California to get the job done right.

● **WHEN:** You are shopping for **oil.**

■ **WHAT TO DO:** "No-name" motor oil has never caught on like no-name gasoline. The reason is a mystery, because the factors that would seem to encourage successful "off-branding" of motor oil are already in effect—only a handful of companies actually make motor oil, although a great many blend and market it; and, the SAE (Society of American Engineers) coding assures at least a degree of uniformity from brand to brand.

Motor oils generally come in three flavors: *normal* (so-called "mineral"-based, although this may be a misnomer), *synthetics,* and *combination* (a relatively new blend which has not caught on).

The sorting out of "normal" vs. "synthetic" oils is a complex and controversial subject. Most agree that the synthetics (a) cost much more, and (b) must be changed as often as normal oil is to maintain the new-car warranty. Obviously, these two facts alone can make a persuasive argument for avoiding them. (They also tend to reduce oil pressure and augment the potential for leakage.) So, while they do have their fans (including the government, by the way, since they were originally designed for the military) this writer recommends strongly that nonsynthetic oil be selected—in a cost-effective brand—and that the filter and oil be changed every three months regardless of mileage. (This is, at least, a proven strategy which has allowed taxi and limousine drivers to put hundreds of thousands of miles on their vehicles without major problems.)

Oils also come in grades (like 5/30) and service ranges, which read something like FOR SERVICE SC. (Single-grade oil such as SAE 10 or SAE 30 is still available—but has little practical application for today's motorists.) For more information about the recent controversy surrounding 10/40 grade oil see page 125. As far as service ranges go, virtually all cars on the road today (except certain antiques and diesels) will do well with a detergent-type oil like type SE or, even better, type SF. (New cars under warranty may require SF—check your manual!) Diesels require a different range—so, again, see your manual. It is permissible to mix brands and even grades, but this is not an advisable long-term habit. For information on oil additives, see page 143.

Some new products are worth considering, such as the new "turbo" oils designed for the extremely rigorous demands of turbochargers. Both turbocharged engines and diesels require changes even more frequently than normal engines.

Generally, change the filter when you change oil; changes on elapsed time, not elapsed mileage. The new "flush" products are recommended for occasional use before an oil change (See page 143.)

● **WHEN:** You are considering alternate fuels (**propane** or **natural gas**).

■ **WHAT TO DO:**

In Canada, where conversions to propane are quite popular, a number of motorists have already lost their lives in alternate-fuel explosions. One such victim had just passed a government check of his propane installation the day of the accident.

From a mechanical point of view, conversion to alternate fuels requires certain basic modifications in the systems of fuel storage (tank) and delivery (carburetors). Cars running on alternate fuels are said to have slightly less power, a shorter cruising range, greater oil consumption, and occasional starting problems in inclement weather. The only advantages are that the fuel bills will be lower and that the emissions will be cleaner. Fleet owners have had greater success with alternate fuels because of economies of scale and because a safety-and-prevention program is easier to initiate when more than one vehicle is involved.

Refueling with alternate fuels, particularly propane, is difficult (the tank must be no more than 80 percent full. An untrained pump jockey can unintentionally endanger the driver and occupants. Also, be sure to check that the climate you live in is compatible with alternate fuels (propane gas, for example, tends to liquefy in under extreme cold).

From a pure *safety* viewpoint, most add-on conversions are of high risk and unproven over the long term. Any part of the system that loosens over time (and, as any apprentice mechanic knows, *all* car parts loosen) can become life-threatening. Between propane and natural gas, propane is the more dangerous fuel because it is heavier than air and, if it leaks, will sink downwards to form dangerous "pockets" of gas in the trunk or cargo area of the car.

If you are thinking of an alternate fuel conversion, have an expert do it. Also, do the conversion only on new vehicles—not on older vehicles where pinhole rust spots could admit deadly gas.

Alcohol fuel blends, another form of "alternate fuels," are having their own problems. See page 162.

● **WHEN:** You want **protection against theft.**

■ **WHAT TO DO:** The only sure way to prevent auto theft by a determined criminal is to chain the axle to a streetlamp—and even then there is no guarantee that you won't come back to find only the axle remaining, and the rest of the car gone.

First, criminals go after some cars more than others. BMWs and muscle cars from the '60s seem to be high on the hit parade these days, but the list changes from day to day.

Second, the manufacturers' built-in theft deterrents (locking steering columns and slippery door latches) are hardly going to stop a serious thief. A slide-hammer can disable most locks in seconds. Nor are thieves forced to rely on brute force. Key blanks are easily available, as are tools that jimmy doors open from the window recess.

How serious are you about car theft? In Boston, harried owners leave their doors unlocked with notes taped to the window begging break-in artists to go elsewhere because there is nothing of value left in the car. Then there are folks (myself included) who go out of their way to drive dirty rusty little cars that most thieves wouldn't take as a Christmas gift. (My '78 Mazda GLC fits in this class. Some days even I don't want to be seen in it.)

Most car owners who have had a major break-in will never again risk purchasing top-of-the-line equipment for the car, particularly sound equipment. But a California cousin of mine decided to "fight back" when a $2000 stereo was taken from his car. His insurance company said another big claim might raise his rates, but rather than switch to a lower-quality stereo, he installed a state-of-the-art alarm system—sensitive microphones in each door post that will activate a beeper on his belt and alert him if someone tries to break into his car. One problem—what if he's not around when the break-in occurs? Worse, what if he is, and the bad guys have guns?

And then there are car alarms—sirens that scream for help whenever someone tries to violate your vehicle. The question is—does anybody care? Pedestrians on the street don't. And, unfortunately, the police don't either. Thousands of false alarms triggered by everything from bird droppings to thermal inversions have left the cops disenchanted with car alarms. In many jurisdictions they won't even answer the call.

Score one for bad guys?

A great many antitheft systems (including the infamous "kill" switch —see suggestion number 1) work by cutting out the ignition switch. But what if the thief had a gadget the size of a small valise that would temporarily bypass the ignition switch and get the car going? These gadgets, originally designed for mechanics and auto clubs, are now getting into the wrong hands. Not hard to get either—about $60 in the current Whitney catalog. This only goes to show that a smart owner has to stay on his (or her) toes *all the time!*

And what about the gadgets that allow the bad guy to get the car out into traffic—and *then* cut the gas or ignition? Good idea, but in most jurisdictions a heavy fine goes to the righteous owner for blocking traffic. *Remember:* the more complex the alarm, the more complex the problems you can expect. My suggestions:

1. The old *kill* switch—a simple hidden toggle switch that cuts the ground circuit to the coil—will still confuse most amateurs. It can be installed in minutes. And—if you are mechanically inclined—you can bring it into the computer age by meshing it with a set of magnetically triggered switches that complete the circuit only when the mating magnet is present (available from Radio Shack for under $5). Wire the kill circuit so that it is hidden from view behind a non-metal part of the dash; placing the other magnet (which you carry in your pocket) on the dash by the hidden switch will complete the circuit.

2. I like simple solutions the most. The old "cane" lock will freeze the steering wheel to the brake pedal. It is very effective against thieves in a hurry. (Most auto-parts stores carry them.) A more sophisticated version of the cane lock is a device that freezes the brake and clutch together (or the gas and brake pedals on automatics). For more information, contact Pedaloc, Box 17107, Pittsburgh, PA 15235.

3. It's national confuse-a-thief month. If your car is stored for days at a time, make a dummy high-tension lead from the distributor to the coil by removing the wire but leaving the insulation in place. It will look correct, but the car won't start. The thief will have to put in some diagnostic time to get the car started, and all you have to do is change wires when you get back.

4. If protecting the *radio* is more important than protecting the car, consider: (1) high-strength casings to bolt the radio to the dash; (2) radios built into slide drawers that you store in the trunk whenever you leave the car (or tuck into your briefcase); (3) radios with built-in security codes so that nobody else will ever play that radio again without the code (more *revenge* than *prevention,* one pundit has said); and (4) dummy radio covers that make your $3000 disc player look like a reject from a '47 Plymouth.

5. Etch the windows with the car's serial number. The thinking here (which most cops support) is that changing four pieces of window glass will discourage most thieves—unless the car is going to a chop shop anyway. Do-it-yourself kits are available from Automark, 3901 Atkinson, Louisville, KY 40218, and Security Etch, 3 Upper Newport Plaza, Newport Beach, CA 92660.

6. Buy a large dog for the backseat.

● **WHEN:** You want to change to **quartz lighting.**

■ **WHAT TO DO:** The jury is in: quartz lighting is at least four times as efficient as normal headlights. (In fact, safety tests show that nonquartz lights are actually a danger at highway speeds: they do not illuminate enough of the road ahead to enable a driver to see an object in time to stop safely.)

For years, the best quartz bulbs have been made in Europe (by Bosch, Cibie, and Lucas). American manufacturers have been hesitant, not to say terrified, of adapting the design to their cars.

Tech wars

European-designed lights generally have replaceable bulbs, but for some reason the U.S. government was unwilling to approve this design. American manufacturers struck back with sealed-beam quartz bulbs, but critics noted quickly that they were lower in quality than the European lights and even more expensive. In the early '80s the U.S. manufacturers started to offer "half-quartz" headlamps—lamps with quartz power *only* on highbeam. This sad compromise didn't find much favor with critics either.

As we move into the late '80s things have become even more complex. New technology created in Europe is leading to bulbs of great power that are the size of postage stamps, while buyers of new American cars get equipment that would be at home on a '52 Chevy. This author is a great believer in seeing where you are going and recommends that, if your car does not have a top-of-the-line quartz high-low unit, you go have the conversion done (under $100). Whether you select the proven replaceable-bulb European design or the new legal-in-all-states bastardized sealed-beam quartz lamps depends on availability, your pocketbook, and your civic conscience. *Note:* Quartz lamps *must be* professionally aligned after installation or you risk temporarily blinding oncoming motorists.

● **WHEN:** You are shopping for a car **stereo.**
■ **WHAT TO DO:** I have a confession to make. I don't approve of car stereos that are more powerful than the stereo in my living room. I am one of those old-fashioned drivers who thinks that it's more important to hear the sounds of the engine and the honking of passing cars than the squeak of Ringo's shoes in an old Beatles tune. I also don't believe in spending more on a stereo than my car is worth (of the four cars I drive, none would fetch $2000 outside of a charity auction).

Now that I've got that off my chest, let's proceed.

Sometime in the last few years (the exact date will turn up as a Trivial Pursuit question) Detroit realized it was missing the potential for tens of thousands of dollars in profit by not making better car stereo packages. The result is that optional factory-installed stereos are now pretty good, which isn't saying much. (The best stereo I've heard recently was in a new Toyota Cressida with a standard-issue 60 watt Technics stereo package.) If you are buying a new car, it's still safe to assume that a proper aftermarket shop can give you a better system for a lower price than Mr. Dealer. But the gap is narrowing.

The new systems cannot be installed by the owner. In fact, they can barely be installed by trained technicians! The working areas are too small, the connections too delicate, and the wiring too complex to let an amateur participate.

New features are coming out every day. By the time this is published, most of my research material will be obsolete. Still, here are some of the more popular features that you should consider:

- *Search.* The ability of the unit, at a push of a button, to locate and lock onto the next-best-received station up the dial. Also called *seek.* Judged useful.
- *Scan.* Like *search* above only, unless you decide you like the station, and push a special button within seconds, it will move on to the next. Silly, and possibly dangerous. The audiophile equivalent of Chinese torture. Can encourage accidents.
- *Boost.* At the push of a button, the power output of the unit doubles, to the point where your socks will start to liquefy. Not to be confused with the *loud* button, which simply adjusts the output curve of the sound and functions as only a mild boost.
- *Quartz lock.* A form of digital tuning that assumes that the radio can tune itself to the station better than your sausage-shaped fingers could.
- *Built-in digital clock.* I've got digital clocks on my waffle iron and my doorbell. I don't need another on my radio.
- *Sensitivity.* Heightens the sensitivity of the unit for hard-to-get stations. These things never work.
- *Graphic equalizer.* What makes you think your graphics weren't equal to start with? Seriously, folks, I know these are the sexiest thing going right now, but I asked a $70,000-a-year radio technician if he knew exactly how to adjust one for optimal listening enjoyment inside his car and he wasn't sure!

Here's the scoop on graphic equalizers

Equalizers have two axes: left-to-right (low to high frequencies) and up-and-down (loudness, with the central position being "neutral"). The big reason for their popularity is that the driver has all those nice levers and knobs to play with! In reality, however, the optimal setting for the equalizer is also the most "boring"—with all the levers at exactly dead center (this will produce the most *accurate* sound). Two tricks: to artificially emphasize the highs and lows on rock music, set the equalizer in a V configuration, with the controls nearest the ends highest and the middle ones lowest. Also, to suppress noise generally on a "bad" or pre-Dolby recording, set all the levers at mid-band, except for the high-frequency controls at the right, which should be down.

- *Fade.* Allows you to choose whether you want the sound to emanate from a point closer to the two front speakers or closer to the two rear speakers. Are you kidding?
- *Dolby.* A useful feature used to remove some of the hiss on cassette-tape playback, but it takes some of the sound away as well.
- *Program locater.* At last—a feature I can relate to! When playing a selection on a tape that you don't want to continue, this button will move on automatically to the beginning of the next song. Nice idea.
- *Auto reverse.* Again, for tape playing, saves you having to flip the tape over while executing a 30 mph double-clutch downshift in your new five-speed Honda CRX. Good feature.
- *Compact disc capacity.* Compact discs—those are the magic words for the next ten years in the audio business. The sound clarity is supposed to be so good you'll throw out your season tickets to rock-and-roll concerts.
- *Antitheft circuit.* A coded program which disables the unit forever unless the right code is pressed. Seems like overkill to me.
- *Skip* and *Repeat.* The most useful cassette controls I've seen on newer models permit you to replay favorite selections automatically by pushing "repeat," and "skip" unwanted sections with the skip control.

● **WHEN:** You are shopping for **tires.**

■ **WHAT TO DO:** Quick: Without peeking at your owner's manual, give the tire size on your car. Mine is P215/70R14. Here's what the numbers stand for: *P* indicates a P-metric tire using the new size coding (as opposed to the older G78-14 stuff) which generally takes a higher inflation pressure (over 35 psi—pounds per square inch) for better mileage. The *215* is the section width. Here, the higher the number, the larger the tire. (215 replaces the old G classification for tires. An old F tire would be a 195 or a 205.) The *70* is the height divided by the width, given as a percent. The lower the number, the wider (and meaner) the tire. (When I get a caller on a radio talk show who wants my opinion on 60 or 50 series tires, I know he's talking about fat racing tires.) The *R* indicates radial construction. There may be a number just before the R which, on certain European and Japanese makes, indicates the performance characteristics of the tire, i.e., maximum speed range. (V-type speed ratings are currently the sexiest, meaning the tire is designed to cruise all day at over 130 mph.) The *14* shows the diameter of the rim, expressed in inches. Diameters of 13, 14, and 15 are pretty standard for all passenger cars. Notice how odd it is to have the section width—215—expressed in millimeters and the diameter in inches. Newer designs, such as the Michelin TRX (originally made for the Ford Mustang III), list the diameter in millimeters as well.

Other information on the sidewall is important too: Sidewall construction tells you what the tire is made of and how many plies. *Load range* tells you how much weight the tire will carry. The tire will be marked as to whether it needs an *inner tube.* The maximum cold (morning) *inflation pressure* of the tire will be marked as well. It is dangerous to exceed this pressure, or to underinflate the tire by too much.

Tires sold in the United States may also have two additional ratings: *heat resistance* in the sidewall (A is best, C is worst); and, *traction* (again, A is best, C is worst).

Here are some more pointers in buying tires: The warranty is important, particularly the so-called road-hazard warranty, which allows you to get some value back on the tire if it wears out prematurely for reasons not your fault (a nail puncture, for instance).

Now that you understand tire sizes, a quick glance at your owner's manual will show you that more than one size will fit on the rims that came with your car and—if you are willing to switch rims—even more exotic sizes can be made to fit. Talk to a tire specialist for help. I recommend purchase of the *largest* size tire that will fit on the rims that came with the car. Switching to fancier rims may be a waste of time and, if they're wrongly matched, they could cause brake or suspension problems.

Tire interchangeability

If your car did not come with P-metric radials, or any radials at all—can you use the new tires? The answer is *yes*. Your tire shop has a table that will show what P-metric size to use. In some cases there is no *exact* equivalent, so you may have a choice of two different sizes. In that case, I recommend choosing the *larger* size and that replacing *both* tires on the same axle at the same time. In any case, never drive with radials on less than all four wheels of the car. Ask your car shop for more details.

What about all-season tires? Do they work? Yes, they do, but they represent a compromise and will not perform as well at either extreme of climate as plain summer or special winter tires. There is also evidence that they wear faster.

Thinking of upgrading your tires? Most cars on the road can benefit from better rubber (virtually all the American companies have now mastered the art of making state-of-the-art high-performance tires but, I warn you, they cost!) and lighter wheel rims.

New tires and rims are a big investment. Get the right ones for your pocketbook—and for your car. Talk to a mechanic *before* you buy to make sure that the set you pick can be mounted, installed, and balanced with the equipment he has (balancing magnesium rims is tricky), and that the new equipment will not damage the suspension. Here's a rule of thumb: never increase wheel offset more than half an inch from the factory original; and never increase tire width more than one inch. To understand "offset," you'll have to chat with the salesman at the rim shop; if you're buying by mail, you'll have to rely on the wisdom of the clerk filling out the order.

Now, as I said, simply keeping your present rims and putting on bigger, wider tires will help some. If, for example, you have 175/70R tires on 13-inch rims, switching to 185/70R tires alone will help. If you go to bigger rims, you must also go to bigger, wider tires. For example, the Goodrich

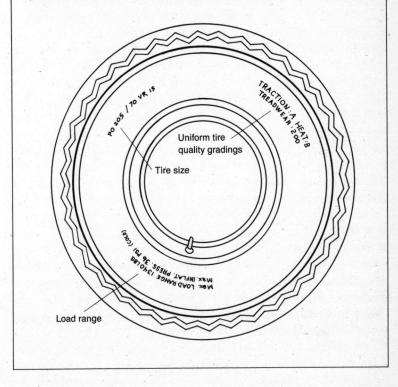

TIRE MARKINGS

Important safety and maintenance information appears on the sidewalls of your tires. For example, P 205/70 VR 15, TRACTION: A, HEAT: B, TREADWEAR: 200, MAX INFLATION PRESSURE: 36 PSI (COLD). Heat and traction are rated A-C. Treadwear (where the rating is used; it is not mandatory) refers to a comparison to a base of 1.0. In other words, a treadwear rating of 200 means that the tire will provide double (or 2.0 times) the tread life typical to its class.

Uniform tire quality gradings

Tire size

Load range

people used to run a series of ads illustrating how an owner with 185/70R tires on 13-inch rims might switch up to 195/60R tires on 14-inch rims or 205/50R tires on 15-inch rims. If in doubt, *ask an expert.*

● **WHEN:** You want a **tire sealant.**

■ **WHAT TO DO:** These are new products, and they come in two types. The *temporary one-time-use sealant* comes in an aerosol dispenser and waits patiently in the glove box for you to call on it. When you have a flat, you can inflate and temporarily seal the tire by jamming the can onto the valve and waiting a few minutes. Generally—in nine cases out of ten—this product will do the job. (I've even seen it inflate large Jeep tires without a problem.) The repair will last several miles, more than enough to get you to a garage.

The so-called *permanent sealants* are installed *before* a problem arises— either by you or by an independent dealer. Generally, the valve of the tire must be removed (a 60-second operation). While the air hisses out menacingly you inject the sealant into the tire body, and then refit the valve and add air. The claims made for these products usually involve: (a) sealing hard-to-stop rim leaks, and (b) ensuring that you don't get flat tires ever again. (The chemicals automatically "seal" punctures as they occur.)

The first products of this type caused some rubber disintegration and froze in winter, but the newer versions seem to work well. This is an exciting new type of product and should be carefully considered, particularly by car owners who do a lot of long-distance driving in isolated areas. The only disadvantage noted so far is that pre-existing imbalance problems within the tire may be accentuated.

● **WHEN:** You are shopping for new **wheel rims.**
■ **WHAT TO DO:** In the old days, all cars came with steel wheel rims. Even the so-called "mag" wheels of the '60s were made of steel. (This is humorous because *mag* is an abbreviation of *magnesium.* Like many other products of the '60s, the domestic version of magnesium rims were completely fake.) Why would anyone want a magnesium (or aluminum) wheel in the first place (aside from looks, of course)?

Steel wheels, although very durable, are heavy. They live at the four points of the car just beyond the suspension points and therefore they contribute to the *unsprung weight,* not the *sprung weight,* of the vehicle. Reducing this unsprung weight even slightly will greatly improve the handling characteristics of your car. Reducing the unsprung weight by using a non-steel rim *and* mounting a larger and/or better-performing tire will improve handling even more! Are there any drawbacks to non-steel rims? Yes:

1. The initial cost is high—over $100 per rim *and* over $100 per tire (installation is extra).

2. They are tricky to install and balance—requiring special weights and lug nuts, and careful torquing. Many reputable tire shops will say they are *not responsible* for their work on mag wheels.

3. They oxidize if not cared for properly. Winter can be very cruel to mag wheels. Also, they are easy to ruin on your own. *Do not* use steel wool, brass wool, or corrosive solvents to clean mags—this speeds up rust. Clean them with a mild nylon cloth or toothbrush. Add a protective wax coating once you're done.

4. They are impossible to fix once bent or damaged.

5. Rim leaks can be a nightmare to fix. I recommend trying the after-market sealants.

6. They are great targets for thieves, and the available anti-theft systems are crude and hard to use.

▪ 5 ▪
NEW AND USED CARS

● **WHEN:** You are shopping the car **auctions.**

▪ **WHAT TO DO:** There are many bargains to be had at car auctions, but first you should learn some basics:

Always get a copy of the rules and regulations *before* you show up. Inspection of the offerings may be permitted only hours or even days before the auction begins, if at all. Sealed bids may be required. Cash or a certified check is commonly required for payment. Often the cars must be picked up or towed by a certain time.

Next, you have to decide what type of auction you want to attend:

Wholesale.   You usually need a dealer's license just to get in the door of a wholesale auction. There are bargains here, but you'll be fighting professional car dealers to get them.

Government.   Various levels of government hold dozens of auctions each year. The best cars often go to those willing to do some homework. All cars leased for government employees (and there are thousands) will eventually go on the block somewhere. So will many vehicles used by the armed forces and the law-enforcement agencies. Contact the major government departments in *your* area to get more information.

Seized cars?

There are bargains to be had in the customs bin: contact U.S. Customs Service, Public Affairs Office, 1301 Constitution Ave., Washington, DC 20229.

Private estates.   Private estates are liquidated virtually every week of the year, and classic-car collectors routinely show up looking for bargains. Check your local papers.

Bankruptcies.   Again, check your local papers. Firms liquidating heavy equipment almost always have a small fleet of cars and trucks—which are usually well cared for.

Local taxis.   As a rule, don't bother.

Airport limousines.   Definitely worth pursuing. Some real bargains here.

Company fleets.   Ninety percent will go back to the leasing company, but it's worth checking.

Bank repossessions.   Here's what to do. Take your bank manager a bottle of Scotch and find out how to track down the repos. Most repos are late-model top-of-the-line sports machines whose monthly payments exceeded the reality quotient of the former owner. Fantastic bargains here for the pure of heart!

● **WHEN:** You want a **convertible**.
■ **WHAT TO DO:** They tried to kill all the convertibles in the late '70s. But it didn't work. Some idiots (let's hope they've been fired by now)

stopped *all* convertible production and tried to sell cars with air condition-
ing and sunroofs instead. They were cheaper to make and the profit was
higher.

When people asked what happened to the convertibles (as some did), the
manufacturers would lie and say that government regulations made them
illegal. (That wasn't true and still isn't.)

But people weren't stupid. The used-car value of convertibles shot
through the roof (no pun intended), particularly VW Bugs, Karmann
Ghias, and early Mustang models. Any of them, if completely restored, is
worth many times its original value. (For more on restorations, see page
184.)

Then, once upon a time, a new leader came to the Chrysler Corporation.
The new leader had new ideas. He looked upon the convertible design and
saw that it was good. He commanded that Chrysler make *more.* And these
"new" convertibles (inferior in many ways to those of the previous decade)
sold like *hotcakes.* The other companies, not to be upstaged by the new
leader, who was always getting his picture in *Time* magazine, started making convertibles of their own. And peace returned to the valley. (For now,
anyway.)

There are differences between the "old" convertibles and the "new"
models:

The older models were designed on cars with frames. Since convertibles
lack a roof, which is part of the overall structure, it's difficult to make a solid
car without a roof on a frame for support, and almost *impossible* to make
a sturdy topless car on a frameless design. Many of the new convertibles,
therefore, wobble and shake like jelly and would be unfixable after a serious
accident.

The older convertibles had glass rear windows which gave about ten or
fifteen years' service. Many new ones have plastic windows, which crack
and discolor after two or three years.

Finally, the initial price of the older models was only about 10 to 15
percent over the base price for a regular model. The new convertibles sell
for 40 to 60 percent over this base. Many of the new ones are not made
by the car company, but rather are subcontracted to smaller firms. Because
of the economics of mass production, many of the new models come off the
line with the regular roof attached—which must be sawn off before the
convertible top can be installed. Obviously, such manufacturing techniques
are wasteful and expensive.

Fraud squad

Because of the extremely high resale value of '60s and '70s convertibles, cars that might otherwise be scrapped because of advanced body rot are being given quickie paint jobs and being sold at prices that would make your eyes water. The trick is to poke underneath the vehicle and examine the floor pan—this will tell you the true condition of the substructure.

Tips for convertible owners:

1. Your top will eventually fall apart but don't fret: many private companies offer replacement units for only a few hundred dollars. Contact your body or trim shop for details.
2. Automatic car washes will shorten the life of the top. So will strong detergents.
3. The hydraulic top-lifters may have to be bled occasionally (see your mechanic). NEVER operate them below freezing temperatures.
4. Custom covers for older models are hard to get, but check magazines like *Cars & Parts* or *Hemmings*.

● **WHEN:** You are thinking of buying a **foreign car.**

■ **WHAT TO DO:** One of my teachers once said that there were no "foreign people," simply "people living in foreign countries." If you find that distinction too fanciful, you'll have a heck of a time trying to find a true foreign car—or a domestic one.

General Motors, the largest car company in the world, owns plants in Britain, Germany, Mexico, Korea, and Japan. In the late '80s, GM sold cars in the United States produced by Isuzu, Suzuki, and Toyota. Chrysler, the last bastion of domestic auto production, makes K cars in Mexico. The company with the name that screams "apple pie"—American Motors—is controlled by Renault of France. Ford owns 25 percent of Mazda and owes much of its success in North America to European engineering (the Merkur is a good example). And the bad old villains of the story, companies like Honda, Nissan, Mazda, and VW, make some of their cars in the good old U.S. of A.

And *all* the car companies are *absolutely terrified* of what the Koreans will do to the market once they get their act together.

Still looking for a foreign car? Here are some tips:

There is a little haggling room left these days on the price of domestic cars, but almost none on the popular foreign models. Be wary of "dealer packs" and unusual items like "special surcharges" or "special markups." (I once saw a Honda dealership in Ottawa, Canada, that posted its prices on the wall like a restaurant menu. There was no bargaining on price, a deposit was required to bind the sale, minimum delivery lag was three months, and there were no demonstrators or floor samples left in the building.)

In spite of internationalized manufacturing, peculiarities of service and parts supply can still lead to long-term headaches for owners. For many years, for example, VW parts cost two or three times what Chevrolet parts cost. That has *changed* in the '80s, as more aftermarket suppliers have been making VW-compatible parts. Conversely, GM, long known for its fair pricing on parts, allowed the replacement costs of parts for its new front-drive cars to soar through the roof. Repair costs for the little front-drive Ford Escort have been consistently reasonable since the car was first introduced. Service and parts costs for the early Ford Fiestas, on the other hand, are a nightmare. Although I love Mazda products for their quality, costs of parts and service remain disproportionate to the car's selling price, and some buyer caution is called for.

One of the best books to help you keep track of overall parts and service costs is *The Car Book,* available each year from the Center for Auto Safety.

Foreign cars are almost beyond the range of the do-it-yourselfer, because special tools are needed for common maintenence operations. These tools are expensive; only a professional mechanic would get enough use out of them to justify the expense.

A recent study published in *Automotive News,* the industry bible, stated flat-out that the Japanese led the world in engine technology and the Germans in suspension technology.

My best "survival" tip: the car you buy is only as good as the service that's available to back it up.

● **WHEN:** You are considering **leasing** a car.
■ **WHAT TO DO:** Leasing has changed—for the better. At first, leasing catered only to those seeking a tax break on the cost of owning the vehicle.

Most experts held that—unless advised otherwise by his accountant—leasing was *not* for the common guy.

So what's changed?

1. Manufacturers' deep discounts for volume buyers, along with some government incentives for the lessor, are bringing lease prices down to where they compare favorably with regular depreciation and maintenance costs. (Bad news though—the dealers are lobbying *against* such discounts!)

2. One-stop shopping (at a lease store that will provide virtually any make or model you choose) allows the lessee to form closer attachments with the salesman. This leads to greater personal service.

3. More economical service and insurance plans are also available.

What are the disadvantages?

1. Leasing may still cost *more* in the long run than buying. It depends, of course, what model you choose and how long you intend to keep it.

2. Early leases gave the lessee the option of buying the car at close to the wholesale price (the *open-end* lease), as opposed to simply dropping the keys off when the whole thing was done (*closed-end* lease). The original idea behind this option was that, if the lessee didn't want to keep or resell the car himself, the lease company would resell it for him, and charge him back for the short fall between the expected sale price and the actual sale price. The open-end-lease didn't turn out to be the hardship on the lessee that people thought it might be. Far from it, in fact. Cagey lessees soon figured out that instead of simply turning the keys in to the agency when the lease was up, it was smarter to run an ad for the car at the retail value, pay off the lease, and pocket the difference (often several hundred or even several thousand dollars). Leasing companies, realizing that in their haste to make a profit on the lease they might be overlooking the potential for profit on the resale, have now smartened up to this—and will likely surcharge the lease if you want this kind of option now. On the other hand, because leasing companies monitor the resale value of cars very

closely, picking a model with a low depreciation pattern (BMW) means that the leasing company may do so well on the expected resale that they may want to pass on some of their good fortune to the lessee. That *could* lead to an exceptionally reasonable monthly lease payment.

3. Leases are, after all, a contract and should be treated with respect. Some restrict the number of drivers or even the age of the drivers, and some insist the lessee cover certain normal maintenance procedures. Some require the lessee to buy insurance; others include it. Some cover repairs and some don't. And some have surcharges for putting too many miles on the odometer. My recommendation: Read the lease carefully and make sure you understand it. A friend of mine recently tried to buy a leased car at the end of his lease for the "final" value written into the contract, but the company argued that, although there was obviously a price assigned to the car, the contract didn't specifically say he could buy it *at that price!* He sued and won.

● **WHEN:** You're shopping for cars **more than ten years old.**
■ **WHAT TO DO:** Hold on—let's talk strategy.

There are only two reasons to go after cars more than ten years old:

1. You have under $1000 to spend and, having read a few guides to used cars, you are convinced an older domestic product is the answer to your prayers.

2. You want to become a collector. You want a car that not only is fun to drive but also will have some collector's appeal. You want a car that might appreciate over time. You want an *investment.*

If you're in the first category, good luck to you. Stick to a popular model (like a Chevy Chevelle, Olds Cutlass, or Dodge Dart). The scrap yards of the world will become your own personal parts trove as the car ages.

If you are in the second category, my friend, beware. The classic-car market has become slightly overcrowded in the last few years. Shopping for a car that is also supposed to be an investment is a dangerous game.

Classified-ad abbreviations

The secret language of car selling:

A/C	Air Conditioning
AT	Automatic Transmission
BO	Best Offer
EC	Excellent Condition
FC	Fair Condition
GC	Good Condition
HD	Heavy Duty
HT	Hard Top
LN	Like New
NR	Needs Repair
PS	Power Steering
PB	Power Brakes
ST	Standard (Shift) Transmission
4WD	Four-Wheel Drive
OO & O	Original Owner and Operator
Rebuilt	Some recent major repair
Conv	Convertible
Mags	Mag wheels (see page 237)
Snows	Snow tires
Posi	Positraction rear axle
Recond	see Rebuilt above
Mechanic's special	Only a mechanic would want it
Tranny	Transmission
Console	Floor-mounted shift

Ask yourself the following questions:

Do you know enough about the car model you are shopping for to tell the real McCoy from a ringer? If not, join an enthusiast's club, pronto. The larger clubs have branches all over North America. (I'm a member of the Cougar Club of America. I have never actually met any of my fellow members, but it *is* comforting to know that they're out there.)

Serial-number roulette

Because of the fanciful nature of the car business, for example, it has been reported that there are more late '60s Z-28s for sale than were actually produced by General Motors. Sound too good to be true? It is. Once you try to sell your "incredible buy" to a *real* collector, the bubble bursts in spectacular fashion. Most of the real muscle cars have special markings all over them—on the registration stamping, on the engine, on the carb, on the manifold, on the transmission, even on the rear axle. To tell if you are looking at the genuine article—you *must* know what to look for. For that, you need an expert!

Do you know enough about car restoration to be able to tell if a good job was done? There is a great variation in the quality of the restoration work being done today. The top-of-the-line restorer will use only NOS parts (see page 239), or factory parts, or verifiable repro parts. *Remember:* every nonoriginal part (that is, not identifiable as part of the original design) *lowers* the value of the vehicle.

Where will you keep it? One does not drive a classic to work each day and leave the keys with the parking-lot attendant. Nor does one leave a '66 Mustang sitting out in the driveway all winter. Do you have a safe parking spot?

Do you have insurance? Classic cars must be insured for their replacement value, not the simple scrap value. This will require a special policy and probably an appraisal. (Which can be very embarrassing if the appraisal is several thousand dollars less than what you paid!) Such insurance may cost even more than a new-car policy—unless you get a rider that says the car will be kept in storage virtually forever. (Whenever you want to drive it, you'll have to call a special phone number to activate the coverage.)

Do you have a source of parts? The car companies consider buyers of ten-year-old cars (as opposed to new) a threat to democracy and the American Way. They will not be helpful in finding parts. (Although I suspect this may change in the late '80s for public-relation reasons.) Not only should you join an enthusiast's club for the car you are buying but you should also subscribe to a good "source" publication like *Cars & Parts* or *Hemmings*.

Do you have a repair manual for the car? True, older cars were simpler, but they were also *different.* Nostalgia aside, no sane mechanic looks forward to taking apart a Holley 4-barrel carburetor! An owner's manual is also useful because: (a) it adds to the collector's value of the car; and (b) it may contain information the repair manual leaves out. (*Hemmings*) is your best starting point.)

What will you do about the rust that has already started in the frame and inner panels of most older cars?

Will you need leaded premium gasoline, or will half-and-half suffice? A car that knocks or pings all the time soon grows unpopular. Major modifications *will lower it's value.* Be careful!

Caveat Emptor!

There are two kinds of classic cars on the market these days. The genuine articles could easily pass muster even in an antique-car show. They are unmodified and have been restored using authentic repro parts or NOS parts. Their value is assured worldwide.

The second group I call the "love classics." They were authentic once but at some point in their checkered past a teenager got hold of them and made whatever silly modifications his fevered brain told him were required. Then, as nostalgia for the '50s and '60s classics grew, someone said "Hey Screech, that old rustbucket of yours could be worth a few dollars." So Screech fixed the car up and sold it. The owner *thinks* he has a genuine classic, but actually it's only a love car. If the owner wants to get his investment back, he'll have to find somebody else who knows as little about cars as he does.

Some sources:

The Paddock (for '60s muscle-car parts)
446 Tennessee St.
Redlands, CA 92373

Cougar Club of America (my club—tell 'em I sent you)
1526 Ericson Place
Bronx, NY 14061

LBM Inc. (for hard-to-find dash-repair kits)
1742 North Case St.
Orange, CA 92667

Automat (for hard-to-find interior panels)
225A Park Ave.
Hicksville, NY 11801

HC Fastener Co. (for hard-to-find nuts, bolts, and trim screws)
1002 Sparks
Alvardo, TX 76009

● **WHEN:** You are buying a **new car**
■ **WHAT TO DO:** Here are the decisions you are facing. (If you're a "typical" buyer, you will usually choose *b*.

1. Why did you pick the car?
   a) Massive research.
   b) You liked the color.
2. Why did you pick the dealer?
   a) Intensive comparison shopping.
   b) Walking distance from your house.
3. How did you appraise your trade-in?
   a) You offered it beforehand to several dealers for cash only—you even offered it to the dealer you ended up buying the new car from!
   b) You accepted the salesman's quote. He had an honest face.
4. How did you arrive at the new car's price?
   a) Fierce bargaining that would make even Kissinger blush.
   b) The dealer got your goat and you gave up.
5. How did you pick the options?
   a) Carefully and thoughtfully.
   b) You took whatever came with the floor model.
6. How much extra stuff did the dealer pack on at closing?

    a) Nothing at all—you held your ground.

    b) You took everything the nice salesman suggested (*but* at least you got 50 percent off list!).

7. If the car was delivered, when did it come?

    a) You insisted that the dealer agree in *writing* to deliver it within eight weeks *or* refund your deposit.

    b) Nothing in life is certain. It got here when it got here.

8. At time of delivery, did you check out the vehicle thoroughly before signing your acceptance on the receipt?

    a) Of course—even though it took about half an hour of work.

    b) Are you kidding?—The wife and kids were *dying* to go for a spin!

Now that we have outlined a typical new-car purchase, let's go into a little bit more detail:

PICKING THE MODEL

Believe it or not, most folks decide on the model they buy for reasons *other than* price and technical characteristics. Common motivations include color, styling, image, nostalgia, familiarity with that make or model, influence of the salesman, recommendation of a friend, and proximity to the dealer.

What will influence *you* when you make *your* $15,000 expenditure? Some years I've done test reports comparing over thirty different cars. *I'm* always surprised how much quality difference there can be within a given price spread. Also, if you keep up with the reviews, you'll find bargains. In the early years, the Nissan 240 sportscars were giveaways. The same is true for the early BMW 2002s, introductory Honda Preludes and CRXs, Toyota Tercels, and Mazda 626s. I'm predicting that the early Hyundai models sold in the United States will be bargain priced as well. To catch the bargains you must do your homework, read the reviews, and use some common sense. On the other hand, there's nothing *wrong* with buying a car for emotional reasons. Just don't fool yourself afterward. Pricing help is available! The publishers of *Consumer Reports* offer a pricing service that gives you the dealers cost of the car you want—and its options! Info from: Consumer Reports, Box 570, Lathrup Village, MI 48076.

PICKING THE DEALER

It's hard to win with car dealers. They're professionals. You're an amateur. They sell ten cars a day. You buy one every ten years. They know the pricing games. You just want the bottom line.

You may choose a dealer based on convenience, but make sure that service, integrity, and value are there as well. There are no easy answers. City dealers say they can offer better prices because of volume—but the fact is that high rents and overhead can keep prices high. Dealers outside the major downtown areas don't have the overhead worries—but neither do they have the pressure to close every deal. These days, many dealers will let you walk out for a bargaining difference of less than $100.

Let's go back to reputation. A happy customer will tell five friends. An unhappy one will tell ten. Try and see what former customers think of the dealer. Don't expect miracles—very few car dealers make it to sainthood. As soon as your check clears, the salesman you were going to invite over for dinner will forget your name. And when you call the service manager (a fellow you will never totally trust, no matter how honest he seems), he will put you on hold.

PRICING STRATEGY
The Trade-in

The first and most important step in the pricing process is getting a fair value on your trade. Warm up to the subject gradually. Be realistic—your old jalopy is not a spring chicken anymore. (Who is?) Give some thought to paying $50 to a detail shop (see page 113) to clean it up. This is the same stunt dealers use to sell cars and—surprisingly—it can be used on them. Watch the local classifieds every day to get an idea of a range of values for your car. Your local librarian or bank manager can be helpful in checking the most recent wholesale value listing on your car (usually from a *blue-book* —a service usually offered only by subscriptions). Go to one or two lots and ask for a *cash* price for your old car. Now you're ready for the big move: go to the used-car lot of the dealer you are considering and—before you let the *new*-car salesman near your old car—have the *used*-car manager give you a *cash price,* as is. That's it—you are now ready to start bargaining, with a *fair* and realistic value for your trade.

What's the Bottom Line?

Once you've got your trade-in all organized, never lose sight of the fact that the *bottom line* cash price is what you're after. The salesman (and his computer) are trained to confuse this issue, so you have to be adamant. It's *not* the trade-in credit, the so-called discount off list, or the easy *monthly* carrying charges that you want to look at, but the *bottom line*—after tax, prep, delivery, license, insurance, financing, and "pack" are figured in (for more about the "pack," see below).

Just You and the Salesman

This is it—*Let's Make a Deal* for adults. The net result is known. You want a new car, you are prepared to swap your old one and some cash for it, and you know roughly what you want to pay (although, like most folks, you underestimated the price of the extras thrown in at closing—see below). The only objective before you now is to bargain the salesman down to save a few hundred smackers.

Bad news, I'm afraid. *The odds are all against you.* The salesman who looks so friendly and naive has taken night courses in closing sales. That helpful computer on his desk is programmed to confuse issues, not clarify them. Many little dramas are played out in bargaining for new cars; here are the most common:

The Emotional Attachment. This is the biggy—if you can beat it, you'll win. The salesman is not stupid. He knows that in your mind you already see yourself driving the car. As far as you're concerned, *it's your car,* and all that stands in your way is a scrap of paper (the contract) and a few dollars. Psychologically, time is on *his* side. The more time you spend bargaining, pleading, or daydreaming, the greater your emotional investment in the car. If you are *not* prepared to *get up and walk out* when faced with an unreasonable offer, counteroffer, or bargaining ploy—then, my friend, you are a chicken waiting to be plucked.

The Legal Reversal. How this upside-down state of affairs ever started I don't know, but according to the way cars are sold in North America, *you,* the buyer, make a legally binding offer the salesman can accept or reject. Then the salesman (playing out the part of the reluctant virgin) agonizes over whether to sell the car or not. *Who's kidding whom?*

The "It's-not-my-job" gambit.   I love this one. You've just spent hours with this stranger discussing intimate details of the purchase, he's bargained you around the room until you're dizzy from trying to read the decimal points, he's persuaded you to sign a legally binding offer at a price the two of you have pretty much agreed upon, and you've given him a down payment as well. He goes out, then he slinks back to the desk saying the manager won't stick by the deal, here's the down payment back, he's sorry, *but for (fill in the blank) hundred dollars more,* it's your car!

Let's Try the Appel Gambit.   If you are made of strong stuff, you can beat the moves above and come back with a devastating counterattack that even Bobby Fischer would be proud of: As the bargaining progresses, begin to say nasty things about the car you picked out—like "probably gets bad mileage" or "bet those seats stain easily." This will *terrify* the salesman because it will show a weak emotional bond between you and the car which *could* blow the deal. After all, the salesman has spent his time on *you* when he could have been making another sale—so maybe he has more to lose after all.

When a salesman and you agree on a price that you suspect will be rejected by the manager, proceed to sign the offer form and write in a *small* down-payment but under your name write in the words "Offer conditional on communication of acceptance to me within twenty-four hours" and (hold on, folks!) *pick up your hat and coat and walk out.* Don't even turn back when the salesman starts crying. Simply go home and wait for the phone call that, inevitably, will come (although they may have to call their lawyer the next morning to figure out exactly what you've done).

Here's the key to Appel's gambit: You have reversed the legal onus in the deal. He is now the one who must chase *you* to close the deal—and he has only twenty-four hours to do it. He cannot come back and say the manager doesn't like it, or that there was a mistake in addition, or that the price has gone up. He can only accept or reject your bottom-line price, or he loses a sale. Since you were prepared to walk out, he knows your emotional attachment to the car is low—he might even worry that you'll go to another dealer. Simply wait for the phone call (it'll be either yes or no, since any other reply cancels the offer) and don't be surprised to find that you've bought a car.

One more twist: if you suspect the salesman of trying to lure you back into the showroom by saying yes when his true intention is to reopen negotiations, ask for a mailgram or overnight letter to be sent, collect, confirming the acceptance of the offer!

And if the gambit fails, what then? Don't fret—you know what car you want, what model, what options, the value of your trade-in, and even the final net cash price of the vehicle to within a hundred dollars or so. Try another dealer!

OPTIONS

I recently got into an argument on a TV talk show about the dealer's true wholesale cost—with a representative of a car dealers' association. My argument was simple—it is generally difficult to pin down the dealer's *exact* wholesale on a given new car because, aside from the normal baseline price per car model, the overall cost will vary depending on the options selected (the markup on options is higher than the markup on the car), the dealer's finance costs, the prep costs, and the special discounts (if any) from the manufacturer for buying either that particular car or any car at that time of year. Since some of the manufacturer's discount might be in the form of a rebate or even a credit, the dealer's true cost (including kickbacks on financing, insurance, and the "pack"—see below) may not even be finalized until *after* the sale. The dealer's rep on the panel became agitated and swore on live TV that all dealers pay exactly the same price for a car regardless of when it is ordered or under what circumstances. I find that position particularly hard to defend. The "loaded" car on the dealer's lot is much more likely to have been discounted by the manufacturer (lowering the dealer's wholesale cost) than the model you special-order when "they build one for you". Still, if you custom-order, you can *avoid* many "invisible" high-cost options that are really pure profit for the manufacturer and dealer alike.

Whenever I am asked what new-car options, I recommend, this is my short list:

- Heavy-duty battery
- Oversize radiator (usually there are two or three levels above standard)
- Automatic-transmission cooler
- Engine-block heater (for winter driving)
- Full-service spare tire (if the manufacturer won't provide this, twist the dealer's arm by threatening to go to a tire store)
- Oversize alternator

- Full instrument-gauge package (see page 25).
- Top-of-the-line radials (Michelin, if possible)
- Sport suspension (better control, better wear)
- Cruise control
- Electric door locks (not for convenience, but for security)
- Whatever light package gets me lights in the trunk and under the hood
- A prewiring package for stereo speakers so that I can have an aftermarket radio put in later

That's it for the dealer. The aftermarket can supply me with the following:

- Fancy pinstriping or vinyl guards
- Floor mats
- Rust protection (see page 46, and "packs," below)
- Stereo radio
- Quartz lighting

Protecting Yourself from the "Pack"

In the late '40s and '50s, when demand for cars began to exceed supply, dealers began adding strange options to the cars they sold, and buyers had trouble avoiding them. The sheer stubbornness of the dealers meant that these high-profit items were turning up on every car they sold, greatly adding to their profit. The "pack" is still with us these days, and the consumer has to be sharp to avoid it. The salesman is *trained* to wait for the *exact point of closing* to hit the buyer with several "small" extras that could easily add $1000 to the bill—and the profit margin on these "pack" items is outrageous! Stay alert for the following "pack" items:

- Financing (talk to your bank manager first)
- Extended warranty (it does offer some peace of mind, but the price is high; your insurance agent might be able to steer you to cheaper plans from private insurance companies)
- Rustproofing (the tar/wax stuff really is a waste of money, usually costs the dealer no more than $30, and can hurt your car—see page 46)
- Paint protection (do you still believe in the tooth fairy?—save your money)

- Fabric protection (buy a can of Scotchguard at the supermarket and do it yourself)
- PDI—pre-delivery inspection (watch out—some manufacturers also *include* this in the retail price)
- Delivery (again, make sure you haven't paid for this twice)
- Antitheft package (see page 167)

THE FINE PRINT CAN GET YOU!

Even lawyers don't look forward to checking each clause in a "standard-form" agreement (that's a fancy name for an agreement which is made out before you get a chance to look at it). It is possible to *legally change* the agreement by writing key terms in ink in the area above your signature. When the dealer signs the agreement, all the clauses you put in then become valid and override the fine print.

Here are some basic clauses I suggest you add in writing (apply to contracts in all jurisdictions):

1. "If the price of the car goes up between now and the time of delivery, I have the option of canceling and getting my full deposit back immediately."
2. "If the value of my trade decreases between now and the time of delivery, I have the option of canceling and getting my full deposit back immediately."
3. "If the car is not ready for delivery to me within —— (fill in) days from signing, I have the option of canceling and getting my full deposit back immediately."
4. "If the car does not come with the options I ordered (and only the options I ordered) I have the option of canceling and getting my full deposit back immediately."

INSPECTION AND ACCEPTANCE

Most buyers are on a "high" when they take delivery—buying a new car is an exciting event. Think back for a moment to the *last* new car you bought —do you remember signing some kind of form as the keys were handed to you? Did you read the form before you signed? Most buyers are too flustered to pay attention, but that form is important. It says the car in front of you is, in fact, the car you ordered, that you are happy with it, and that you accept delivery. From the time you sign that form, buddy, it's your car!

What you want to do is inspect the car thoroughly *before* signing. Check to see that the options you ordered are there. Play the radio, open the windows, push the buttons, open the hood, move the seats, start the engine, and go for a spin. (Don't be surprised if the shocked salesman goes with you!) Check the paint and interior carefully. Check alignment on the tires and balance of the wheels. Anything wrong? Ask that it be fixed *immediately!*

Some may think this ploy is hard on the dealer, but I disagree. After all, you're paying the $15,000—you're entitled to some courtesy. Also, this could be the last time you will ever see the salesman—once you sign the form, you belong, heart and soul, to the service manager.

If you refuse to sign until repairs are done, you'll be amazed how fast you get service. They'll pull four mechanics off a Cadillac-engine rebuild just to make you happy. And you know what? You deserve it!

How big a deposit?

Would you believe that $1 is enough? It is. That's why there's a contract in the first place—to make sure that you pay for the car when it arrives. The deposit is simply a throwback to the horse-trading days —when they used real horses. Lay down a small deposit—this makes it less likely the dealer will try to "stall" you and try to play off your fear of losing the deposit.

What's a TO?

TO stands for "take over." It's what happens when you give your salesman such a hard time (by following the advice here, for example) that he suddenly remembers a dentist appointment and brings in a new face to take over—and a new deal. If this happens, put on your marching shoes, brother, and hit the road!

● **WHEN:** You want to **sell your car.**

■ **WHAT TO DO:** Read the section on classified ads (page 185) and see what works for you. Tell your friends the car is on the block. Post a notice on your apartment bulletin board and in the laundry room. Put a FOR SALE BY OWNER sign in the side window. Visit a detail shop (page 113) to improve your car's looks (and value).

Drop by a few car lots and see what kind of cash price you can get. Make *your* asking price $1000 higher.

Learn a few useful phrases for the bargaining process:

- "I'm not a mechanic but it's running well as far as I'm concerned."
- "Is the price negotiable? Yes, I guess I'll take more."
- "Do I know it needs work? Yep—that's *already* figured into the asking price."
- "No, I'm not in a rush to sell it, but first fellow to my door with cash or certified check drives her home."

If you have a mechanic who's been looking after the car all along, don't be afraid to give his name to prospective buyers. He'll be truthful about the car and might even pick up a new customer.

New wrinkles

There's a *lot* new in the used-car business these days. Here's the latest—some of these options may be available in your area:

- *Listing agents.* Your car will be put on a computer list, and interested buyers will be referred to you. You will be charged only on sale.
- *Dealer consignment.* Local dealers trying to get a bigger piece of the pie will take your car "on consignment." If it sells, you get a prearranged price. Watch out for hidden fees in consignment contracts.
- *Park-and-sell lots.* You rent space on a lot for a day, and any buyer that walks up to your car is fair game.
- *Private-consignment lots.* These guys are not car dealers at all but they do have a lot of vacant land. They'll let you leave your car and keys there. If they sell the car, they either take a fixed commission or all the excess over an agreed price.

● **WHEN:** You are shopping for a **used car.**
■ **WHAT TO DO:** Why buy a used car?

- Somebody else gets the "depreciation surprise," an economic oddity that makes your new car worth 30 percent less than you paid for it thirty seconds after you take delivery.
- A used car is probably broken in, with the little repairs already taken care of.
- Mechanically, an older car is simpler than newer models. Parts and service are widely available. Most corner garages will know how to service it. You are not tied to a dealer.
- The strengths and weaknesses of the model are "known" to the marketplace. So are the year-to-year depreciation and the likely resale value.
- The car may have "collectible" value in addition to its day-to-day value as transportation (see page 184).
- You'll save big bucks.

Where do you shop for a new car?

Local classifieds. These are a good place to start because they provide extremely accurate local values for all the cars you might be interested in. (Classifieds that are free to the advertiser may show higher prices, because the seller can wait for a response without running up a bill.)

Long-distance classifieds. Magazines like *Hemmings* have antique and collectible cars at good prices, but you'll have travel and insurance costs to consider.

Used-car lots of new-car dealers. Aside from the fact that 99 percent of these cars are "detailed" to hide the signs of abuse (see page 00) and that the asking prices will be 100 percent of retail (or higher), these shops are generally not a bad deal if you do your homework.

Car lots—used only. Nope—not for this little black duck! With a few exceptions (quality lots that take in only quality vehicles), these guys know even less about the prior history of the cars they sell than you do!

Car-dealer strategy

Let the dealer know that you want only cars taken on trades, not from auctions or other dealers. Insist that he let you see incoming cars *before* they're detailed. Tell him that, if you like what you see, you'll make an instant cash offer *and* save him the price of the detailing. Pick the dealer carefully. Lots in ritzy neighborhoods tend to have a great many customers who get rid of their top-shape late-model cars because they've got nothing better to do that day.

Friends and neighbors.   Why not?—there are great deals to be made. Somebody somewhere is thinking of a trade-in. Maybe the lease is coming up on your dentist's or lawyer's car. (Many leases let the old lessee pick up the car at the "wholesale" price—although this trend is slowly fading away.)

Auctions.   (See page 178.)

Rental car lots.   There's nothing wrong with this approach at all. The cars are generally well maintained, well warrantied, and the service records should be available. Most firms comply with the industry convention that cars with more than $750 damage are not sold to the public (although they *may* turn up on a gypsy lot!) The cars that get a lot of use at airports are usually not displayed either. Here's a trick: look at the exhaust manifold. If it's excessively corroded relative to the mileage on the car, the car was probably used for stop-and-go city driving. Forget it!

How important is mileage? In reality, a well-maintained four-cylinder engine is capable of 100,000 trouble-free miles (except maybe for a VW Bug), and a larger engine can go about 150,000. Obviously, the lower the mileage, the higher the asking price. Do odometers still get rolled back? Yes, they do. (Some actually get rolled *forward*—the rear end is jacked up and the car is run until the odometer rolls on past 100,000!) And the so-called antitampering gadgets from the Big Three are a joke among the pros. If you can *prove* you were misled as to real mileage you can get damages—not only based on fraud, but also from a federal law that has been on the books since

1972. Proving it may be tough, so be careful. All used-car sales should specify the odometer reading in the contract!

HOW LONG SHOULD IT TAKE TO FIND A CAR?

Allow at least seven full days to find a good used car, bargain for it, and check it out before purchase.

BARGAINING

The most effective bargaining gambit in buying a used car is reducing the price by the expected repair costs. To play that game, however, you must first know what repairs are required. That means checking out the used car. Do you need a mechanic to check out the car? Of course you do. Be prepared to spend a few dollars checking it out *properly*. No matter how much the checking costs, it's still cheaper than getting a bad buy.

Checks you can do on your own

1. Check for underbody leaks. Find out where the car is usually parked and see what fluids are leaking out of it. (Make notes to discuss with your mechanic later).

2. Pass a dime-store magnet (wrapped in tissue) around all the sheet metal and note where the magnet won't stick (This indicates a bad rust repair or a major accident.) Note any bubbling in the paint (this indicates rust). On the other hand, if the paint is new, find out why. (A quickie job done to help sell the car probably won't last.) Does one end of the car hang lower than the other? This could mean suspension problems. Walk to the rear and see if one side of the car *leans* over more than the other (an uneven car indicates an accident). Examine the two front tires carefully. The wear should be even. If not—you could have major suspension problems. Examine the rear tires for unusual wear patterns—sellers often try to hide badly worn *front* tires on the *rear* of the car.

3. Hop in the driver's seat and look for signs of abuse—like a sagging door on the driver's side, broken springs in the driver's seat, a driver's seat that won't move up and down smoothly, unusual stains on the dash, cigarette burns, etc.

4. Pop open the hood and poke around a bit. Was the engine detailed (see page 113)? If so, you could be dealing with a seller far more

sophisticated than you realize. Pull out the oil dipstick and have a look at it—is there a rainbow varnish buildup at the bottom? Any obvious signs of leakage? Any unusual smells? (See pages 50 and 218). Any wiring that doesn't seem to go anywhere? (This usually means the car has had either a succession of different owners or had a major collision.)

5. Go for a test drive with the owner. Listen to the explanations the owner volunteers without being asked—this will give away a lot about the car. If the owner says a part needs an "adjustment," assume it needs an overhaul. If he says a part needs a repair, assume it has to be replaced. If he says that a certain procedure will be due in a few weeks, assume it should have been done yesterday. And if he says that some repair was done recently to get the car ready for sale, assume it was done *badly,* using *cheap* parts, and will have to completely reinspected by a *pro!*

6. Ask the owner if anything presently in the car is *not* included in the sale price. You may be shocked to find that the radio, CB, and mag wheels were not going to be part of the bargain.

Arrive at a price "subject to mechanical inspection"

This is a sound practice from the buyer's viewpoint, because it commits the seller to a *maximum* price before any money is spent on an independent mechanical evaluation. If the mechanic turns up problems (and he will) you, the buyer, can use this as a lever to reduce the price or, if the seller won't budge, walk away from the deal. On the other hand, if the mechanical examination shows nothing (and the seller may not be 100 percent certain of the mechanical condition of the car), at least the price is not going to go any higher. The legal phrasing (this can also apply to buying from a car lot) can be as follows: "The sale and sale price stated are conditional on the car passing a reasonable mechanical inspection at a place of the buyer's choosing and at the buyer's expense, which inspection must show no repairs to be done in excess of a value of $25 per repair, or $100 in all."

Now the hard part—the inspection

The mechanical inspection is the most unpleasant part of buying a used car. Human nature being what it is, most people don't bother.

Tough. The problems of owning a "bad" car far exceed the nuisance of the inspection. If you take shortcuts in buying a used car, you'll get hurt!

Which mechanic to use? I'll tell you a secret: Mechanics aren't beating down your door to make the $50 you'll spend on the check-out. There is a lot of other more profitable work they could be doing. Reputable shops will check out a used car as a courtesy to regular customers or their families. Your best bet is to use a mechanic who knows you (and wants your patronage) or a friend's mechanic who will treat you right.

A tip: Have all the test results put down *in writing.* This keeps the mechanic from getting sloppy and also gives you some recourse if he takes shortcuts that end up costing you money.

Don't leave the choice of tests to the mechanic. Mark down the following *essentials* on a sheet of paper and ask for a written report on each:

1. Completely inspect the underbody. Check the frame and floor for rust. Check the shocks, muffler, front suspension, and springs. Look for signs of major accidents. Check the driveshaft and U-joints. Look for leaks anywhere in the engine area, transmission area, radiator, brake lines and cylinders, gas lines and tank. Check and spin tires by hand, from underneath, looking for wear and bulges in the sidewalls. Check for deterioration in the undercoating. Check for shiny-clean parts that indicate recent major repairs.

2. Remove the tires and completely check all four brake cylinders or calipers by eye. Also check brakes from the driver's seat, making sure the system holds pressure. Double-check for leaks. Look into the master cylinder reservoir for signs of fluid contamination. Check pad and lining wear. Check for unusual scoring of drums or discs. Look for signs of contaminated wheel-bearing seals.

3. Hook up the scope and exhaust analyzer to the engine and crank it up. Check for the available battery current, alternator output, starter draw, ignition output and pattern, secondary wire patterns. Look for missing at speed. Check the cylinder balance electronically (only a scope can do this), and use the exhaust analyzer to verify that the proper air-fuel mixture is being burned.

4. Follow the scope test up with a vacuum-gauge test and a compression test. Pull two or three plugs at random to check for unusual deposits. Watch the stem of the EGR value move during rapid throttle.

5. With the engine on, listen for unusual noises (see page 41) and pinpoint unusual smells. Check the condition of your belts and

hoses. Pop open the oil filler cap and see if blue smoke billows out (it shouldn't). Peer into the oil filler tube with a flashlight and look at the condition of the rocker arm or cam area. Sludge or discoloration means the car has been subjected to infrequent oil changes and other abuse. Pull the automatic transmission dipstick and rub the fluid in your fingers looking for grit (there should be none). Smell it (it should not smell burnt).

6. Make a test drive. Verify straight, accurate steering that returns to center after turns, normal play in the clutch and steering wheel, positive braking action, and smooth shifting of the automatic transmission without unusual noises. Acceleration should be positive and smooth, without hesitation, knocking, or pinging. The steering wheel should not move when the brakes are applied hard. When moving the transmission from drive to neutral to reverse (on a manual or on an automatic) there should be no unusual noises.

7. Finally (on a front-wheel-drive vehicle), find an empty parking lot and do a tight series of figure-8 turns with the window open so that you can hear what's happening. You should *not* hear any clunks, thunks, pops, or clicks coming from the front wheels. (This can indicate the need for expensive and complex repairs.)

Also, your mechanic should be alert to signs of sabotage or tampering. For example, one way to hide a major oil-pressure problem is to disable the oil-pressure light (a rushed buyer would not remember to check that all dashboard lights and gauges activated when the ignition key was turned) or pour some thickener into the sump. Oil problems are particularly serious, because they can lead to major repairs—so be cautious. If there is any doubt, it might be prudent to change the oil *at your expense* to get rid of the masking agents, and then have a oil-pressure check done with a mechanic's pressure gauge. (Engine rebuilds can cost more the purchase price of the car, so this advice is far from extravagant!)

One more expert?

If the above tests raise any suspicion of the car having been in a recent accident (a very serious consideration with the new front-drive econoboxes) leave the car at a body shop and ask the owner (a $10 "incentive" will help) to look it over for a minute or two. *A body man will spot clues that even a top mechanic may overlook.* If the car was in a serious accident—forget it! (Yes, there are competent shops out there, but the odds are *against* your getting a car that's been fixed correctly.)

CLOSING THE DEAL

If you still want the car:

- Make sure your insurer knows you'll be taking delivery (see page 115).
- Make sure that the local registry shows the transfer, or you may end up getting parking tickets from places you've never been.
- Get any extra keys the former owner may have. Also politely ask for spare parts, touch-up paint, extra tires and rims, old repair slips, owner's manuals, recall notices, and anything else that may be of value.
- If there is any possibility of an outstanding lien or a prior ownership in the car, ask your lawyer or auto club how to check this.
- Certain jurisdictions will let you contact the former owner(s) to verify mileage.
- Call the NHTSA in Washington to see if there have been any major recalls on the car. (You may not be able to see if *your* car was repaired, but at least you can ask your mechanic to inspect the area later.)

One final tip: Don't buy cars from your great-aunt Mary in Sacramento if no one in your family can recall having a great-aunt Mary in Sacramento.

■ 6 ■
TO PREVENT PROBLEMS

● **WHEN:** You want your **battery** to live forever.

■ **WHAT TO DO:** First, make sure which type of battery you own: the older kind (with caps) that requires the addition of *distilled* water every few weeks, or one of the newer so-called low-maintenance batteries that also requires water every few months—although it's harder to pry off the caps —or a maintenance-free type.

Is the battery properly secured? Bouncing around is not good for a battery. Most auto-parts stores have replacement hold-down kits for a few dollars.

Are the terminals clean? Acid around the top of the battery eats through the connectors, increases circuit resistance, and can cause shorts. It's also dangerous to human skin. Wash the battery down with a mixture of baking soda and water; rinse off with water from a pressure hose. Let it dry. Remove the lugs with the right wrench, clean the posts with sandpaper, reattach the lugs, and smear them with petroleum jelly.

Battery tools are cheap!

Here's what's in a good do-it-yourself battery tool chest: a lug wrench, terminal pullers, terminal spreaders, a clamp carrier or carrying strap, sandpaper, and Vaseline.

If the water is disappearing too fast, the battery is being overcharged by the alternator. See a mechanic.

Some other tips:

- A battery warmer is a good idea in winter and kind to the battery.
- If your battery has a built-in color eye (hygrometer) check the manufacturer's directions on how to use it.
- Always use the correct boost procedure.

> ### Boost tip
>
> When boosting a battery with side terminals instead of top terminals, positioning the clamps is tricky and can lead to dangerous shorts. Most auto-supply houses sell special extensions that give a greater biting area for the clamps—for under $5

- Don't use battery additives indiscriminately.

● **WHEN:** You want to go **four-wheeling**—safely!

■ **WHAT TO DO:** If you are serious about four-wheeling (using vehicles with four-wheel drive off-road), join an off-road club. You will probably be given a refresher course in off-road maneuvering.

Keep in mind that the higher center of gravity in the four-wheel drive vehicle, combined with the driver's desire to climb or descend major inclines, raises the very real possibility of a rollover. In a case that made headlines recently, a young girl who was part of an off-roading club lost her life during such a rollover.

Make sure that:

- You understand the shift controls for your particular vehicle.
- Your vehicle has a quality roll bar (to brace the chassis and roof in case of a roll).
- You never ascend or descend at an angle—always approach an incline straight on. If you get stuck going up, simply come down in a reverse straight line, using the brakes and the reverse gear compression to slow your descent. Never veer off at an angle to get traction. (Sometimes twisting the wheels fully to the left and right in sequence will help you get a grip.)

Freeplay checks. These checks are sometimes different for different cars—read your owner's manual for the specific information for your car.

Free play is
left–right
movement—
See your manual.

- **WHEN:** You want to do your own **freeplay** checks
- **WHAT TO DO:** Most cars permit the following freeplay checks. See your owner's manual for more detail:

Steering gear. With engine off and the front wheels pointing straight ahead, try to move the wheel in either direction. Play should not exceed ½ inch in either direction.

Clutch. With the engine off apply pressure to the clutch until you feel resistance. The play here should not exceed ¾ inch (on most cars—see your manual).

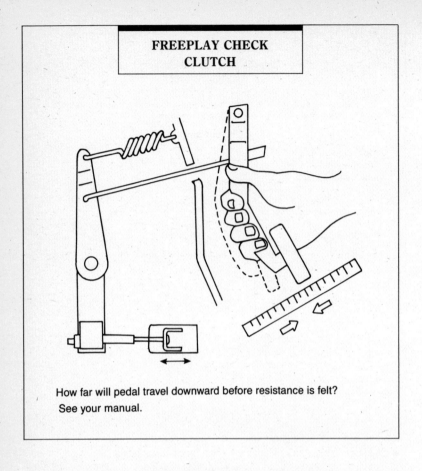

FREEPLAY CHECK
CLUTCH

How far will pedal travel downward before resistance is felt?
See your manual.

Parking brake. Pull up on the parking brake until you feel resistance. The play should not exceed 3 inches.

Brake pedal. Turn on the engine and let it warm up. With the transmission in DRIVE (or neutral on a manual) stomp the brake pedal to the floor with your right foot. You should be able to fit the toes of your left foot under the depressed pedal. Automatics with power brakes only: apply the brakes hard with the engine running and the selector at NEUTRAL. Shift to DRIVE. You should feel the pedal move slightly toward the floor. If it doesn't move at all, the booster is defective. If it goes right to the floor, there is a pressure leak in the hydraulics.

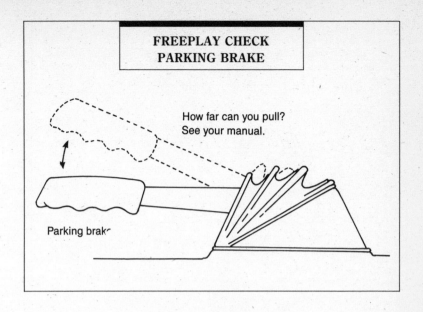

FREEPLAY CHECK
PARKING BRAKE

How far can you pull?
See your manual.

Parking brake

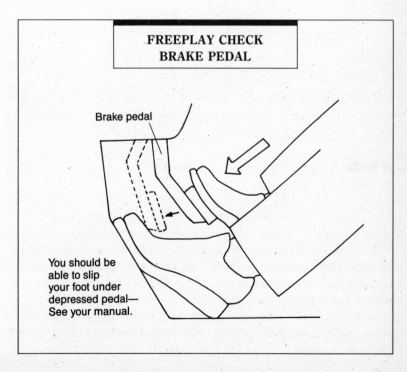

FREEPLAY CHECK
BRAKE PEDAL

Brake pedal

You should be
able to slip
your foot under
depressed pedal—
See your manual.

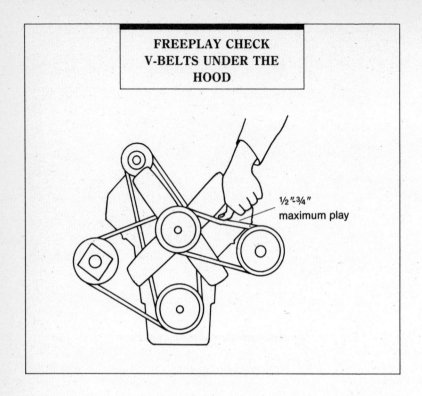

**FREEPLAY CHECK
V-BELTS UNDER THE
HOOD**

½″–¾″
maximum play

V-belts under the hood. Locate the midpoint of each V-belt (the central point between any two pulleys) and push hard with your index finger. The belt should not depress more than ½ inch.

● **WHEN:** You want to care for your **front-drive** car.
■ **WHAT TO DO:**

1. Have the constant-velocity boots checked by a mechanic every six months. At the first sign of a broken seal, replace the boot.
2. Have the alignment on all four wheels checked at least once a year —at a shop with all the latest equipment. Have uneven tire wear or leaks at the steering rack attended to promptly.
3. Learn where all your "fluid check" areas are. Check them regularly, especially the automatic transaxle (if you have one).
4. Maintain proper front-tire inflation. Do not drive into curbs.
5. If your car is to be used to tow another car or a trailer, follow the

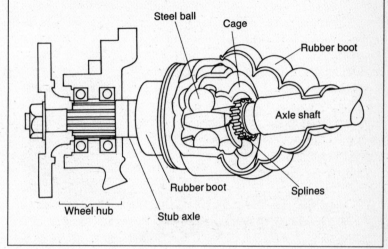

CV BOOT

Most front-wheel drive cars have four of these fragile-looking connections. They wear out about twice as fast as the U-joints that were common on rear-drive cars, and cost up to fifteen times as much to replace.

Steel ball

Cage

Rubber boot

Axle shaft

Splines

Rubber boot

Wheel hub

Stub axle

manufacturer's recommendations for placement of the hitch, load distribution, and other specifications. Don't be surprised if the manufacturer says your vehicle *cannot* be used for towing at all.

6. If your car needs a tow from a tow truck, don't let the front wheels remain on the ground. See that they are either lifted by a tow truck with a new "wheel cradle" bar or, if the tow is from the back, insist that a dolly go under the front wheels.

7. If you are doing emergency car-to-car towing, fasten the chain according to manufacturer's instructions: usually around an axle, not a bumper.

8. If you get stuck in snow, do not spin the front tires needlessly.

9. If you get into an accident, go to a properly equipped shop (see page 105).

10. Be on the alert for the telltale noises that CV joints make as they deteriorate:

- The outboard joints will make clicking and popping noises during tight turns.
- The inboard joints will make a thunk or clunk when accelerating from rest or coasting down from a higher speed.

See a mechanic as soon as you hear these sounds! Compared to the traditional U-joints on a rear-drive vehicle, CV joints cost 15 times as much to repair—and you have twice as many of them!

● **WHEN:** you are planning a **highway trip.**
■ **WHAT TO DO:** The good news about highway driving is that it gives your engine a chance to clean itself out. The bad news is that it puts a strain on all the other systems of the car. Worse, the failing systems will often not show themselves until you pull off the highway, or stop for a toll.

Tips:

1. Change the oil before a long trip. Contaminants in your present oil will burn off quickly in highway driving, leaving little genuine oil in the sump. A flush and fill before you go will help avoid this problem.
2. Check all the fluid levels, particularly in the radiator. A slow leak in the city could mean big trouble on the highway. If in doubt have the system pressure-tested (this costs about $15).
3. Make sure your tires are inflated to the right pressure. There is no need to add air on modern tires, but a low tire will build up dangerous sidewall heat quickly.
4. Carry extra windshield-washer fluid and a sponge. Bugs have no pity at high speed.
5. Verify that the gauges are working correctly. Even the idiot lights should wink at you when you turn the key.
6. Carry some extra V-belts in case one breaks. Parts are often hard to get away from home.
7. Verify that your spare tire is in good condition, and that all the parts of the jack are present and accounted for.

e. See the sections on emergency kits, on page 156, and on highway breakdown, on page 70.

● **WHEN:** You want a general **preventive-maintenance** program.

■ **WHAT TO DO:** Here's a realistic program that you should be able to live with:

- Engine oil and filter—Change every three months, regardless of mileage. Grease if the fittings will accept it. (Newer cars won't.)
- Transmission (automatic)—Change oil and filter every two years. Be sure to use the correct fluid—see your manual, or see your dipstick (the right fluid is usually marked on the edge).
- Transmission (manual)—Change oil every 4 years.
- Brake wear—Inspect once a year.
- Ignition and emission system—check once a year.
- Spark plugs—Change every two years.
- Spark plug wires and cap—Change every three years.

Here's a strange test

For purists only—Keep track of excessive acidity in your antifreeze by taking a standard VOM meter, setting at the low voltage setting, and sticking one lead in the antifreeze and the other to a ground. If the reading is above $8/10$ volt, you've waited too long between changes.

- Brake fluid—Replace every three years.

Air contaminates brake fluid

It absorbs water from the air. Use a new unopened can or one that was opened in the last few months and then tightly recapped. Use a fluid with a DOT rating that meets or exceeds that originally used by the manufacturer. Brake fluid can damage paint and rubber, so wipe up spills quickly. If you're converting to lifetime silicone fluid, flush the system first or you risk a harmful combination of incompatible fluids.

- Rear brakes and parking brake—Adjust every six months.
- Freeplay adjustments—Check every six months (see page 207).
- Alignment—Check once a year.
- Valves—Adjust (if needed) once a year.
- CV joints (front-wheel-drive)—Check every six months.
- Universal joints (rear-wheel drive)—Check every two years.
- Front suspension—Check for wear every year.
- Front bearings—Grease (where possible) every brake service.
- Air filter and breather—Change once a year.
- PCV valve—Change every two years.
- Charcoal canister filter—Change every two years (see your manual).
- Engine—Inspect area for gas leaks (they look suspiciously shiny and clean) every time the hood is opened.
- Engine fluids (oil, transmission, brakes, washers, radiator)—Check at least once a month.
- Tires—Check pressure, including spare, at least once a month.
- Wiper arms and blades—Change once a year.
- Exhaust system—Inspect once a year.
- Underside of car—Check for leaks once a year.
- EGR valve and oxygen sensor—Change as recommended in your manual.
- Inner panels and underside—Oil yearly.
- Lock cylinders—Lubricate with WD-40 before winter.
- Radiator—Flush and fill every two years.
- Radiator—Change cap and pressure-test every three years.
- Radiator hoses and V-belts—Replace, every three years.
- Radiator thermostat—Change according to your manual.
- Parking-brake cable—Lubricate before winter.
- Battery terminal and body-to-ground connecting strap connections —Clean once a year. This is a cheap way to avoid hard-to-find starting problems.
- Fuel filter (this is particularly important on fuel-injected cars— Change yearly—or as per owner's manual.
- Clutch reservoir—top off every six months (If your clutch is hydraulic, of course—brake fluid will do the trick).
- Points and condenser—Replace (if needed) once a year.

● **WHEN:** You'd rather be safe than sorry (general **safety** considerations).

■ **WHAT TO DO:** There are many hidden danger areas around the modern motorcar:

Seatbelts. It is indeed ironic that one of the biggest safety advances in cars can also be dangerous, but this is true nonetheless. The major problem is that slack can build up inside the rolling mechanism. When an accident finally comes and the seat-belt inertial lock is triggered, the years of built-up slack allow the occupant to travel several inches forward before stopping—and just a few inches can make a deadly difference. Have this checked by a mechanic.

In addition, check the securing bolts every few years and the replace belts completely on cars more than ten years old.

Air bags. More irony—air bags are not even in regular use and already reports are in of air bags detonating in error and bruising 250-pound police officers! It's the author's recommendation that children not be left alone in the front seats of airbag-equipped cars.

Rust. Rust kills, says the *Wall Street Journal.* Rust holes in the floor can admit deadly carbon monoxide fumes into the passenger compartment. Rust's attack on the infrastructure of the vehicle can render it less likely to withstand a serious accident. Rust can also weaken brake-fluid lines, making the braking system less able to sustain a panic stop without rupturing. (Police in salt-belt jurisdictions scare drivers of unsafe vehicles off the road by asking for a demonstration of emergency braking. This test usually ends in a ruptured brake line and a wiser owner.)

Electric fans. These units, which have replaced belt-driven fans, can start by themselves—even when the engine is shut off. Fingers could be lost if they're in the way of the fan when it turns on.

Air-conditioner refrigerant. Gas escaping from these lines under high pressure could blind an eye or freeze a finger.

Catalytic converters. They're a source of extremely concentrated heat. Early models used in tests by the U.S. military reportedly ignited the tall grass they were parked in.

Exhaust leaks. These can release carbon monoxide—see above.

Fuel injection. Many of the newer systems keep the lines pressurized to 50 or 60 psi even when the engine is off. This can be dangerous if idle hands tamper with the line, or in the event of a collision. Some electric fuel pumps—lacking an emergency cutout—may continue pumping gas under pressure even after an accident has occured.

"Once-only" suspension bolts. This is a major threat to uninformed backyard mechanics and do-it-yourselfers—new suspension nuts and bolts are designed by the manufacturer to stretch when installed, and are not under any circumstances to be reused after a repair or adjustment to the suspension. If an amateur mechanic reuses one of these unintentionally, the steering or suspension could fail at any time.

Cramped battery-mounting areas. As underhood space shrinks, cramped battery trays with side terminals increase the likelihood of sparking or shorting during boost-starting. This in turn increases the likelihood of a hydrogen-gas explosion.

Improperly installed propane tanks. Since propane is heavier than air, a small leak in an improperly installed system will collect and form a pocket of death waiting for a spark to ignite it.

Picking the wrong jack point. On unibody cars, picking the wrong point at which to place the jack could result in the body collapsing during a tire change.

● **WHEN:** You want to survive the **self-service** station.
■ **WHAT TO DO:** Read and reread the manual that came with your car. Know your tire pressures, where to check fluid levels, what brand of oil and gas to buy, and under what conditions to check your automatic transmission fluid.

Tires. Get a good tire gauge and keep it with you at all times. Dial gauges are far superior to pencil gauges and cost under $5. Always check tires when *cold* (or first thing in the morning), because air expands as it heats up. During extremely cold weather, check tires first thing in the morning and add air as needed. Attend to slow leaks before they become big leaks (see page 34). Don't forget to check your spare.

Oil. If you are following my recommendations for oil and filter changes (every three months regardless of mileage) you should not have to add oil between changes. If you are losing oil, find out why.

Radiators. Check the radiator at the overflow tank, not at the cap (which is scalding hot, sealed, and pressurized). While all radiators lose a little fluid in normal operation, you should have to add your 50-50 mixture of antifreeze and water only occasionally. Use the proper antifreeze (see your manual). If the fluid in the overflow bottle becomes cloudy or milky, see a mechanic. If you are adding fluid often, see a mechanic.

Brake fluid. A little fluid loss is normal between brake jobs—maybe a few tablespoons a month. More than that and you should see a mechanic. Don't allow dirt to get into the master-cylinder reservoir, don't leave your can of fluid open and exposed to air (which ruins it), and don't let the fluid touch the paint (it's corrosive to paint).

Power-steering fluid. Should require little if any topping off throughout the car's life. Otherwise, see a mechanic.

Transmission fluid. This should require little if any topping off during a car's normal life. Periodic changes are recommended—see your manual. Fluid may get lighter over time (as it weakens) but it should not get darker or pick up any unusual smells or particles. Nor should it foam or form varnish on the bottom of the dipstick. See a mechanic at the first sign of trouble. If you top it off, be sure to use the correct brand. See your manual for details. The information is often written on the dipstick as well.

V-belts. The new ones are hard to inspect visually, but look for obvious cracks or tears. Belts should be replaced every two or three years. Once they are properly installed (and re-tightened after they set) they should not require further adjustment. If you have a serpentine belt system, carry an extra belt with you at all times, or risk being totally incapacitated. The correct tightness is about ½ inch play downward (using your thumb) at the midway point between the two pulleys.

Clutch fluid. Not all cars have this—see your manual. Fill it with brake fluid.

Magic eye hygrometer in the battery. See your manual to find out what color it's supposed to be and whether or not your battery requires regular topping off. Be careful—many so-called easy-maintenance models still have a procedure for adding distilled water.

General leaks. Look sharp—any unusual moisture can indicate a leak that gets worse when the engine is running. See pages 34–37 for information on how to identify and fix specific problems.

Washer fluid. If your area freezes in winter, I recommend using washer fluid antifreeze all year round. The extra cost is only a few dollars, the odds of being caught in a freeze are reduced, and there is a detergent mixed with the alcohol which will give you some cleaning effect even on a hot summer day.

Wipers. Wipers should be changed once a year. Their useful life can be greatly prolonged by regular cleaning. Run the window squeegees (kept at most service stations) along the length of the refill blade—this will remove a surprising amount of dirt and grease.

Smells. Three smells are of concern to us:

- Gasoline—has its own distinctive smell. When you smell gas, trouble is never far behind.
- Rotten eggs—on most modern cars, this is a natural, no-extra-cost benefit of the catalytic converter.
- Burning plastic—almost always means a wiring problem in the making. Track it down with your nose before it disables the car or causes a fire.

● **WHEN:** You want to shift for yourself (**shifting techniques**).
■ **WHAT TO DO:** I prefer manual transmissions to automatics because they give greater control under difficult driving conditions; permit "compression braking" (the use of the natural backpressure of the engine to slow the car down by downshifting); and generally cost less to repair.

In the '80s little upshift lights on the dash—to remind the driver when to shift—have become trendy. I'm old-fashioned: if you're not sure when to shift, you've got no business driving the car.

Here are some tips:

- The kindest way to downshift, reduce wear, and maintain smooth engine power without risking a skid is to *double-clutch*—clutch in, shift to neutral, clutch out, rev engine, clutch in, shift to lower gear, clutch out, and engage gear.
- To stop in an emergency, downshift through the gears without touching the gas.
- To start on snow or ice, use second gear and gradually let out the clutch.
- To drive for power and acceleration, keep a heavy foot on the gas and stay in each gear until red-line.
- To drive for economy, shift to a higher gear as soon as you are able to without "lugging," or straining the engine.

Controversy

Several years back, BMW took exception to the above generalization and published data showing that better mileage is achieved only when you stay in the lower gears longer and upshift when the torque runs out. Although traditional vacuum-gauge tests showed this method to be inefficient, BMW developed a new computerized vacuum gauge that showed other engine variables besides vacuum. The final results supported the BMW hypothesis—that it was possible to get better mileage in the city with more aggressive driving and with more time spent in the lower gears. Practically, however, unless you have a computerized fuel gauge (which can be bought and installed for under $125—they tie into the fuel line and speedometer cable), you are better off simply getting to the higher gears as soon as you can.

- For a racing start, rev the engine and hold it at a high rpm before releasing the clutch.
- Never downshift on glare ice—it'll throw you into a skid that not even a pro could get out of.

- To save wear, never downshift at all. Shift to neutral, let the clutch out, and coast to stop signs. (This leaves you with no control of the drivetrain, which is considered dangerous).
- The red line on the tach is there for a reason—stay away from it.
- Check the play in your clutch pedal from time to time according to your manual. Waiting too long to replace a friction plate risks damage to the flywheel as well.
- When parking pointed uphill, leave the gear shift in first and the parking brake firmly on. For downhill parking, select reverse with the brake firmly on. Failure to use the brake puts strain on your transmission and may damage it.
- If you have an old VW Bug, lubricate the floor-mounted pivot linkage before and during each winter.
- Check your gearbox oil periodically according to your manual. The same applies to a "wet clutch"—if you have one. (Check the reservoir.)
- A friction-reducing additive such as Molyslip or Tufoil is a good idea for the gearbox and differential.

● **WHEN:** You want to **store your car.**

■ **WHAT TO DO:** Legend has it that when Edsel Ford took a liking to a car, he would have it wrapped in a large plastic bag and shipped to Australia to keep it fresh and new. Whatever truth there may be to the story, a plastic bag wouldn't do the trick—unless the air was pumped out before sealing, of course. The car you want to store has to "breathe" or you'll return to find a smelly, rotting, rusty relic with mushrooms growing out of the carpeting and water in the fuel and brake lines.

A garage with some heating and lots of ventilation is best. Storing outdoors, particularly in winter, is hard on a car (worst on the side of the car exposed to wind, weather, and sunlight) so a "breathing" car cover is recommended.

There are really only two ways to store a car:

Long-term storage. This is a serious business, indeed. First, the car goes up on blocks to take strain off the tires and brakes. All fluid tanks (gas, radiator, and brake) are flushed first (to remove contamination) and filled to capacity. (Some experts prefer to drain the gas tank, however, to avoid gasoline decomposition.) The radiator is filled with 100 percent antifreeze instead of the usual 50-50 mix. Dry-gas and "gum-rid" are added to the fuel. A few tablespoons of motor oil are poured down the carburetor throat and the engine is turned over to distribute the oil. The battery is removed and put on a wooden block. Arrangements are made to slow-charge it every few months for forty-eight hours at a time. The inner panels and underside of the car's body are oiled (see page 49). The paint is waxed. The vinyl roof and tires as well as the dashboard are treated with Armorall or equivalent. All linkages and hinges (including accelerator and transmission) are soaked down in WD-40. V-belts are loosened, to prevent setting or stretching (they should be replaced anyway once you start the car up again). The carburetor and intake bolts are tightened down, to minimize warpage. A large open box of baking soda is left in the driver's seat to minimize odors. Purists will empty the tires and refill them with bottled nitrogen—it's kinder to rubber over the long haul.

Warning

Restarting the car after a long storage is the single most harmful part of the procedure. Disconnect the ignition wire at the coil and crank the engine for 60 seconds or so to build up some oil pressure inside the engine and camshaft areas before final ignition.

Short-term storage.   You can safely leave up a car alone in a heated, ventilated garage for up to two months at a time without risking anything worse than a dead battery. The following steps, similar to those for long-term storage, are recommended: hook up a trickle charger and timer to the battery (with a one-amp charger, thirty minutes a day should do it); fill all fluid tanks to capacity; add dry-gas and gum-rid; and be cautious about restarting as explained in the box. Expect restarting to be rough, because the carburetor and manifold will be gummy with gasoline residue. (Cleaning the carburetor will help, but the job is complex and expensive.) Things will clear up once the car gets back into normal use.

- **WHEN:** You want your **tapes** to last.
- **WHAT TO DO:** Are you a music-lover? Do you spend more time trying to decide what to play next than what to have for lunch? Do you drive an

$800 car with a $2500 stereo? (Don't laugh—I've seen it!) Then you may want the following quick tips to keep your tapes longer:

- Tapes don't exactly melt, but direct sunlight can cause problems. Keep them away from direct heat and light.
- Extremes of temperature can weaken the oxides and make tapes brittle.
- Don't buy the thinner long-playing tapes—they stretch.
- Keep dirt and contaminants out of the mechanism.
- Tighten the spools (with your finger or a pencil) before loading.
- Demagnetize and clean the player's heads periodically.
- Make sure the labels are secure or they'll jam the auto-eject mechanism. All the king's horses and all the king's men won't be able to find your tape ever again.

● **WHEN:** You want to **test-drive** your own car.

■ **WHAT TO DO:** Why test-drive your own car? Because *somebody* has to—that's why! Most owners are so out of touch with their own vehicles that, in a crowded parking lot, they often discover they've been trying to unlock the door of somebody else's car! Regular test-driving of your *own* car will bring the two of you closer together spiritually. (If you don't buy this, consider that spotting problems before they require serious repairs can save you a bundle!)

Start the car, listening intently for unusual noises or excessive starter strain. The sound of the engine turning over before it catches should be smooth, like a kitchen blender. If the engine turns slow and then fast before catching, there is either an electrical failure, a problem in the starter, or a damaged cylinder in the engine. A camshaft problem is also possible.

Walk around the car while it's warming up. Check the tires by eye. Look for signs of leaks on the ground. Watch the color of the exhaust smoke (see page 24). Look beneath the car for dangling pipes or hoses. Open the hood and listen to the engine (see page 41).

Accelerate uphill to check the ignition and fuel systems. Apply the brakes hard on an empty road to check braking. Try to stop at a stop sign using only the parking brake to see if it works. On an empty road, release the steering wheel at about 40 mph and see if the car holds a true course. Find an empty parking lot and do a series of figure-8 turns while listening for front end noises (especially important on a front-wheel-drive car). Drive through a tunnel slowly with the windows down and listen to the engine and drivetrain sounds that get bounced back at you—make a note of anything unusual for your mechanic.

With the vehicle at rest and the engine on, turn the steering wheel from lock to lock and listen for strange noises. (A clunk or snap means trouble—see your mechanic.) Jam the brake pedal to the floor hard while parked with the engine on, and hold it there for at least 60 seconds—it should not sink down at all. Shift from neutral to drive to reverse and listen for slippage in the automatic transmission and wear (thunking) in the U-joint.

Check all dash gauges and make sure they work (even the idiot lights should blink at you when you turn the key.)

Next, do all your freeplay checks (see page 207). An old test that still works: To test the clutch, pull on the parking brake (while the car is standing still), clutch in, put it in the highest gear, and let the clutch out. The motor should stall right away—if not, you've got trouble.

With a helper, make sure that your brake lights and turn-signal lights are working. Check for headlight alignment by pulling up about 15 feet from a garage door and switching from brights to dims. The patterns should be reasonably symmetrical and will appear to the eye to be slightly higher than the actual headlight level, and slightly to the right.

Stand behind the car while a helper accelerates briskly down an empty street. Note the color of the exhaust. (See page 24.)

Check the front tires for differences in wear between left and right; also check the rear tires on a late-model car. Double-check the belts and hoses under the hood. Check for leaks and unusual smells, make sure fluid levels are right, and you're done.

● **WHEN:** You are pulling a **trailer.**

■ **WHAT TO DO:** First, see your manual. You can't *assume* that the cars of the '80s can pull a trailer. A great many front-drive economy cars specifically caution *against* pulling any kind of load.

If your car *will* accept a load, contact your dealer or manufacturer to see what the maximum weight it can tow is, what kind of hitch is recommended, what special precautions must be taken (for example, some Cadillacs use aluminum extensively—hooking a steel trailer hitch to an aluminum sub-frame could result in galvanic corrosion), and what the recommended *tongue* weight distribution is for the trailer.

Tongue weight

Tongue weight is the weight of the forward part of the trailer, (whether loaded or not) in front of its wheels. Generally, tongue weight should be at least 10 percent of the total trailer weight (verify by separately weighing the whole trailer and then the tongue) but manufacturer's recommendations may differ.

What's your GVWR?

GVWR stands for Gross Vehicle Weight Rating—the maximum weight your car is engineered to move. The GVWR is likely to be found in both your owner's manual and on your car's VIN nameplate. Never exceed it. When calculating your GVWR, you must include the tongue load of the trailer. Here are some other weights to check (see your manual for details): TTW (Total Trailer Weight), the maximum weight permitted for the trailer; GCW (Gross Combination Weight), the maximum combined weight of the trailer and the vehicle; and GAWR (Gross Axle Weight Rating), the maximum permissible weight per axle. If in doubt, phone your local manufacturer's representative for details. Overloading a vehicle is *dangerous.*

Towing with your car may require a better grade tire than you have, or stronger shock absorbers or struts. Automatic-transmission coolers should be installed for long-distance towing—an oversize radiator is a good idea as well. Towing is considered *severe service* by *all* car manufacturers. Engine, transmission, and differential fluids require changing two or three times as frequently as normal if you do a lot of towing.

When you remove a hitch from a late-model unibody car, have a professional body shop reseal the underside of the car to keep out water and exhaust fumes.

> ## Towing taboos
>
> Do *not* tap into your vehicle's hydraulic braking system to run trailer brakes—unless specifically permitted by the manufacturer. Most cars cannot handle the extra volume of brake fluid. Making the connection imprudently could be disastrous.
>
> Do *not* install just any hitch on a car with an energy-absorbing bumper—make sure that the hitch is compatible with the bumper, or a rear-end accident could bypass the bumper and damage the whole subframe.

Have you ever driven with a trailer before? Practice in an empty parking lot before going on the road. Backing up with a trailer is quite different than backing an unburdened car, and it takes some getting used to.

● **WHEN:** You want to be a good **winter driver.**

■ **WHAT TO DO:** Ever notice how, on the day of the year's first big snowfall, folks who have endured winter all their natural lives seem to forget what snow is? Better be safe than sorry: Brush up on your winter survival strategy:

- Have you got your snow tires on? (Or, in milder areas, all-season tires?) Snow tires work best when installed on *all four wheels.* Also, a narrower tread will "cut" the snow better than a wider one.
- Extra *weight* in rear-wheel-drive cars should be installed by a mechanic under the rear seat. Putting weight in the trunk can affect handling negatively.
- CV boots (page 246) should be checked on front-wheel drive cars before winter.
- Carry a good winter emergency kit with you (see also page 156) that includes mittens, a sweater, a hat, snow scrapers, shovels, battery cables, lock deicer, waterproof matches, WD-40 to dry wiring, an aerosol tire inflator, a heat source (use candles or the new chemically activated heat packets for warmth), a flashlight, and flares.
- Don't make any fast moves on icy roads—no fast starts, no fast turns, no sudden braking, and no sudden downshifting.

- What's the best way to brake on ice? Even the experts are divided. One controversial technique taught at the Goodyear Advanced Driving School involves jamming on the brakes to the point of a four-wheel skid, unjamming them to steer for a split second, jamming them on to stop, unjamming again to steer, etc. A more reasonable technique for most drivers is to gently apply the brakes to the point of skidding, ease up when the skid starts, and then reapply the brakes. On an *automatic* transmission, shifting from drive to neutral at the beginning of the braking action will dramatically increase control on ice.
- If stuck in snow, see page 95.
- When going uphill on ice in winter, use a lower gear and steady pressure on the gas. Do not accelerate in spurts and do not stop on the hill if you can avoid it.
- Going downhill on ice in the winter requires a light touch on the brakes—too much braking and you'll lose steering control. In dire situations, use the hand brake instead of the brake pedal—that gives you about 40 percent braking and doesn't affect the steering. Pick a lower gear, but without sudden downshifting.
- In snowstorms, periodically clean out the snow that packs behind the front wheels—or you may get a nasty surprise when you try to turn the wheel.
- If you have hidden wipers, get in the habit of turning the engine off when the wiper is still halfway up the window. Wipers that park under the hood recess in snowy or icy weather could freeze there. Use composition plastic (non-metal) wipers in winter.
- Remember that air contracts in cold and that you may have to add air to your tires during the winter. (Conversely, you should bleed air as the weather gets warmer again.)
- Battery output decreases as temperatures fall. If your battery is no longer a spring chicken, either use an electric blanket on it or bring it into the house with you in the evening.
- Do *not* use any VI (viscosity index) modifiers like STP oil treatment during the winter. Thickeners will only make the car impossible to start.
- Adding about eight ounces of dry-gas to the gasoline every two weeks is a good preventive measure.
- Tire chains may be your only answer to bad roads. Before you buy

the old-fashioned kind that require special installation, check out the newer, lighter models, which can be installed with the wheels still on the car. When you drive with tire chains, assume reduced braking efficiency in the event of a panic stop.

- Consider a four-wheel-drive vehicle. In the top-of-the-line models with the axles set to EMERGENCY LOCK, you can (theoretically) get out of a jam even if only *one* wheel has purchase. (In real life, however, this doesn't often work that neatly—ask any four-wheel-drive owner!)

The many flavors of four-wheel-drive

Four-wheel drive is an idea whose time has come. The benefits of four-wheel drive go far beyond traction through mud and snow—the incredible $40,000 Audi Quattro proved that the four-wheel-drive technology can outperform a two-wheel-drive vehicle even in a race! Models available in the '80s run the gamut in terms of convenience. On the one hand, you can still buy the old-fashioned macho vehicles that require the driver get out and lock the front hubs to use the four-wheel drive; on the other hand, you can buy the super-luxury models that let you switch to four-wheel drive from the driver's seat. Most models permit switching to four-wheel drive while in motion. The future of four-wheel drive is in fully automatic units that activate at the touch of a button (such as the Subaru system). The higher repair costs of four-wheel drive are generally offset by the exceptional traction, dependability, and road worthiness of the systems.

7

INFORMATION AND SUPPORT

● **WHEN:** You want to contact the major **automotive associations** and car-oriented **government agencies**.

■ **WHAT TO DO:** Here's a starter list. For more information check with the reference librarian at your local library.

Clubs:

The AAA is the great-grandfather of all the car clubs:
American Automobile Association
8111 Gatehouse Rd.
Falls Church, VA 22047

Fact-Finding.
Automotive Information Council
29200 Southfield Rd., Suite 111
Southfield, MI 48076

Tuneup literature:
Car Care Council
600 Renaissance Center
Detroit, MI 48243

Friendly advice:

A first stop for advice on where to turn for many car-related problems. Legal aid information when needed. Individual memberships $15 a year. *Highly recommended.*
Center for Auto Safety
2001 S St. N.W., Suite 410
Washington, DC 20009

Consumer tests and literature:
Consumers Union
256 Washington St.
Mount Vernon, NY 10550

CU is the dauntless producer of *Consumer Reports,* the bible of consumer journalism, and a host of other publications and services (including a new-car wholesale price analysis).

If they can't solve your problem here, no one can (see also NHTSA, below):
Dept. of Transportation
400 7th St. S.W.
Washington DC 20590

Trying to find the closest skid school?
Driving School Association of America
245 East Shore Rd.
Manhasset, NY 11030

For the famous EPA mpg list, or general emission information:
Environmental Protection Agency
401 M St. S.W.
Washington, DC 20460

These people look out for "unfair selling practices" for all cars, new and used, as well as for car gadgets and accessories:
Federal Trade Commission
6th St. and Pennsylvania Ave. N.W.
Washington, DC 20580

For insurance information and referrals:
Insurance Information Institute
110 William St., 8th floor
New York, NY 10038

The foremost fleet association has good information on the problems fleet owners experience with many popular makes and models:
National Association of Fleet Administrators
295 Madison Ave.
New York, NY 10017

To find out about local wholesale auctions (but you had better be a licensed dealer—or at least a friend of one):
National Auto Auction Association
5701 Russell Dr.
Lincoln, NE 68529

These guys keep track of which cars move the fastest—with the engine off:
National Auto Theft Bureau
10330 S. Roberts Rd.
Palos Hills, IL 60465

Aftermarket parts are as good as or better than OE (Original Equipment). For more information:
NAPA
2999 Circle 75 Parkway
Atlanta, GA 30339

And, finally, the automotive "throne room" in Washington:
NHTSA
400 7th St. S.W. Room 5232
Washington, DC 20590 HOTLINE: 800-424-9393 (or 202-426-9550)

This is the number 1 car hotline in the USA. It's the first government agency to "shop" when you suspect a safety or recall situation on your new or used car. (Non-safety problems are supposed to go to the FTC (see above but it's best to start here first).

● **WHEN:** You want to know more about **arbitration, lemon laws,** and **other defenses** open to you.

■ **WHAT TO DO:** Although most states have them, lemon laws are *lemons.* Only Connecticut and Vermont have created an arbitration system to put teeth into the laws. Getting a lawyer on a minimal retainer (he gets the rest of his fee if you win) might be your best bet.

Both arbitration laws and lemon laws are being used as political footballs these days. Instead of the statutes which vary widely from state to state and province, a more unified approach is needed very much. In the meantime, here's the state of the game at half-time:

Your game plan

Getting satisfaction from a car dealer is no longer simply a matter of challenging him to a duel with pistols at twenty paces. There are a lot of laws to play with—and many are on your side. The strategy you should follow in the event of trouble is: (1)Have a serious chat with the dealer's manager or shop foreman. (2)Send the dealer a formal letter (via registered mail) outlining your case. Lawyers will often help draft this kind of letter for under $50. (3)Consider launching a *simultaneous* action in small-claims court. (Why simultaneous? Because the cost is reasonable, most of the arbitration and lemon laws don't prevent you from doing so, and the trial takes so long to be heard anyway that you may as well get an early start.) (4)Go into arbitration (as outlined below). Finally, (5)take the first steps required by the local lemon law, if your state or province has one.

Read your owner's manual

Complaint procedures and arbitration rules are laid out in this manual. Don't overlook this valuable source of information.

ARBITRATION

The concept is simple: instead of a long, expensive legal proceeding, you present your case as best you can (either in person or in writing) to a group of presumably impartial arbitrators or mediators who listen to both sides and render a decision.

Even though it *sounds* simple, it isn't. First, different companies subscribe to different arbitration programs and the program you have to follow is dictated by the kind of car you own, and possibly even by how long you've had it. (Ford and Chrysler have their own programs, in most areas General Motors uses an arbitration process offered by the local Better Business Bureaus, and many foreign manufacturers use a private organization known as Autocap.)

To get started with the arbitration procedure for your car, you must first find out which program the manufacturer subscribes to—and then get a written copy of the rules and regulations for that program. You should also request information on the parties that will be doing the arbitration *and* copies of the documentation submitted by the other side. In most events it should be possible to bring in an outside mechanic for support or at least to enter his opinion into the written proceedings.

New-car arbitration?

If you have a problem with a brand-new car, the rules may be slightly different. The FTC, which governs new-car warranties (see page 229), has become quite involved in the arbitration programs and is publishing guidelines for new-car arbitration. If you are in this situation, contact the FTC. (For example, the old rule—laid down by the manufacturers—that prevented the consumer from going to court to overturn the result of the arbitration no longer applies.) The question also comes up—can you ignore the arbitration provisions totally and go directly to a small-claims court? Experts feel the answer is yes, because small-claims courts and warranties are governed by essentially different sets of laws. However, if arbitration is available, you are best advised at least to try it.

Do consumers benefit from arbitration? One out of two complainers is likely to emerge with a better "settlement" than without it. The odds are significantly lower, it seems, for Chryslers and Fords than for other cars.

LEMON LAWS

This a rapidly growing area of legislation—perhaps too rapidly. The original thought was noble and just. The result in most areas is chaos.

Formerly, the return policy of the automobile manufacturers was graven in stone—if we can't fix it, we'll keep trying until we get it right, or until the warranty expires, whichever comes first.

The policy was ridiculous, but remained unchallenged for almost three-quarters of a century. Lemon laws basically say that provided (a) you follow the exact legal procedure set down by the legislature of your state or province, (b) you act within the time set out by the law, (c) you correctly notify the manufacturer and the other parties the law specifies, (d) you have given the dealer a certain minimum number of chances to fix the problem, and (e) he has failed to fix the problem (or the car has been out of service for a minimum time)—*then* you can return the car and get a refund (whew!). In many cases, however, these laws have been found to be effective *only* where the claimant is prepared to launch a formal lawsuit immediately. Relying on the so-called arbitrators to enforce this legislation outside of a courtroom has produced very unsatisfactory results. Contact your state or provincial attorney general's office for more information.

Used cars and repairs

Recently "lemon laws" have been expanded to cover used cars—the state of New York and the province of Quebec are two good examples. Certain of these laws have rather interesting provisions regarding all auto repairs and special rules about estimates and phone authorizations for repairs which make them fascinating reading and well worth tracking down.

Don't forget small-claims court

Small-claims courts remind me of the "Little Engine That Could." They are tiny (the most impoverished part of the legal system); many are short of real judges and have to use justices of the peace or even lawyers to decide cases; they take a fair amount of time to get things done; they seem cluttered and unorganized compared to full trial proceedings—but *they work*. Consumers who have used the small-claims systems have come away with a sense of "having had their day in court." Before you get too involved in the the glamorous new *arbitration* or *lemon* laws, don't forget where it all started—small-claims court.

● **WHEN:** You want the best automotive **books, magazines,** and **other publications**.

■ **WHAT TO DO:** There are lots of publications to choose from. You've already shown excellent taste by looking at mine. But there are others.

My own reference library consists of a *Motor* or *Chilton* service annual (addresses below) plus my owner's manual—and subscriptions to *Car and Driver* and *Motor Trend.*

The service annuals give me hard data and specification for all the new cars, and keep me up to date on the latest repair procedures for all late-model cars—including my own. The owner's manual often provides valuable information that simply can't be had anywhere else. If you've lost yours, check the classifieds in *Hemmings* (also below).

The two magazines are the best, are great fun to read, and overlap in many areas. Their hundreds of small ads and classifieds are a treasure trove of information for the serious car survivalist.

Sources are:

Auto Body Repair magazine
65 E. South Water St.
Chicago, IL 60601
Monthly information on body repair.

Automotive News
1400 Woodbridge
Detroit, MI 48207
If it's not reported in the *News,* it didn't happen.

R.Bentley Books
872 Massachusetts Ave.
Cambridge, MA 02139
For connoisseurs of service manuals only.
Write for catalog.

Black Book
Box 758
Gainsville, GA 30503
Used car-prices and predictions—by subscription only.

Car and Driver
3460 Wilshire Blvd.
Los Angeles, CA 90010

Cars and Parts
911 Vandemark Rd.
Sydney, OH 45367
A good back-up to Hemmings, below.

Chilton
Chilton Way
Radnor, PA 19089
Publishes annuals plus individual handbooks.

Consumer Reports
256 Washington Street
Mount Vernon, NY 10550

Hemmings
Box 76
Bennington, VT 05201
A must if you own a car more than 10 years old.

Motor
555 W. 57th St.
New York, NY 10019
Publishes annuals plus an excellent monthly magazine.

Motor Trend
8490 Sunset Blvd.
Los Angeles, CA 90069

New Car Cost Guide
2001 The Alameda
Box 6227
San Jose, CA 95150
A subscription service.

The following extremely large mail-order book shops are especially good for first-timers:

Carbooks
181 Glenn Ave.
Sea Cliff, NY 11579

Classic Motorbooks
Box 1
Osceola, WI 54020

● **WHEN:** You want to get the most from your **library.**
■ **WHAT TO DO:** The library has two distinct advantages for car buffs: a lot of information has accumulated (particularly for older cars) and it's free.

The main disadvantage is the time lag in getting books stocked. Seeking information on current models in the library may be frustrating, unless it's available in a magazine or newsletter.

Books. Libraries using the decimal filing system on open shelves will have all the car books together, so you can pick the ones that interest you. (Libraries that keep books "in the stacks" expect you to know what book you want in advance—use the subject catalog to orient yourself.)

Annuals. Most good libraries carry either the *Motor* or *Chilton* repair annuals for both current and past years. The extremely valuable feature of these annuals is that they offer complete specifications on older models— including hard-to-get information like ignition part numbers, radiator and gas capacities, torque specifications for all parts of the car, and detailed diagnostic techniques for emission controls. The disadvantage is that the repair instructions were written for Class A mechanics. Simple procedures like "(1) Disconnect battery ground cable. (2) Remove engine. (3) Disassemble cylinder head. . . ." may leave you speechless.

Magazines. Current issues of magazines are always available in the library. Monthly visits with old standards like *Consumer Reports, Popular Mechanics, Popular Science,* and the like can really keep you up to date.

Research. Libraries were meant for research, and if you're thinking about suing a dealer or repairman, research might be just what you need. Ask the librarian to introduce you to the government-documents section so that you can get copies of the relevant state or local legislation. A few minutes spent with the *Index to Periodical Literature* will turn up any articles on your car or your problem that have appeared in major magazines. Older magazines will be in the stacks and you will have to request them.

Community Services. Most good libraries have information on local groups and clubs. If there are any antique-car groups, enthusiast clubs, racing associations, or consumer-action groups in your area, the library would know.

● **WHEN:** You want to go right to the top (the **manufacturer**).
■ **WHAT TO DO:** There's an old saying that the manufacturer will give you everything but satisfaction. They'll answer polite inquiries about recalls, production statistics, sources for old parts, parts codes, enthusiast clubs featuring their cars, technical service bulletins (see page 240), and replacement owner's manuals and service manuals.

You can address your letter directly to the president of the company, but don't hold your breath.

AUTOMOBILE MANUFACTURERS

American Motors
2777 Franklin Rd.
Southfield, MI 48034

Chrysler
Box 1919
Detroit, MI 48288

Ford
American Rd.
Dearborn, MI 48121

General Motors
General Motors Bldg.
Detroit, MI 48202

BMW
BMW Plaza
Montvale, NJ 07645

Fiat
777 Terrace Ave.
Hasbrouck Heights, NJ 07604

Honda
100 West Alondra Rd.
Gardena, CA 90247

Mazda
3040 East Ana St.
Compton, CA 90221

Mercedes-Benz
1 Mercedes-Benz Dr.
Montvale, NJ 07645

Nissan (Datsun)
18501 Figueroa
Carson, CA 90245

Saab
Box 697
Orange, CT 06477

Subaru
7040 Central Parkway
Pennsauken, NJ 08109

Toyota
19001 S. Western Ave.
Torrance, CA 90519

Volkswagen
888 W. Big Beaver Rd.
Troy, MI 48099

Volvo
1 Volvo Dr.
Rockleigh, NJ 07647

● **WHEN:** You want to join an **owner's club**.

■ **WHAT TO DO:** First sober up: If you are driving an '84 Chevette, the only social gathering willing to give you a forum will be the Happy Hour boys at the local watering hole.

On the other hand, if you own virtually any foreign sports car, or any antique car (which now usually means pre-1955 cars), or any muscle car of the '60s, or (God Bless You) a '60s or early '70s Mustang—get ready to make new friends! (There is even a "Slant Six" owners' club for early Dodge Darts and Valiants. Honest.)

Why would you *want* to join an owner's club? Because owning an older car can sometimes get unreasonably complex. When that happens, it's nice to have friends. Aside from the expected yearly meets and trophy-hunting, the regular club bulletin will feature useful articles on everything from unusual mechanical problems to sources for hard-to-find parts and trim. You can expect insurance tips, gossip, and lots of interesting trivia.

One of the first things I did after purchasing my '68 Cougar GT was to join the Cougar Club of America. I then proceeded to cry my eyes out when I found how many *other* GTs were still alive and kicking—and looking even better than mine! (All right—club membership can be depressing sometimes as well!) Still, I have no regrets. The article in their bulletin on repairing the sequential turn-signal box was very useful—it convinced me to never, under any circumstances, even *attempt* the repair on my own. I'm always learning about new inexpensive outlets for repro parts.

Pick up virtually any back issue of *Road and Track* and you'll see ads for dozens of clubs. If you don't see one that interests you, send a half-dozen letters to clubs that feature similar cars and some nice fellow will write back with the address you want. (I originally got in touch with the Cougar Club by corresponding with a Mustang Club. They couldn't convert me, so they sent me on my way.)

Dues average about $40 a year. The combined activity of all members insures an ongoing source of parts and supplies—which, in turn, means that the long-term value of the cars will stay high.

● **WHEN:** You need NOS **parts for older cars**.

■ **WHAT TO DO:** NOS usually stands for "New Old Stock." (It can also mean "Nitrous Oxide System" as well, so be alert!) That means that someone is selling the manufacturer's original stock parts for that car. The stock is *old* (it was made about the same time as the car), but it is *new* because it has never been used. (Other sources of stock are scrap yards (page 146) and new suppliers making "authentic" reproduction parts—called "repros" —for classic older models. Many '60s Mustang parts are repros, not NOS.)

Hemmings is your best source for NOS parts (see address page 235). The following sample entries only illustrate the range of available NOS parts:

Carpeting:
Auto Carpets
316 Greenbrier Rd.
Anniston, AL 36201

Chevy parts, '55–'69:
Cars Inc.
1102 Conbermere
Troy, MI 48083

Convertible tops:
Hydroelectric
48 Appleton St.
Auburn, MA 01501

Dash repairs and coverups:
Sun Marc
Box 4026
Riverside, CA 92514

Detachable tops for
sportscars:
Parrish Plastics
5309 Enterprise Blvd.
Bethel Park, PA 15102

Mustang specialist
Eastern Mustang
646 South Rd.
Poughkeepsie, NY 12601

Old Pontiac owner's manuals:
Peter Ross
5009 Winthrop
Austintown, OH 44515

Rechromed plastic:
Mister G
5613 Elliot Reeder Rd.
Fort Worth, TX 76117

Rubber parts:
Metro
11610 Jay St.
Minneapolis, MN 55433

Volvo specialist:
IPD
2762 N.E. Broadway
Portland, OR 97232

● **WHEN:** You are looking for **service bulletins.**

■ **WHAT TO DO:** Once again, definitions are important here: "Service bulletins" relate to problems common to all production models of the particular make and year which are *not safety-related* and therefore not subject to recall by the NHTSA. In fact, non-safety-related problems are handled by the FTC.

Whether or not there is a "secret warranty" (a free repair based on the service bulletin) depends on a lot of factors—contact your manufacturer, your dealer, the FTC, the Center for Auto Safety, and your local consumer action group.

Policy on service bulletins changes almost daily. Formerly, the large companies hardly even admitted issuing them at all. Now, some companies will actually sell them to the owner as they come out! Contact your vehicle's manufacturer for more information. At this writing, unfortunately, the only central source for all the service bulletins was the Department of Transportation library in Washington, D.C. One interesting, and controversial, method of obtaining this information is to write to the DOT or the NHTSA —a division of the DOT—using a freedom-of-information request. Simply mark *Freedom of Information Request* on the outside of the envelope. In theory, the government must respond within ten working days—(see also page 91). You can also call the Center for Auto Safety at 202-328-7700 for information.

● **WHEN:** You want a **service manual** for your car.

■ **WHAT TO DO:** There are two routes to follow here:

Official Manuals. The manuals authorized by the car's manufacturer may be hard to get, expensive, and hard to understand—but they're the genuine article. That's got to be worth something!

For official American Motors, Renault, and Jeep manuals, write to:
AMC
37200 Amrhein Rd.
Livonia, MI 48150

For Buick:
Tuar Co.
Box 354
Flint, MI 48501

For Cadillac, Chevrolet, Ford, Lincoln, Mercury, and Pontiac:
Helm Inc.
Box 07130
Detroit, MI 48207

For Chrysler:
Chrysler
20026 Progress Dr.
Strongville, OH 44136

For Oldsmobile:
Oldsmobile
Box 23188
Lansing, MI 48909

For foreign makes (and others not listed) call the manufacturer's representative for more information.

Unofficial Manuals. The competition here is fierce and fast. Major names in this field include *Bentley, Chilton, Motor, Haynes, Petersen,* and half a dozen others.

The unofficial manuals all have a friendlier format (and price), better illustrations, and a willingness to share shortcuts the manufacturers never bother to mention. (For example, there are two ways to repair the head gaskets on certain old VW Bugs. The official way involves dropping the engine. The unofficial way doesn't!)

● **WHEN:** It's time for **small claims court**
■ **WHAT TO DO:** Get a copy of the rules and regulations governing the small claims system in your area. (This is a state or provincial matter, *not* federal.) Find out:

- What is the maximum amount you can sue for?
- What is the cost of the suit?
- Do you need a lawyer?
- Can the other side use a lawyer?
- How long after the problem arises can you sue?
- What happens if the other party doesn't show up?

- Can you force third parties (others involved as witnesses only) to show up?
- Can you compel the other party to bring certain documents?
- Will your case be heard by a real judge?
- Do you have a choice of night court?
- If you win, how can you enforce the judgment?
- If you settle out of court, can you enforce the settlement with the court's help, if need be?

The answers to these questions differ from place to place, but generally small-claims courts are designed to allow you to plead your case without interference from lawyers. Rehearse yourself in advance (practice cross-examining your wife, neighbor, or pet) and bring all relevant documents, service records, and repair estimates with you. Most claims come up in court within twelve months of the action being started. Don't be surprised if the other side offers to settle as soon as the papers are served.

Consider also arbitration and lemon laws—see pages 231–34.

● **WHEN:** You want to know what parts from one kind of car can be **substituted** for **parts** of another kind of car.

■ **WHAT TO DO:** The major source of information on parts substitution (for example, whether a five-speed gearbox from a '68 Torino will fit in a '71 Mustang) is:

Hollander Interchange Manual
Box 9405
Minneapolis, MN 55440
Send for their catalog.

● **WHEN:** You want to decipher your **VIN number.**

■ **WHAT TO DO:** On your car, usually near the door pillar, is a stamped plate with a lot of numbers. The longest of these—seventeen digits—is your VIN (Vehicle Identification Number). The interpretation of the VIN code varies from manufacturer to manufacturer and from year to year. The coded information is *valuable* in future recalls, court actions, repairs, part replacements, vehicle modifications, paint and body work, and plain everyday curiosity. Your authorized service manual will explain the codes. Here, for *example* only, is what the GM VINs for 1984 models show:

DIGIT	MEANING
1st	Country where car was built
2nd	Corporate division
3rd	Vehicle make
4th	Restraint system
5th	Model series
6th and 7th	Body type
8th	Engine type
9th	(n/a)
10th	Model year
11th	Plant
12th through 17th	Production sequence history

The VIN is not the only source of production information, however. Here are additional places to look for more production and capacity data:

- Ignition key
- Glove-box labels
- Door pillar
- Carburetor air horn
- Intake manifold
- Engine block
- Dashboard
- Transmission body
- Rear-axle housing
- Tire sidewall
- Inside trunk lid
- Inside hood
- Engine firewall
- Cylinder reservoirs (brake, steering, clutch, radiator)
- Gas tank cap
- Fuse-box lid
- Radio housing

APPENDIX
HOW TO TALK CAR

Discussions of the newest developments in car design and technology often depend on a wide range of confusing abbreviations, acronyms, and special meanings.

If you suddenly have trouble following the articles in your favorite car magazine, or if your mechanic sometimes seem to slip into speaking a foreign language, see if the following explanations don't bring speedy relief:

■ **ABS (Antilocking Braking System)**. This system keeps the brakes from locking, stops the car quicker than even a professional driver could, and puts an end—forever—to skids. All cars will probably have ABS (either the computerized version or the less expensive mechanical form) by 1990. Worth its weight in gold.

■ **Airdam.** Airdams are used on different parts of the car (the hood, front underskirt, side fenders, and trunk) to improve the aerodynamic flow for improved mileage, and greater stability at high speeds (they keep the car from lifting). Airdams were popular as add-ons in the '70s, but in the '80s they come as standard equipment on most sports models.

■ **Alloy.** *Not* made of steel or steel alone. Instead, alloys (primarily of such metals as magnesium and aluminum) are used. Iron and steel are excellent materials for car components, but heavy. Inside the engine, on the body and suspension, and even on the wheel rims, excess weight can exact a penalty in performance and economy. Most new cars have alloy engines and wheel rims. Body panels are usually alloyed steel or plastic, and suspension parts are being made of graphite and synthetics.

■ **Arbitration.** A new legal procedure to settle disputes out of court. See page 231.

■ **Black box.** A catch-all name for the computer "brains," usually enclosed in small rectangular metal boxes (not black) under the hood. They are expensive and must be replaced, not repaired.

■ **Block.** The single largest chunk of the engine except for the valves and cylinder heads. It's a **short block** if it comes without the head (including the valve train) and other attachments. A **long block** is almost the whole engine.

■ **Boots.** Generally means **CV boots,** the single most important maintenance item on front-drive cars. The boots cover and protect the CV JOINTS.

■ **Cap.** Usually, the **distributor cap,** which controls the timing of the electrical impulses sent to the spark plugs. Up to now the distributor has been almost sacred (it's been around forever), but newer cars don't have a distributor at all—timing is controlled by crankshaft-position sensors and a computer.

■ **Catalytic converter.** This part of your exhaust system looks like a large coffee can (not the muffler, which is larger) and cleans the exhaust gas as it goes through. Catalytic converters are not trouble-free, as originally thought—they rust, clog, bend, and generally wear out. They are also expensive.

■ **Cd.** Usually means **coefficient of drag** and refers to how cleanly a car cuts the wind. Lower numbers are better, because less fuel is wasted fighting through the air. Used to compare one car to another. For example, a Cd of about 0.4 or lower is considered excellent.

■ **Chuggle.** This is the jarring sensation common to late-model cars with "lock-up" torque converters in the automatic transmission. (There is no cure for this.)

■ **Clinometer.** An interesting picture-gauge on the dash of some four-wheel-drive vehicles which shows you the *angle* your vehicle is at, both from the front and the side. Actually, this is a silly device—originally meant to encourage *safety* by warning the driver of a too-steep ascent, it had just the *opposite* effect by encouraging daredevil drivers to try steeper and steeper hills to get higher readings on the gauge. One note of caution—your own vehicle, unlike the little fairy-tale image on the gauge, can easily turn over and crush you if you abuse it.

■ **Clipped car.** Two cars that have been damaged so badly they were written off as "not repairable" have the damaged parts clipped off and the rest meshed together by a body shop and resold as normal merchandise. Is a good clip job possible? There is disagreement, but body experts feel that a proper job of splicing two car halves together *can* be made to last —if the bodywork is professional and the proper welding points are chosen. Still, the average buyer is well advised to *stay away* from clipped cars.

■ **Compression.** The oldest car test is the compression test, which gives you a good idea of the wear on your valves and rings. What is good compression? Generally the readings across the board should be *even*— with the lowest within 20 percent of the highest. For example, on a four-cylinder engine, 80-100-80-100 is a good reading. Compression tests aren't everything, however. An older engine (over 100,000 miles) can have good compression but still need an overhaul.

■ **Cradle.** Today's UNIBODY cars don't have frames under them, so the engine must sit on a special kind of subframe called a cradle. Cradles on some FRONT-DRIVE cars allow engine removal only from *underneath.*

■ **CV (Constant-Velocity) joints.** Most front-drive cars have four—and they need constant loving attention. (Also see BOOTs.)

■ **CVT (Continuously-Variable Transmission).** A future transmission without gears. (Most of the technical diagrams I've seen remind me of a hamster running on a treadmill. I think the physics are similar.) It gets better mileage and it drives more smoothly. Expect it to be a reality by the late '80s.

- **Daylighters.** Drivers who keep their lights on in daylight. Statistics show that daylighters average 22 percent fewer accidents than the rest of the population.

- **Dead pedal.** A fake pedal at the far left of the footwell for resting your left foot. These oddities were once found only in the finest racing machines —drivers used them to brace their bodies during sharp turns. Today many trendy cars come with a dead pedal as standard equipment, although I hate to think that any of the owners might actually turn corners fast enough to need the thing!

- **Discs and drum.** These are the basic parts of your braking system. At the beginning of time (as we know it) cars had drums on all four wheels. Now most have discs in front (where the brake grabs a moving disc) and drums (where the brake expands outward to slow a drum spinning around it) in back. The next step (late '80s) is four-wheel discs, which provide optimal stopping power.

- **Double-clutch.** The best method of downshifting: Clutch in, shift to neutral, clutch out, rev the engine, clutch in, shift to the lower gear, apply gas and release the clutch.

- **Driveaway.** This is either "something you say to someone you don't like" *or* "a service that provides drivers to take cars from anywhere to anywhere." See your Yellow Pages. The drivers are usually people who want to get to their destination so badly they will pay the gas to do so. Generally costs the owner about one-third as much as simple freight. Insurance requirements vary.

- **EFI (Electronic Fuel Injection).** Can mean almost anything. The only thing you know for sure about fuel-injected systems is that there is no carburetor (on GM's **throttle body injection** system, even *that* explanation seems suspect). Fuel injection systems can operate mechanically, electrically, with or without a computer; they can inject fuel into the manifold or right into the cylinders. Cylinder fuel injection requires more injectors (one for each cylinder) and is the best. It's usually called **ported fuel injection.** (See illustrations on pages 250 and 251.)

■ **EGR (Exhaust Gas Recirculation).** A valve, controlled by a long series of other valves, injects some of the cylinder exhaust back into the air-fuel mixture for reburning. These are, even today, considered a crude and undesirable form of emission control (although they are in wide use). Newer motor designs will show ways of keeping the air clean without them.

■ **Electronic scattershield** (a.k.a. **idiot circuit**). Many modern cars have built-in circuits (hidden in the computer controls) to control drivers who, for whatever reason, decide to take a kamikaze run down to the local deli at 100 mph in first gear. Similar to the old governors used on commercial vehicles, these devices will cut out fuel or ignition if a preset speed is exceeded under certain conditions. Mazda RX-7s, for example, simply cannot be over-revved because of the idiot circuits.

■ **4WD (Four-wheel drive).** All four wheels get engine power. **Full-time 4WD** means that all the hidden drivetrain equipment that drives the front wheels turns all the time—even if the actual front wheels themselves are not engaged in the system. (Engaging the front wheels usually involves turning a lever in the car or on the front hubs themselves.) **Part-time 4WD** means that, when the system is disengaged, so are the parts of the drivetrain that would otherwise transmit power to the front wheels. In other words, no power is wasted. A drawback to part-time 4WD is that it can be engaged only in **lockup** (with both wheels moving at the same rate, since there is no extra differential) so that the 4WD can be used for short periods of time only and never on paved roads. Full-time 4WD usually has a front differential so it has a wider range of uses. 4WD is getting *more* complex in the '80s, not less. Read your manual. (See illustrations on pages 252 and 253.)

■ **Front drive, FWD,** or **Front-Wheel Drive.** A car which has the engine in front and the drive wheels in front. Of course, that means the transmission and differential as well as the steering and suspension are in front too. Does it get crowded in there? In a word, yes.

■ **G.** Measure the roadholding ability of the car when the suspension is pushed to its limit. Car magazines run test cars as fast as they can around a track—just to the point of losing control—and the one that "pulls the most Gs," usually expressed as decimal like .80, is theoretically the best handler.

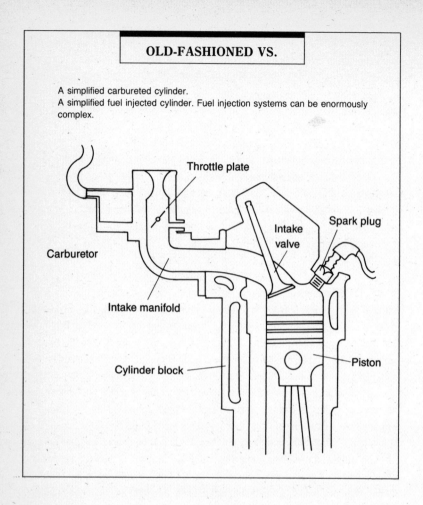

OLD-FASHIONED VS.

A simplified carbureted cylinder.
A simplified fuel injected cylinder. Fuel injection systems can be enormously complex.

Throttle plate

Intake valve

Spark plug

Carburetor

Intake manifold

Cylinder block

Piston

Some sports cars had G-meters on the dash but, for the immature driver, this seems like little more than an invitation to mayhem.

■ **Glow plug.** A diesel engine doesn't need spark plugs, but they do need a little extra help to get started. That help comes from glow plugs. Starting procedures vary in diesels, so if you are borrowing a friend's diesel for a heavy date, find out how it works before you tear off down the street. Glow plugs, by the way, are a weak area on diesels, because they can short out (and cause major problems) without adequate warning to the driver. Many mechanics recommend testing all glow plugs at each tuneup (a twenty-minute job).

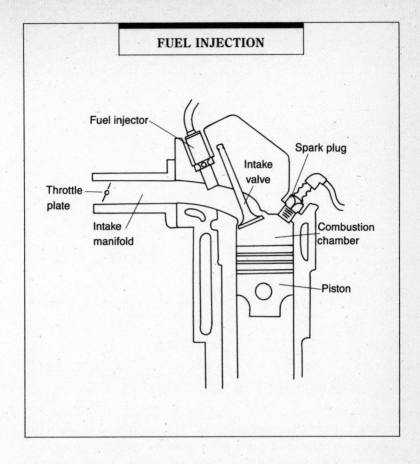

FUEL INJECTION

Fuel injector

Spark plug

Intake valve

Throttle plate

Intake manifold

Combustion chamber

Piston

■ **Gray-market cars.** There are shades of gray. The "dirty" gray cars are cars that snuck onto the market via the back door: damaged cars that were supposed to have been destroyed after insurance settlements, or imported one-of-a-kind vehicles that were supposed to be given EPA tests again before going out on the road (but never were). At the other end, some grays are really street-legal (properly registered) but suffer a loss of prestige (and possibly warranty coverage) because they were imported by nonauthorized discount dealers.

■ **Halon.** A type of gas used in the newest and trendiest fire extinguishers. Although excellent at putting out fires without damaging neighboring components, there is some doubt as to its safety if inhaled by humans.

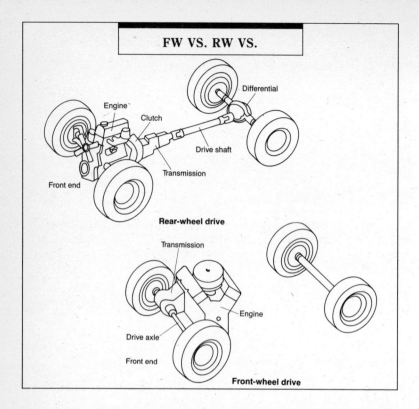

Rear-wheel drive

Front-wheel drive

■ **HDLA (High-Density Low-Alloy** steel) or **HSS (High Strength Steel).** A steel used a lot in new cars. It's thinner and lighter but supposed to be just as strong—and is until it gets into its first accident. Then all it is is trouble. HSS steel rusts easily, it can't take stress or bending, and welds must be done with a MIG welder.

■ **Heel-and-toe.** A proper driving technique calls for a lot of down-shifting and DOUBLE-CLUTCHING. But what if you have to brake while clutching and feeding gas? You'd be a foot short, wouldn't you? Not if you heel-and-toe: press the brake pedal with the ball of your right foot and the accelerator with the heel. Don't try it on a crowded freeway, please.

■ **High-tension wires.** The wires that run from the distributor cap to the spark plugs.

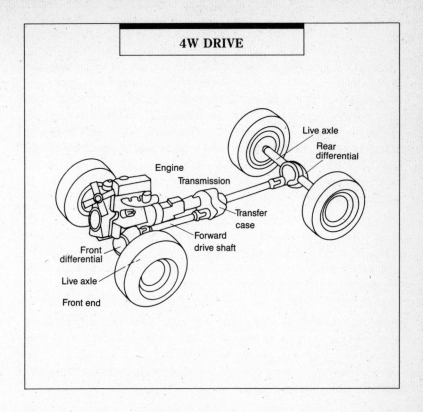

4W DRIVE

Live axle

Rear differential

Engine

Transmission

Transfer case

Forward drive shaft

Front differential

Live axle

Front end

- **Jackpoint.** When you jack up a FRONT-DRIVE car or a UNIBODY car, you must place the jack only at certain reinforced points on the underside or you risk catastrophe. See your manual.

- **Limp-in.** When the $800 computer BLACK BOX (above) on your $15,000 car goes on the fritz, you could theoretically be left stranded. Most new models have a limp-in mode built into the computer so, that instead of shutting down, the computer realizes it is sick (which, doctors say, is half the battle) and finds a way to keep the car running long enough to get you to a service bay. Read about the "Check Engine" light in your owner's manual.

- **Metric.** As the metrication of North America proceeds, the old "standard" or "Imperial" measures (miles, gallons, inches) are slowly giving way to metric measures (kilometers, liters, meters). In metric, for example, one doesn't refer to miles per gallon, but rather liters per hundred kilometers. Since 100 kilometers = 62 miles and about 4 liters make a U.S. gallon (or 5 per Canadian gallon), a metric fuel-economy rating of 6 is great, 9 is average, and 14 is a gas guzzler. Many newer cars need metric tools to make even small adjustments, so check your manual and double-check with your corner mechanic to play it safe—using standard (SAE) tools instead of metric tools can damage fittings. Metric bolts and fasteners are usually marked slightly differently than SAE and, once you get the hang of telling them apart (metric nuts and bolts have numbers on them), you should have no further difficulty.

■ **MIG (Metal Inert Gas).** A fancy kind of welding system (requiring special training) that *must* be used on the new lighter steels in UNIBODY cars if the repair is to last. Any body shop doing major repairs on a unibody car should have a MIG welder.

■ **Module.** Modules and sensors are part of the great computer conspiracy to control the world as we know it. You may hear your mechanic cursing out a defective ignition control module, BLACK BOX, or MAP (Manifold Absolute Pressure) sensor. Take heart—what he's really saying is that he's not sure what they are, either.

■ **NOS.** (New Old Stock, usually). New to the car, anyway (see page 239). Can also stand for **nitrous oxide booster,** a short-duration but devastatingly impressive power-enhancement system (and expensive, too).

■ **OEM.** In the beginning, there was the OEM **(Original Equipment Manufacturer)**, tied in some way to the original manufacturer of the car. And the OEM made good parts and accessories, and the people were thankful. And there was no competition, and the OEM companies were thankful. And then the OEM companies raised their prices so much that nobody was thankful. And then came the **aftermarket**, a tireless, hard-working group of companies (selling hundreds of millions of dollars' worth of products a year) dedicated to the simple proposition that there is money to be made by supplying better products than the OEM's at fairer prices. And, while not everybody is ecstatic, at least the arrangement seems to be working.

- **Open loop and closed loop.** Computers again. When everything is working properly, the computer gets lost in its own little world of perfection, called a **closed loop**. However, when the computer senses a problem —perhaps the car has not warmed up, or perhaps a wire is loose somewhere—the computer shuts itself partly off. This is called an **open loop** and is only slightly different from LIMP-IN as above.

- **Oversteer and understeer.** Generally used to define different types of skids, but can apply to the general performance characteristics of the car as well. **Understeer** means the car turns slowly, slightly, or not at all when the driver turns the steering wheel. Obviously too much understeer is not desirable. One car magazine rates all cars it tests in terms of degree of understeer, with only moderate or less being acceptable. **Oversteer** is the other extreme—an oversteering car would respond too well to steering input. This could cause the back end to try to trade places with the front (the *oversteer skid*—see page 93). A car that oversteered all the time would be unstable and flat-out dangerous.

- **Oxygen sensor.** It's possible to understand $100 million of emission-control technology by simply understanding this: You want to get the leanest possible air-fuel mixture (as little gas as possible) into the cylinders that lets the car performs properly; if it's *too* lean, the cylinders will misfire. The best way for the computer to keep track of the mixture and of the spark adjustments is to monitor the emissions from the last combustion cycles so that it can make changes (at the rate of dozens of times a second) to the *next* cycle. The oxygen sensor looks like a spark plug and screws into the exhaust manifold near the engine. It senses the amount of oxygen in the exhaust gas, so the computer can make its adjustments. Now someone has invented a better mousetrap. The oxygen sensor will soon give way to a specially developed **sensing wire,** which does the same thing but takes up less space.

- **Push start.** Starting the car without using the starter motor. On standard-shift cars this can usually be done by pushing the car at about 10 mph, turning the ignition "on," and releasing the clutch with the car in second gear. Not usually possible with automatic transmissions; consult your owner's manual.

- **R&R.** In the army, this means rest and recreation—and is a *good* thing. In the secret language of cars, it means **remove and replace** and it's a bad thing—generally very expensive. See your last major repair bill for details.

- **Serpentine.** See also V-BELT. It is estimated that the one-piece serpentine belt powering all the subsidiary equipment will replace the more usual series of several different V-belts by 1990.

- **Shoe & pad.** In *drum* brakes, **shoes** are the parts that expand outward to catch the revolving drum in which they are enclosed. (Spin a deep bowl over a closed fist and open the fist—the bowl will stop spinning.) The portions of the shoes that would actually contact the drums (the same way only part of your fingers touch the bowl) are covered by replaceable **linings**. In *disc* brakes, where the **caliper**, a stationary, clawlike grabbing device, seizes a disc which spins between its opposed fingers, *pads* refers to the parts of the grabbing device (caliper) which wear down over time from constantly grabbing the disc.

- **Specs (specifications).** Ever try to bake bread without knowing how much of each ingredient to use, or how much dough will fit in the pan, or how hot the oven should be? Those are specs. Your car has lots—capacities for the radiator, gas tank, and oil sump; torque (tightening) specs for the head bolts and wheel lugs; temperature specs for the thermostat in the radiator—hundreds of specs in all. Your service manual will give them to you, but only a few will be vital for your day-to-day driving survival. (For example, to mix antifreeze, you need 50 percent water and 50 percent antifreeze—but how much of the total mixture do you want to make? See the spec for "cooling-system capacity" in your manual.)

- **Spoiler.** Another word for AIRDAM (see above).

- **Strut.** Just when people were getting comfortable with the various types and flavors of shock absorbers (regular, gas-filled, heavy-duty, non-adjustable, adjustable, air type, and overload, to name a few) along came struts. The MacPherson strut is a new kind of suspension design—new to North America, anyway. It has fewer moving parts than older designs and appears on virtually all front-drive cars and some of the newer rear-drive cars as well. The **cartridge** portion of the strut assembly is similar to the basic old-fashioned shock, but repairs on the strut are costly—some designs require replacing the whole assembly (ouch!); some permit changing just the cartridge (still much costlier than changing shocks). The reasons for repairs are the same, however—you renew struts when the ride deteriorates.

■ **Supercharger.** A supercharger takes outside air, compresses it, and forces it into the engine; the "compressed" charge picks up more fuel and burns more powerfully. It differs from a TURBOCHARGER (below) in two main ways: turbocharging runs its compressor from the exhaust pressure, while supercharging runs its compressor with a V-belt; and turbocharging needs a lag time to build a charge, based on engine speed, where supercharging kicks in almost immediately.

■ **Tall rear end.** Refers to rear-axle gearing, usually expressed in ratios like 3.25:1 (where it takes 3.25 revolutions of the driveshaft to turn the rear wheels once). "Taller" ratios like 3.00:1 deliver better mileage but poorer acceleration. In the '60s, buyers had the choice of a multitude of rear ends (whether they *knew* what they were buying is a different matter), but in the '80s such options are rare.

■ **TBI (Throttle Body Injection).** A cheapjack form of fuel injection (see EFI above) so pathetic that it could only have come from American bean-counting design practices. Most cars produced in the late '80s will have abandoned TBI almost totally, moving ahead to real "ported" fuel injection.

■ **T-cup.** No, this isn't a new kind of undergarment. Smaller cars have led to smaller oil filters—a breakthrough many mechanics think we could have done without. The tiny new filters are called T-cups. (It's not clear whether this name was given because they're about the size of a teacup or because they had a parts code that started with the letter *T.*)

■ **Torque lock.** In a car with automatic transmission, parking on a hill without engaging the parking (or hand) brake before shifting to "Park" will place the entire weight of the car against the small pawl in the transmission that locks the rear wheels. On a steep hill, this weight can be so great that you will be unable to move the lever from "Park." You'll need help to rock the car an inch or two before you can free the lever.

■ **Torque steer.** In a front-drive car, this refers to the tendency of the steering to "alligator-wrestle" the driver during hard acceleration. It can and has caused accidents. The newer models are better than the old ones, but try out a turbocharged front-drive car sometime and you'll swear you're back in the Everglades wrestling the 'gators.

■ **Torx.** Now that you're finally comfortable with the three common kinds of screws (those with the basic straight slot, the x-shaped Phillips slot, and Robertson), they've invented a new kind! Torx drivers look a little like the stars your third-grade teacher used to put on your spelling tests—but have six "points" instead of five. They're not cheap, but they're cheaper than trying to make do with the wrong bit—and stripping the screw.

■ **Transaxle.** In the old days the engine (which powered the car) was separate from the **transmission** (which transmitted the power and allowed you to shift gears for different ratios), which was separate from the **differential** (which allowed the two drive wheels to share the power, and to turn at different rates as the car turned corners). Since front-drive cars don't have a lot of extra room under the hood, the transmission and differential on a front-drive car are combined in one unit—the **transaxle**. And it's all wine and roses until your first major repair bill hits you . . .

■ **Turbocharger.** In a turbocharger, the power of the exhaust gases is used to turn an impeller (compressor) which crams a denser, more powerful air-fuel mixture into the cylinders. There are two types: suck and blow. The **blow** type (the air blows directly into the carburetor) is rare. The **suck** type (air is sucked into the carburetor from a point *under* the carburetor) is very common. Here's turbocharging in a nutshell: (1) It works—it makes a four-cylinder engine perform like a V-8. (2) It's fun. (3) It sounds great. (4) It *accelerates* certain types of internal engine wear. (5) Using the turbo a lot produces mileage as poor as a V-8's. (6) Repairs and maintenance are quite costly. (7) Improper driver conduct or owner abuse (like turning off a hot engine *immediately* after a long highway drive) can *seriously* damage the turbo—see your manual. (Also see SUPERCHARGER.)

■ **Unibody.** If you bend down to peek under a modern car to look for the traditional two-beam frame, you won't see it. *There isn't one.* The car is fitted together like a three-dimensional jigsaw puzzle. As long as all the pieces are in place and fitted correctly, the structure remains safe and integral. (Also see JACKPOINTS.)

■ **Upshift light.** A dashboard indicator light (pioneered by Volkswagen) that tells you when to shift up for better mileage. Although theoretically a sound idea (they work fine on paper), they are really just one more form of idiot light. If you don't know when to shift, you have no business driving a standard transmission in the first place.

■ **V-belt.** All the rubber drive belts under the hood are properly called V-belts. The one-piece belts with lots of wiggles over lots of pulleys are called SERPENTINE belts.

■ **VI (Viscosity Index).** A measure of the viscosity, or thickness, of oil. A **VI modifier** will make the oil thicker, for example. See the discussion of multigrade oils on page 218.

■ **Wankel (or rotary) engine.** Instead of pistons, which go up and down in the cylinders, the Wankel engine spins like a clothes drier. Instead of individual separate cylinders, the Wankel moves the air-fuel mixture through different doorways, where it is mixed, compressed, and burned— then the whole cycle repeats. The only mass-production rotary-engine car in the world now is the Mazda RX-7—which is an *extraordinary* car. Wankel engines require more emission-control devices than piston engines. One of the great unanswered automotive conundrums is, "If the Mazda RX-7 is so powerful even *with* all those extra antipollution controls, then what, pray tell, could it do if they took the controls away?" (No one has ever been able to find out, as far as I know.)

■ **Zombie gauge.** Any dashboard gauge that, when the engine is shut off, does *not* return to zero but instead stays in the exact position it was when "alive."

INDEX

Horn, jamming of, 85
Hoses, leaking of, 85–86
Hot wax treatment, 112
HSS (High Strength Steel), 252

Idiot circuit, 249
Idiot lights, 32–33
 battery light, 32
 brake light, 32–33
 flickering/dimming lights, 33
 oil-pressure light, 32
 temperature light, 32
Idle, rough, 25
Ignition
 do-it-yourself test, 23
 scope test, 99
Inspection
 new car purchase, 195–96
 used car purchase, 201–3
Instrument panel gauges, 25–33
 ammeter, 29
 gas gauge, 29
 oil-pressure gauge, 26, 28
 temperature gauge, 28
 turbo-boost gauge, 31
 vacuum gauge, 30–31
 voltmeter, 25–26
 See also Idiot lights.
Insurance, 62, 115–19
 antique cars, 119, 186
 body shop work, 105–6
 companies versus brokers, 117
 discount programs, 118
 no-fault area, 117
 types of coverage, 116
Intake backfires, 12
Interior, vinyl repair, 136–37

Jack point, 79–80, 253
 precautions, 216
Jacking, 79
Jumper cables
 quality of, 98
 use of, 67–68

Keys, locked in car, 86

Leaded premium gas, 160–61
Leaded regular gas, 160
Leaks, 34–39
 automatic transmission fluid, 35
 brake fluid, 37
 engine oil leaks, 35
 gas leaks, 37
 gearbox/steering gear/rear axle fluids, 35
 hose, blowing of, 85–86
 leak sealers, 142
 power-steering fluid, 35
 radiator fluid, 34
 tires, slow leak, 54
 water leaks, 37–39
Leasing, 182–84
 disadvantages of, 183–84
Lemon laws, 231, 233
 used cars, 233
Library, use for automotive information, 236–37
Lighting, quartz, 169–70
Limp-in, 253
Locks, freeing of, 87–88
Lock-up torque converter, 11
 chuggle and, 11

INDEX